THE EMPTY MEN

THE ANCHOR BIBLE REFERENCE LIBRARY is designed to be a third major component of the Anchor Bible group, which includes the Anchor Bible commentaries on the books of the Old Testament, the New Testament, and the Apocrypha, and the Anchor Bible Dictionary. While the Anchor Bible commentaries and the Anchor Bible Dictionary are structurally defined by their subject matter, the Anchor Bible Reference Library will serve as a supplement on the cutting edge of the most recent scholarship. The series is open-ended; its scope and reach are nothing less than the biblical world in its totality, and its methods and techniques the most up-to-date available or devisable. Separate volumes will deal with one or more of the following topics relating to the Bible: anthropology, archaeology, ecology, economy, geography, history, languages and literatures, philosophy, religion(s), theology.

As with the Anchor Bible commentaries and the Anchor Bible Dictionary, the philosophy underlying the Anchor Bible Reference Library finds expression in the following: the approach is scholarly, the perspective is balanced and fair-minded, the methods are scientific, and the goal is to inform and enlighten. Contributors are chosen on the basis of their scholarly skills and achievements, and they come from a variety of religious backgrounds and communities. The books in the Anchor Bible Reference Library are intended for the broadest possible readership, ranging from world-class scholars, whose qualifications match those of the authors, to general readers, who may not have special training or skill in studying the Bible but are as enthusiastic as any dedicated professional in expanding their knowledge of the Bible and its world.

David Noel Freedman, GENERAL EDITOR

THE ANCHOR BIBLE REFERENCE LIBRARY

— THE —

EMPTY MEN

THE HEROIC TRADITION

OF ANCIENT ISRAEL

Gregory Mobley

DOUBLEDAY

New York   London   Toronto   Sydney   Auckland

THE ANCHOR BIBLE REFERENCE LIBRARY
PUBLISHED BY DOUBLEDAY
a division of Random House, Inc.
1745 Broadway, New York, New York 10019

THE ANCHOR BIBLE REFERENCE LIBRARY, DOUBLEDAY,
and the portrayal of an anchor with the letters ABRL are
trademarks of Doubleday, a division of Random House, Inc.

Book Design by Leslie Phillips

LIBRARY OF CONGRESS CATALOGING-IN-PUBLICATION DATA
Mobley, Gregory.
The empty men : the heroic tradition of ancient Israel /
Gregory Mobley.—1st ed.
p.   cm.—(The Anchor Bible reference library)
Includes bibliographical references and index.
1. Heroes in the Bible.   2. Bible. O.T. Judges—Criticism, Narrative.
3. Bible. O.T. Samuel—Criticism, Narrative.
I. Title.   II. Series.
BS579.H4M63 2006
222'.32066—dc22   2005051905

ISBN 0-385-49851-9

WITH MY GOD, *I can leap a wall.*

II SAM 22:30 = PS 18:30 (18:29 ET)

Contents

Preface

Many scholars directly or indirectly contributed ideas and modeled approaches that helped me write this book. I first worked on these ideas in my dissertation on Samson. Lawrence Stager put me on his trail. David Bynum wrote the essay that opened the gate to the arena of folklore and adventure literature where I would engage my subject. Peter Machinist invited me into the circle of his ancient Mesopotamian acquaintances: Gilgamesh, Enkidu, Erra, the Sibitti; and made me feel at home in a world that once seemed foreign. John Huehnergard sent me a note about the name "Delilah." Jo Ann Hackett suggested that I use my thesis on Samson as the foundation for a broader examination of heroes. Lawrence Wills stimulated my thinking about heroes, the Bible, and storytelling through the course of many conversations. Allan Emery shared with me his expertise on Iron Age Israelite weapons. Matthew Myer Boulton helped me clarify my approach to Gideon and Abimelech.

Two scholars who wrote about the book of Judges while at my school, Andover Newton Theological School (née Andover Seminary), were models for me. I imagined they were close by, working like fiends in offices down the hall as I wrote. George Foot Moore still reigns, after a century, as the best commentator on Judges. Phyllis Trible's scholarship on Judges and her tender attention to details in the biblical text were models I attempted to emulate.

Students in classes at Harvard Divinity School, Union Theological Seminary, and Andover Newton Theological School allowed me to preview my ideas. Their critiques and comments have stayed with me. Many of them will see ideas of theirs reflected in these pages. Among them, I must single out Katherine Layzer who gave me the lines from Rilke, Edie Howe who recommended that I read *The Rock,* Charles F. Eastman III who checked my biblical references, and Jason Larson who gave the entire manuscript a thorough and expert reading.

My twin brother, Jeffrey Mobley, reminded me about the chaos monsters in *The Cat in the Hat.*

A few words of clarification are in order.

The translations of biblical passages, unless otherwise marked, are mine.

I have chosen to render the divine name as YHWH, adopting the format of the NRSV. Though it strikes me as cheeky for scholars, especially Christian, to vocalize the Tetragrammaton, I have retained its (hypothetical) vocalization when quoting those who do. A couple of times I have employed the impossible form "Jehovah," aware of its brokered, misbegotten origins, but also appreciative of its energy; for me, it connotes God in the Old Style.

I realize that the phrase "empty men" in my title will trigger associations among readers with T. S. Eliot's "hollow" and "empty men." Though I covet any association with such a giant, I must alert readers that my empty men are not the same as his hollow men. To borrow a German idiom I heard in English from Dieter Georgi, "you could steal horses" with the men and women described in my book. I do not think you could with Eliot's; they would be too tied up in knots of modern alienation to be of much help when it was time to get to work.

While I am indebted to many for inspiration, I assume responsibility for any errors in this book.

The three persons who helped me the most with this project were Marsha White, Andrew Corbin, and David Noel Freedman.

Marsha White read every line, provided me with bibliography and comments based on her expertise on the Deuteronomistic literature, and supported me with friendship. I first met Andrew Corbin when he was a student of mine at Union Theological Seminary. After he graduated, he took a job at Doubleday where he remembered his former professor. He gave me this opportunity and then was a model of encouragement and wise counsel as he edited this book. It was a special privilege to have David Noel Freedman, the editor of the Anchor Bible series and the dean of American scholarship on the Hebrew Bible for the past half century, tutor me both in biblical scholarship and English grammar.

There was a time in the course of writing this book when I got shaky and needed steadying. I got over that rough stretch and was able to complete the book. In the hours before that daybreak, I imagined—was it a dream or a reverie?—that two figures had visited me. My dead grandfather winked at me and said, "You rascal." My mother smiled at me and said, "I always knew you could do it." So this book is dedicated to Elmer Mobley and to Carole Ann McDaniel Mobley. And also, to Mary Page, my wife, my Defender, who always did and continues to stand by me.

Abbreviations

AB	Anchor Bible
ABD	*Anchor Bible Dictionary*
ABRL	Anchor Bible Reference Library
ATANT	Abhandlungen zur Theologie des Alten und Neuen Testaments
BA	*Biblical Archaeologist*
BAR	*Biblical Archaeology Review*
BASOR	*Bulletin of the American Schools of Oriental Research*
BBB	Bonner biblische Beiträge
BHS	*Biblia Hebraica Stuttgartensia*
BJS	Brown Judaic Studies
BN	*Biblische Notizen*
b. Soṭah	Babylonian Talmud Soṭah
CAD	*The Assyrian Dictionary of the Oriental Institute of the University of Chicago*
CANE	*Civilizations of the Ancient Near East*
CAT	*The Cuneiform Alphabetic Texts from Ugarit, Ras Ibn Hani and Other Places*
CBC	Cambridge Bible Commentary
CBQ	*Catholic Biblical Quarterly*
COS	*The Context of Scripture*
DDD	*Dictionary of Deities and Demons in the Bible,* 2nd edition
DJD	Discoveries in the Judean Desert
ErIsr	*Eretz-Israel*
ET	English translation

HALOT	*The Hebrew and Aramaic Lexicon of the Old Testament*
HDR	Harvard Dissertations in Religion
HSM	Harvard Semitic Monographs
HSS	Harvard Semitic Studies
HTR	*Harvard Theological Review*
HUCA	*Hebrew Union College Annual*
ICC	International Critical Commentary
JAOS	*Journal of the American Oriental Society*
JBL	*Journal of Biblical Literature*
JEOL	*Jaarbericht van het Vooraziatisch-Egyptisch Gezelschap (Genootschap) Ex oreinte lux*
JNES	*Journal of Near Eastern Studies*
JPS	Jewish Publication Society
JQR	*Jewish Quarterly Review*
JSOT	*Journal for the Study of the Old Testament*
JSOTSup	Journal for the Study of the Old Testament: Supplement Series
JSS	*Journal of Semitic Studies*
KJV	King James Version
LXX	Septuagint
LXX^B	Septuagint Codex Vaticanus
MT	Masoretic Text
NCB	New Century Bible
NJBC	*The New Jerome Biblical Commentary*
NRSV	New Revised Standard Version
OBT	Overtures to Biblical Theology
OCD	*Oxford Classical Dictionary,* 3rd edition
ODCC	*Oxford Dictionary of the Christian Church,* 2nd edition
OEANE	*Oxford Encyclopedia of Archaeology in the Near East*
OTG	Old Testament Guides
OTL	Old Testament Library
RevQ	*Revue de Qumran*
RlA	*Reallexikon der Assyriologie*
SBLDS	Society of Biblical Literature Dissertation Series
SBLEJL	Society of Biblical Literature Early Judaism and its Literature
SBLWAW	Society of Biblical Literature Writings from the Ancient World

SSN	Studia semitica neerlandica
TDOT	*Theological Dictionary of the Old Testament*
UF	*Ugarit-Forschungen*
VT	*Vetus Testamentum*
VTSup	Supplements to Vetus Testamentum
WBC	Word Biblical Commentary
ZAW	*Zeitschrift für die alttestamentliche Wissenschaft*

THE EMPTY MEN

THE EMPTY MEN

1

MUSTER

THE EMPTY MEN

The phrase, "empty men," *'ănāšîm rêqîm,* occurs only three times in
the Hebrew Bible, twice in Judges (Judg 9:4; 11:3) and once in
2 Chronicles (2 Chr 13:7). Nearly empty of context and ambiguous
in meaning (lacking *what?*), the phrase barely registers amid the
noisy precincts of Judges and its neighbor Samuel, with their ethnic
donnybrooks, tournaments of the twelves, and genital mutilations.
Empty men are pulled into the orbit of the renowned warriors
Abimelech and Jephthah but remain anonymous amid the colorful
roster of heroes and villains—Slasher, Sunny, and Scabby versus
Double-Trouble, Baby Bull, and Wolf—in Judges and Samuel.
Empty men, probably the portionless runts of early Iron Age Israelite kinship litters, are bequeathed little room to stand in a narrative landscape crowded with turreted urban fortifications and
temples, rural tented encampments, and competing territorial
claims.

I

Who were these "men with nothing," *'ănāšîm rêqîm*, who attached themselves to Abimelech (Judg 9:4) and Jephthah (Judg 11:3), and those men, "in straits, in debt, embittered," who gathered around David (1 Sam 22:2)? Early Iron Age Syro-Palestine was a society in which social identity was rooted in kinship networks and inherited land. Second sons and sons of secondary wives, misfits and mercenaries, outlaws and outlanders: these are just some of those who fell between the kinship cracks. The also-rans in their natal groups, these empty men compensated by forming pseudofamilies under the patronage of warlords, trading their services for portions of martial harvests and brigandage.[1]

The phrase "empty men" denotes only a fraction of the warriors attested in Judges and Samuel but it connotes an entire Israelite heroic tradition submerged in biblical texts about, in story time, ancient Israel's frontier era. The Bible itself, as well as subsequent Jewish and Christian cultures, has a deep ambivalence about these heroes, the *gibbôrîm*.[2] Though the *gibbôrîm* left a substantial literary legacy through their war chants, heroic elegies, prayers and thanksgivings for divine protection, and roles in battle accounts and anecdotes, the corpus of and about this subculture was absorbed into the work of Exilic priestly historians who wrote in the wake of two centuries of quixotic military resistance to the incursions of, respectively, Assyrian and Babylonian imperial forces.

For these historians, who produced the scrolls of Deuteronomy and the Former Prophets (Joshua, Judges, Samuel, Kings), Israel's future did not lie along "[the] way [of] the multitude of *gibbôrîm*" (Hos 10:13). The Exilic historians who collected and redacted these stories about the frontier era had seen too much of siege and defeat in their lifetimes. The prophetic scrolls available to these historians presented chillingly authentic depictions of martial carnage from the eighth to sixth centuries B.C.E.[3] The survival of the community who worshipped YHWH depended on correct cultic practice and obedience to Mosaic teaching, not on violent resistance to the next imperial superpower in the Levant. The ideal king of the generation that went into exile had been Josiah, their David, who incarnated the *Shema*, "turn[ing] to Yhwh with all his heart, with all his soul, with all his might" (2 Kgs 23:25). Still, for all his Mosaic piety and Davidic pedigree, Yhwh was not with him when he went out to the plains of Megiddo against the Egyptians. Josiah, the great king, the second David, fell (2 Kgs 23:29).

Hopes for military deliverance were eventually projected into the cosmic sphere, as in Daniel's vision of the four great beasts, the chaos monsters that symbolized the parade of Near Eastern empires, receiving their ultimate comeuppance from the Ancient of Days seated on his heavenly throne (Dan 7:1–18). But that vindication lay only in the "forever and ever" (Dan 7:18, NRSV). In the mean times in between, in history, the Judahite community had daytime stories about angels that rescued the faithful from fiery furnaces and lions' dens and nighttime dreams of eschatological reversals to keep hope alive under Persian and Hellenistic rule. As Richard Marks noted in a study of rabbinic attitudes toward the *gibbôrîm*, the age of the warriors largely was confined to the past or projected onto the future.[4] But between the times, the *gibbôrîm* were dangerous role models. Martial adventurism amounted to tilting at windmills.

For the Judahite sages, who produced a corpus of wisdom sentences (i.e., Proverbs) and essays (i.e., Ecclesiastes), and a philosophic adventure story about a man named Job, the way forward also lay not along the martial paths of glory but along the path of righteousness. "The path of Yhwh" was the only enduring defense (Prov 10:29) for their culture. You can almost conjure the image of the sages' legendary patron, King Solomon, who claimed to rule on the basis of wisdom rather than battle-tested valor, from this adage, this *māšāl*, in Prov 24:5, "The man of understanding is mightier (literally, "more the *geber*") than the one hardened with strength."[5] Though Qohelet acknowledged that martial hunting seasons were among the times that characterized mortal life (Eccl 3:8), the author of Ecclesiastes concluded that "wisdom (ḥokmâ) is superior to heroism (gĕbûrâ)" (Eccl 9:16).

Biblical heroes, as surely as their names, live still. In addition to being our namesakes, they function as our imaginary companions, religious mentors, and symbolic ancestors. The protagonists of biblical narratives, from Noah to Nehemiah and from Eve to Esther, are too diverse to characterize with a single set of generalizations, but their most enduring qualities are neither physical nor martial. Above all, Jacob, the personification of "Israel" in all its meanings, seems most characteristic of the heroes of the Hebrew Bible. Though he does not lack for physical vitality or cunning, Jacob prevails over a nocturnal adversary not primarily because of strength or even wisdom but out of a stubborn refusal to let go until he has wrested a blessing from an unyielding universe (Gen 32:23–33 [32:22–32 ET]). This same quality can be seen in a Job, who will not be deterred from an audience with the Architect of the Universe, or in a Ruth who, beyond custom, steadfastly clings (√dbq) to Naomi (Ruth 1:14–18). The peregrinations of the patriarchs, the brooding intensity of the prophets, the devotion to learning of the sages: these require a measure of physical vitality but, more than that, of spiritual tenacity (cf. Dt 11:22), of a refusal to abandon hope and faith in spite of centuries, eventually millennia, of tragedy. This is the kind of biblical heroism we know best.

But there are adventure stories in the Bible, and this genre is densest in Judges and Samuel. Apart from Bible stories prudently bowdlerized for the religious education and entertainment of children, however, the tales of the gibbôrîm largely have been read through the didactic filters of biblical redactors and interpreters who have fashioned moralisms from the raw material about these crude warriors. Only a couple of gibbôrîm, for instance, Samson and the youthful David in his combat against Goliath, have escaped the clutches of their parochial minders to join their rightful peers, the league of universal heroes.

The purpose of this book is to read portions of the Bible as adventure stories. It is an attempt to recover something never wholly lost but often neglected. It is an attempt to pull together disparate bits of evidence and reconstruct the outline of early Iron Age Israelite warrior culture, and to analyze the conventions and appreciate the structure of biblical adventure stories. It is an attempt to isolate the heroic tradition of ancient Israel, as one might speak of Greek or Irish or Indo-Aryan heroic tradition, and to open this tradition up to comparisons with other heroic literatures.[6]

LITERARY SETTING

Since the middle of the twentieth century, thanks to the literary analysis of Martin Noth, scholars have recognized that all of Judges and Samuel, the books that contain the heroic material analyzed here, are embedded in a longer literary work (Deuteronomy through 2 Kings) completed during the Babylonian Exile. Through reference to its characters' obedience or disobedience to the standards of the book of Deuteronomy, this work sought to explain how the destruction of Solomon's Temple by the Babylonian army in 587/6 and subsequent Exile had been punishment for infidelity to divine teaching. At the same time, in the particular idioms of these Exilic writers, this work admonished present and future generations to "get right with God," as the Appalachian road signs phrase it.[7] Noth referred to this literary work as the "Deuteronomistic History."

These historians did not begin from scratch but utilized older poems and stories, annalistic records from the courts of Israelite and Judean kings, genealogical records, oddly shaped bits of ancient royal *administrivia*, lists of geographical boundaries and of officials, legends about prophets, and priestly teachings, many of which must have already been shaped into literary documents. To this extent, the historian(s) was conservative and, often, his point of view was expressed only through the arrangement of these older sources. For instance, the episodic arrangement of the heroic tales in Judges, beginning with Ehud and Deborah and ending with Jephthah and Samson, may or may not reflect the order of the chronological parade but certainly, in its present order, profiles the progressive degeneration of tribal leaders and of a society in decline from a Mosaic ideal.

Such an analysis as Noth's is subtle, for it rests on the subjective enterprises of isolating smaller, preexisting sources and of divining the authorial or editorial intent of their present arrangement. Less subtle are the repetition of certain words and phrases in accounts which appear in Deuteronomy through Kings, a more or less consistent chronological framework imposed on the entire work, and a specific set of speeches placed in the mouths of important characters—Moses, Joshua, heavenly messengers, Samuel, Solomon—that speak in the same voice, the voice of Moses from the book of Deuteronomy. These elements, intact, constitute Noth's strongest evidence that this span of scrolls represents a single, coherent work.

The Deuteronomistic History pays its respects to the legendary frontier heroes, including Ehud, Gideon, Samson, Saul, David, and Joab, men wild enough to tame a wilderness and secure the territory that became the Iron Age kingdoms of Israel and Judah. But the story that began in the book of Joshua with an entrance into Canaan finished in the book of Kings with an exit to Babylon. In the aftermath of the destruction of Solomon's Temple and the deportation of Judahite elites to Babylon in the early sixth century B.C.E., these Jewish historians asked "What went wrong?" and found the answer in a legacy of prophetic critique initiated by Hosea and Amos in the eighth century B.C.E. and continuing through the oracles of Jeremiah and Ezekiel into the sixth century. Israel, and then Judah, were sinners in the hands of an angry God. Their history represented a long decline from a Mosaic ideal and no era or personages—except for perhaps the first and last heroes of the Deuteronomistic History: Moses's hand-picked successor, Joshua, and the Judahite king, Josiah, royal patron of the Deuteronomistic historians—were left out of the indictment.[8] Over time, the history spanning the biblical books of Joshua through Kings came to be imbued with the authority of a prophetic oracle, a message from the divine court.

But before the material in Judges and Samuel became God's holy words, there were stories. There were stories about an era when warriors fought solo, in pairs, in threes, and in twelves; when trophies were taken and kills counted; when dueling was described as manly "play." There were stories about a left-handed assassin named Ehud and his solo mission in and out of an inaccessible fortress, about the improbable triumph of Gideon and his band over a vast swarming enemy, and about Samson, long hair flowing, the original Hell's Angel, rambling through Philistia like a one man army.[9] These heroic stories, and others, were turned into sermons and history lessons by later redactors. Julius Wellhausen commented on the friction between the celebrative, constitutive tenor of many of the individual adventure stories in Judges and the didactic goals of the larger history in which they became embedded. Read on their own terms, "the heroic figures of the judges refuse to fit in with the story of sin and rebellion" chronicled in what we now refer to as the Deuteronomistic History. To the contrary, "[the judges] are the pride of their countrymen, and not humiliating reminders that Jehovah had undeservedly again and again made good that which men had destroyed."[10]

Some of the narratives in Judges may have been bundled together in a pre-Deuteronomistic heroic anthology. Wolfgang Richter referred to this hypothetical document as the *Retterbuch*, or "Book (or Scroll) of Rescuers."[11] Richter's *Retterbuch* included what we now know as the middle section of the book of Judges, chapters 3–9. This block of material shares the same general geographic arena, the central Samarian highlands; a common tone of triumph as Ehud, Deborah, and Gideon retire from their contests undefeated; and a consistent editorial framework, a set of formulas: the people did evil; the deity allowed them to be oppressed; the people cried out for help; a rescuer emerged; the land had rest.

I prefer the view of Richter to that of Barnabas Lindars who contends that the stories of Judges emerged in literary form only through the historical work of the Deuteronomists.[12] But I have chosen not to focus this work on the literary evolution of Judges, or on reconstructing documentary precursors to the extant biblical texts. The archipelago of scholarly islands sighted in Genesis through Kings—J, E, D, P, Dtr, to say nothing of J^1, J^2, L, Dtr^1, Dtr^2, Dtr^N, and more—is now oceanic and I will neither map any new discoveries nor contest the claims of other explorers to any of this hypothetical turf. The heroic material in Judges and Samuel—however these scrolls emerged in literary form—is on the surface level of the text. Its examination does not require a reconstructed text. All that is needed to hear this material anew, as adventure stories, is a temporary suspension of the moralistic voices at the boundaries of the stories and in the religious imaginations of their readers.

The oldest literary stratum of Judges, whether it is imagined as an anthology of heroic narratives (Richter) or as a set of independent stories (Lindars), celebrates, for the most part, Iron Age martial heroism, which in those days included the ceremonial slaughter of enemy leaders, blood feuding, and trophy taking. But the putative scroll, the Book of Rescuers, that first contained these *gestes* has been turned into a Book of Vices, and the actions and motivations of the *gibbôrîm* susceptible to second guessing at every turn, in every age. The aim of this book is to dig out some of this Israelite heroic material submerged in Judges and Samuel.

THE LIMITS OF THIS STUDY

The purpose of the second chapter, "Heroic Culture," and the third, "Heroic Conventions," is to change the backdrop behind the adventure stories and anecdotes in Judges and Samuel from that of a religious history by Exilic theologians to that of early Iron Age martial practice and heroic storytelling, allowing these heroic materials to emerge as more than object lessons, their protagonists as more than exemplars, knights of good (or bad) faith. In subsequent chapters, I will retell the stories of certain heroes—Ehud, Gideon, Abimelech, and Samson—from Judges, hoping to capture the heroic qualities in stories that have been turned into sermons and history lessons.

I will make reference to other texts in Judges and Samuel, but I will not devote chapter-length treatments to them. The poetry and prose of Judges 4–5, concerning Deborah, Barak, and Jael, and of Judges 10–12, concerning Jephthah and his daughter, have been the subject of many treatments in recent years, most notably Susan Ackerman's historical and literary treatment of female characters in the book of Judges, and, for Jephthah and his daughter specifically, studies by Phyllis Trible and Peggy Day.[13] The heroic material in Samuel will be referred to throughout the study, but I have not included individual treatments of its legendary warriors, such as Saul, Jonathan, David, and Joab, though it was my original ambition. The style, as much as the content, of the stories about Ehud, Gideon, Abimelech, and Samson captured my attention; and the stories about the warriors in Samuel, though equally memorable, do not lend themselves to the same kind of treatment because they are braided together into a single, multi-textured narrative. The heroic material in Samuel draws on the same repertoire of motifs as that in Judges, but the texture of Samuel prevents us from clearly distinguishing one story from another. It is impossible to isolate the story of, say, David from that of Saul or of Joab. Two recent books about David, by Steven McKenzie and Baruch Halpern, are recommended to those interested in historical reconstructions of the events and personages of the Davidic era.[14]

THEOLOGY

One thing I fear is that a focus on the Israelite heroic tradition could be misconstrued as an ideological charter for aggression, whether by communities that respect biblical authority or by social groups or individuals who see themselves as the spiritual—or even genealogical—descendants of the biblical *gibbôrîm*. I feel compelled to declare my irenic intentions and append testimonies to my good citizenship. But I will resist that urge.

Others have written and are better suited to write more persuasively and programatically than I about the peaceful goals of the versions of Judaism and Christianity which they wish to champion, and about interpretive strategies for dealing with the violence in the Bible that often seems to contradict its highest ideals.[15] I have religious commitments—I sit on the back pew of Christendom—and do not pretend that I can hide behind the mask of objective historian or that of detached literary critic, naive about the significance of biblical interpretation in history. But the pile of writings inscribed with pious censure and ethical disapproval of the *gibbôrîm* is high enough already. I want to retell their stories; readers can decide for themselves whether boyish enthusiasm overrides literary discrimination and moral responsibility.

I have an even greater fear. Since I am Christian, this unapologetic profile of ancient Israelite martial heroism could, perversely, be perceived as further evidence of some variation of a popular Christian canard, namely, that "the God of the Old Testament is a God of Wrath while the God of the New Testament is a God of Love." The *bad* example; the antithesis in need of a synthesis; a first, failed cosmic experiment: the dominant theme of much Christian interpretation of the Hebrew Bible, of the *Old* Testament, has been to accentuate the negative. I once heard the Jewish educator David Gordis quip, "Jewish people read the prophets as recounting the failure of the Jews. Christian people read the prophets as recounting the failure of *the Jews.*"

There are, to use Phyllis Trible's phrase, "texts of terror" in the New Testament: household codes that condone the institutions of slavery and the patriarchal family (e.g., 1 Pet 2:18–3:7; 1 Cor 11:2–16) and texts that demonize and scapegoat "the Jews," such as in John 18–19 where, over and over again, the Jewish people are blamed for Jesus' death while the Roman governor, Pontius Pilate ("Would you like me to release him?" "I find no fault in him"), is absolved of responsibility. The final book of the Christian canon, the Revelation to John, stages an apocalyptic drama in which the Pale Galilean is transformed into a cosmic superhero, the Lamb, who engages in combat with yet another avatar of our ancient foe, here the Great Red Dragon, though liberal Christians since the nineteenth century have striven unsuccessfully to distance their moral champion Jesus from New Testament apocalypticism and to downplay the sangfroid of these early Christian eschatological scenarios.

Knowledge of social contexts helps us put the sexism, tribalism, and apocalyptic revenge fantasies of the Jewish and Christian Bibles in perspective. The Jesus movement began as a sect of first-century Palestinian Judaism. As a result, these sibling faiths, both issuing from Second Temple Judahite religion and a common grandparent, the religion of ancient Israel, exaggerated their differences and emphasized distinct themes of their common heritage, like biological twins seeking individuation. The New Testament, which emerged when this rivalry between followers of Jesus and other communities within Judahite circles, especially the Pharisee movement, was in full pitch, enshrines the regrettable but inevitable polemics of an era when both Christianity and Rabbinic Judaism were forged. The virus of anti-Semitism entered the Body of Christ during this period and, under stressful conditions, has erupted in fevered oppression and pogrom throughout the Common Era.[16] But my purpose here is not to practice a kind of chronocentrism and take issue with the ethical sensibilities of the ancient communities that gave us the Bible and, when not trying to survive, managed to leave us this literary legacy that at times seems so narrow and small minded and then, in the next line, broad and big enough to contain our dreams. We bear responsibility for interpreting these texts in healthy ways.

But what about the relative density of descriptions of violence and violent rhetoric in the Hebrew Bible in contrast to the irenic ideals espoused by Jesus in the New Testament? The Hebrew Bible emerged over the course of centuries, the New Testament over decades. The New Testament community did not have to deal with the messy problems of territoriality, statehood, and civil defense. The Iron Age kingdoms of Israel and Judah did. Subsequent configurations of empire and church would; and Christendom—paradoxically but understandably, given the vicissitudes of history—has its own bloody chronicles.

Many modern readers of the Bible, whether Jews, Christians or neither, are put off by the violence in Judges and Samuel. They are not the first. In the fourth century C.E., Bishop Ulphilas (Ulfilas, Wulfila) omitted the books of Samuel and Kings from his translation of the Bible into Gothic from Greek.[17] According to his chronicler, Philostorgius, the good Bishop omitted the Books of Reigns because they were "a mere narrative of military exploits, and the Gothic tribesman especially were fond of war, and were in more need of restraints to check their military passions than of spurs to urge them on to deeds of war."[18]

The present book might neither have passed the Bishop's muster nor will it reassure contemporary readers made uncomfortable by the violence in the Bible. Often it may seem as if I consider ancient Israel as one more Iron Age warrior culture. All of the nouns in that sentence—ancient Israel, Iron Age, warrior culture,

culture—are slippery and I will not try to handle them any longer than necessary. To generalize: yes, ancient Israel included a warrior subculture. I will grant the Bible's critics that much. Still, any religion that was not invented five minutes ago has to deal with history, and history is messy. "History," in Fredric Jameson's words, "is what hurts."[19]

Part of our problem, as Jewish and Christian interpreters, is that our canon has roots in the Iron Age, and the God we (and, indirectly, Muslims) worship was classically conceived, however accurately or not, in another time. As Walter Burkert writes, "The ancient gods—with the single exception of Jahweh—are no longer powerful nor represented in living belief; they do not demand cult and no longer spread awe."[20] But YHWH is exceptional. No one has to apologize for Erra or Seth or Ares anymore. Since YHWH is the only surviving deity from that era, YHWH must face interrogation. Jews, Christians, and Muslims, if so inclined, must apologize for their texts of terror.

We know Jehovah's faults all too well, whether expressed in conquest narratives in Joshua or in Crusaders' ideology.[21] But neither Judaism nor Christianity is special in this regard. Violence does not spring from these systems. Neither religious culture invented human cruelty nor the reflex to find cosmic validation for social rivalries nor the overpowering human need for transcendent reassurance in boundary situations such as combat. Kali and Ogun have blood on their hands too. These are questions that can be addressed theologically by myths about the Fall, or by rhetorical constructs about the "evil impulse," *yēṣer hārāʿ*, and "virtuous impulse," *yēṣer haṭṭôb*, competing in the human heart, or nontheologically by theories of sociobiology and anthropological social identity formation.

There are new species of religious commitment in this and every age which, in their creation, implicitly claim Edenic, prelapsarian purity. In order to pull this off, they must demonize history and tradition, and effectively cut themselves off from the ancestors, or hypothesize an ideological fantasy of some Golden Age to which they will return us. Only time will tell, but in time, holy wars may very well be launched in the names of their new improved, or old rediscovered deities. I prefer my messy religion, deeply rooted in human culture and history, ever open to reform and reformulation, to a pure, pristine, but shallow one.

Where is this going theologically? I am not sure. Perhaps this represents the musings of someone so immersed in violent biblical adventure stories to have become inured to their barbarities. Fervently do I pray that this work would not be construed as a warrant for warfare and for an uncritical reappropriation of warrior culture and its ideals. I am realistic enough to know that conflict is inevitable, that, as Lincoln said in his second inaugural address, "offences . . . must needs come," but, still, "woe to that man by whom the offence cometh."

Still, could this argument open a door to a larger discussion of, in Christian terms, Divine Love, a love that includes the food chain and a divinity who, in the terms of William Blake, is both Tyger and Lamb?[22] This view of Divine Love is hinted at in the divine speeches in the book of Job, where even the brutal economy of life on earth, illustrated in the image of a vulture eating the remains of fallen warriors, is declared to be part of the cosmic design, ʿēṣâ (Job 39:26–30). Without falling into the trap of romanticizing or endorsing the warrior subculture of ancient Israel, I could not help but be affected by the biblical acknowledgment of the energy and ferocity of life on earth, and how that reality inevitably issues in times of war, and its attempt to channel this energy in constructive ways rather than to demonize or deny it. Ancient Israelites understood the role of ritual, not to blindly authorize warfare, but as a means to, provisionally, control and channel it. The recitation of chants and martial psalms fortified men crossing the threshold into this grim zone. Conventions of homecoming described in Judges and Samuel, the group rites when the women met the men at the city gate (1 Sam 18:6–7) or the family scenes at a domestic threshold (Judg 11:34), provided for integration of warriors back into civilian life. The solitary, mundane release of a man beating a sword back into a plowpoint against an anvil provided a ritual catharsis as the killing point was beaten out of the weapon and the fury out of the warrior.

I am attempting to articulate a small truth; an enduring, small truth. I did not attempt to solve the problem of evil or to apologize for the violence in the Bible. I wrote this book, in the end, not for the church or the synagogue or the academy, though I have them all in mind. I wrote this book for personal reasons and for persons. The small truth mentioned above resists formulation but it has something to do with a third sense of the term "empty men." Its primary referent is in Judges and serves as a term for men alienated from kinship networks. I have given it a secondary referent as a term to describe the entire tradition of Israelite heroic storytelling that has often been lost in the moralistic matrix of biblical interpretation. There may also be something else in the term, something universal, something about the perennial friction between civilian and warrior cultures, and about how our disgust with the sins of warfare often leads us to disinherit the poor sinners whom we draft to perform our dirty work. Mainly, then, I wrote this book for Samson and Ehud. I wrote this book for each and every underdog soldier in the night. I wrote this book for my uncle, Joe Lester Mobley, whom our extended family welcomed home from Viet Nam on the tarmac of the Cincinnati airport in 1968. I wrote this book for the empty men.

> If only,
> oh if only I were a boy with the unknown yet before me
> as I sat propped on my future's arms, reading about
>> Samson,
> how his mother bore nothing at first, then—everything.
> (Rilke, "The Sixth Elegy")[23]

NOTES

1. For more on "empty men," see pp. 36–38.

2. R. Marks, "Dangerous Hero."

3. Perhaps the most graphic is Nahum's imagined description of the fall of Nineveh (Nah 2–3); see also Isa 5:26–30; Jer 4:19–21, 29; 5:16–17; 6:1–6, 23–24; 8:16; 9:21 (9:22 ET); 14:18; Ezek 7:14–17; 23:23–30.

4. R. Marks, "Dangerous Hero," 190.

5. Reading the first line of the verse with the LXX, *kreissōn*, i.e., Hebrew *gābar*, rather than the MT *geber*.

6. Scholars who have described the era depicted in Judges and Samuel as Israel's heroic age include C. Gordon, J. Blenkinsopp, and R. Bartelmus. Gordon, inspired by the parallels he found among Ugaritic, Greek, and Israelite literatures to articulate his theory of a common Eastern Mediterranean civilization in the Bronze Age from which Hellenic and Hebrew cultures emerged, catalogued a number of comparable features between Homeric and biblical heroic traditions in "Homer and Bible." Gordon described an Israelite heroic age that began in the era of Judges and culminated in the Davidic period (p. 55). Blenkinsopp noted his impressions of an Israelite heroic milieu from which the stories about the judges and David arose ("Some Notes on the Saga of Samson and the Heroic Milieu"). The most extensive study of Israelite heroic traditions is that of Bartlemus who contended that the materials about Samson, David, and the *gibbôrîm* were a creation of the Davidic dynasty, designed to legitimate its regime. Since David's throne was not bequeathed to him in the ordinary way, through inheritance, his legitimacy had to be based on something extraordinary, the surpassing favor granted to him by the deity and evidenced by the nearly superhuman feats that he and other Judahite warriors performed (*Heroentum in Israel und seiner Umwelt*).

The present study is indebted to these studies but is primarily focused on specific texts in Judges and on their literary structure, adducing the heroic parallels with other cultures and literatures as a means of explicating details in the Bible rather than combing these texts for examples of heroic themes and motifs.

7. M. Noth's hypothesis is in *The Deuteronomistic History*. For recent surveys of the discussion, see S. McKenzie, "Deuteronomistic History"; and A. Mayes, "Deuteronomistic History."

8. For the view that the first edition of the Deuteronomistic History was written during Josiah's reign, and later revised in the Exile, see F. Cross, *Canaanite Myth and Hebrew Epic*, 274–89.

9. On my use of the term "Hell's Angel," see the discussion of Samson as Chaos Monster on pp. 200–204.

10. J. Wellhausen, *Prolegomena to the History of Ancient Israel*, 234.

11. W. Richter, *Traditionsgeschichtliche Untersuchungen zum Richterbuch; Die Bearbeitungen des "Retterbuches" in der deuteronomistischen Epoche*.

12. B. Lindars, *Judges 1–5*, viii.

13. S. Ackerman, *Warrior, Dancer, Seductress, Queen*; P. Trible, *Texts of Terror*, 93–116; P. Day, "From the Child Is Born the Woman."

14. S. McKenzie, *King David*; B. Halpern, *David's Secret Demons*.

15. S. Niditch, *War in the Hebrew Bible*; P. Craigie, *The Problem of War in the Old Testament*; M. Lind, *Yahweh Is a Warrior*.

16. If I may be permitted a homily in a footnote: it could be that contemporary Christians and Jews, by preserving and celebrating their distinctive identities, provide a special service for their sibling faith. For each community, in the process of differentiation, preserved special configurations of a common heritage that the other group lost or deemphasized. In this way,

interfaith dialogue could be a *tikkun,* the recovery of scattered fragments of our respective traditions from the other faith.

17. "Ulphilas," *ODCC,* 1654; J. Birdsall, "Versions, Ancient (Gothic)," 804.

18. Philostorgius, *Historia Ecclesiastica* 2:5; as seen in G. Stokes, "Ulfilas," 1059.

19. F. Jameson, *The Political Unconscious,* 102.

20. W. Burkert, *Creation of the Sacred,* xi.

21. The medieval Knights Templar ate their meals in silence while a brother read portions of the book of Joshua to them (D. Seward, *The Monks of War,* 32).

22. W. Brueggemann in *Theology of the Old Testament* has already opened the discussion with his insistence that negative aspects of YHWH's characterization in the Hebrew Bible are theologically significant; see pp. 359–403. Along these lines, I am impressed with the formulation of D. Akenson: "Yahweh personifies . . . ultimate reality exactly. Life is bounteous, so too is Yahweh; life is unfair, so too is Yahweh (just ask Job). Yahweh is the name for reality invented by Hebrew religious geniuses who paid attention to the way the world works" (*Surpassing Wonder,* 98).

23. R. Rilke, *Duino Elegies* (trans. E. Snow), 39.

2

HEROIC CULTURE

CULTURE AND CONVENTION

This attempt to profile the blood feuders, warlords, and raiders from the settlement and early monarchical periods of Israelite history is provisional and incomplete. First, it rests on an uneven foundation of extrabiblical evidence, mainly of whatever archaeologists have happened upon, such as a few dozen inscribed arrowheads from the period and the literary remains from ancient Israel's antecedent and neighboring cultures. Second, the evaluation of biblical evidence, though ample, is subject to infinite scholarly second guessing. The accounts in Judges and Samuel, in story time, take place in "the days of the Judges" (Ruth 1:1) and in the initial decades of the monarchical era. This era corresponds in historical time to the early Iron Age, ca. 1200–1000 B.C.E. But if Noth's analysis is correct, these traditions about early Israel could not have achieved their present literary form (or something approximating it, given the larger and more complicated story of how biblical manuscripts were edited and transmitted for centuries) before the Exilic period, since the concluding chapter of the entire Deuteronomistic History, 2 Kings 25, is an account of events in the early sixth century B.C.E.

In historical terms, then, how much of the tenth-century David can be found in a sixth-century account?[1] In literary terms, there are some empirical grounds for isolating the oldest sources of the Deuteronomistic History, poems like the Song of Deborah in Judges 5, because they are preserved, as it were, in dialect, in an earlier stage of the Hebrew language, which evolved over a span of more than half a millennium.[2] But for the most part, the Hebrew text of the entire History, the bulk of which is prose, reflects the same stage of the Hebrew language. As such, despite more than a century of intense scholarly activity devoted to isolating discrete literary units and assigning them compositional dates relative to each other, the varied results of these experiments—impressive, ingenious, inconsistent—remain hypothetical.[3]

Still, the stories in Judges and Samuel, indeed the entire Biblical corpus, clearly have a precanonical history, a checkered past, as evidenced by their uneven generic texture and contradictory and redundant details. Even if we lack reliable empirical filters for separating early from late stages, there are clear signs of development within stories. Stories grew like onions, with cores of oral or written tradition accreting layer upon layer of detail and narrative shaping over time, or, in Steven McKenzie's image, like peaches, with a basic solid core, encased in something soft and often penetrable, representing intermediate literary development, covered by a thin exterior skin of editorial or chronological formula created by the final editors, such as the Deuteronomists.[4] I assume that the narratives of Judges and Samuel began in some form long before the postexilic production of the scrolls of Judges and Samuel, and that the biblical materials themselves, read in concert with extrabiblical texts and historical and archaeological data, can be utilized as sources in understanding the heroic culture and literary conventions of early Israel.

The trickiest problem for this analysis, however, is not the literary complexity of biblical texts. Rather, it is the distinction between culture and convention. How can we distinguish between the historical phenomenon of Iron Age warriors and the later narrative conventions in accounts about them? For example, later we will discuss the motif of a warrior experiencing the "rush" of divine breath as the prelude to a feat. On one hand, this can be seen as narrative convention, comparable to descriptions of battle fury in many heroic literatures. On the other hand, this idiom of the heroic dialect reflects something entirely real and wholly human: those occasions when men closed in battle and—inspired by ritual? hardened by occasion or training? fueled by adrenaline or intoxicants?—fought fearlessly, ferally.

The biblical emphasis on the inferiority of Israelite arms also illustrates the ambiguities of distinguishing between martial practice and narrative custom. On one hand, it is likely that Israelite highland militias in the era of the Judges were at a technical disadvantage to urban, lowland Canaanites and Philistines.[5] On the other hand, as best seen in the signature account of 1 Samuel 17, David against Goliath, the repeated emphasis of this motif elicits suspicions that—as evidence of divine support? as claim to the perennially attractive status of underdog?—the contrast in weaponry was exaggerated.[6] Aware of the subjectivity of literary stratification of biblical texts and of the artificiality of separating medium and message, I will soldier on, working back and forth between extrabiblical materials and biblical stories, acknowledging but leaving unresolved the conundrum of distinguishing history from literature, culture from convention.

SOURCES

Bronze arrowheads inscribed with the names of Iron Age Lebanese warriors; war oracles and bragging inscriptions in Akkadian, Egyptian, Aramaic, and Hittite; ancient battle scenes on relief panels and heroic profiles on seals; Bronze Age Syrian myths about divine warriors, female and male; heroic materials inside and outside the Bible: all of these provide windows into the historical phenomenon of premonarchical warrior groups in Syro-Palestine. To use the names of martial groups mentioned in the Bible and ancient inscriptions, what might we reconstruct about the following: in Judah, David's "heroes" (gibbôrîm); in Lebanon, the sons of Anat (banū ʿanat) and the sons of Ishtar (banū ʾaštart); in Philistia, "the votaries of Rapha" (yĕlidê hārāpâ); (2 Sam 21:18) or in Moab, "the sons of Ariel" (following the Greek of 2 Sam 23:20)?' Here we first will consider extrabiblical literary sources, including myths about ancient Levantine divine warriors, in order to understand better the ideology of these human warriors, as well as a set of inscribed bronze arrowheads from Syria and Palestine that offer hints about the warriors' social organization. Then we will consider certain biblical texts in light of these extrabiblical sources.

The biblical sources include, first of all, the major accounts in Judges, about individual heroes such as Ehud or Samson, and in Samuel, where, unlike Judges, its heroes—Samuel, Saul, David, Joab—do not take the stage one at a time, but act as rivals, mentors, donors, comrades, and nemeses in material that moves beyond the episodic to the epic. For the most part, however, I will defer the analysis of these materials to later chapters. In this chapter, the primary biblical source considered is a set of minor traditions, the anecdotes about and catalogue of warriors in 2 Samuel 21 and 23.

Anat

Narrative poems dated to 1400–1350 B.C.E. inscribed on clay tablets in a Bronze Age Syrian language, Ugaritic (a Northwest Semitic cousin of Hebrew), tell about Anat, a goddess of war, and offer hints about the heroic values of a people who lived two centuries prior to, and a little more than two hundred miles north of earliest Israel in the highlands of Ephraim. Anat, as shown in the studies of Neal Walls and Peggy Day, and as seen in her epithet, *btlt*, "maiden," is eternally pubescent.[8] Developmentally, she appears to be in between stages, between menarche and motherhood, and this location gives her the freedom to invert the conventions of the patriarchal cultures both of West Semitic mythology and Ugaritic society: she is female but not a fertility goddess; she is not male but she is a warrior.[9]

A single episode from a collation of the texts from Ras Shamra, Syria, the site of the city of Ugarit, introduces us to the Maid of Ugarit and, crucially for our topic, to the mythology of warriors in the Levant in the era immediately preceding the earliest heroic materials preserved in the Bible. As the episode begins, Anat has prepared for the transition from civility to hostility: she has undergone some kind of physical transformation (probably the removal of cosmetics) and has descended from her palace—like so many West Semitic deities, she dwells on a mountain, Mt. Inbubu—to the battlefield.[10]

Then, in Mark Smith's translation:[11]

And look! Anat fights in the valley,
Battles between the two towns.

She fights the people of the se[a]shore,
Strikes the populace of the su[n]rise.

Body parts fly as she delves into action.

Under her, like balls, are hea[ds,]
Above her, like locusts, hands,
Like locusts, heaps of warrior-hands.

Next she gathers her souvenirs—in Wall's words, "a sash of severed hands and a garland of human heads"—before continuing.[12]

She fixes heads to her back,
Fastens hands to her belt.

Knee-deep she glea[n]s in warrior-blood,
Neck-deep in the gor[e] of soldiers.

With a club she drives away captives,
With her bow-string, the foe.

Then, the scene changes, signaled both by content and through repetition of the phrase that began this section of the poem, "And look!": "And look! Anat goes to her house, / The goddess takes herself to her palace." The subsequent scene will also be framed by a repetition, the contrast of "unsated" with "sated."

Unsated with her fighting in the valley,
With battling between the two towns.

She arranges chairs for the soldiery,
Arranges tables for hosts,
Footstools for heroes.

Hard she fights and looks about,
Battling Anat surveys.

Her innards swell with laughter,
Her heart fills with joy,
Anat's innards with victory.

Knee-deep she gleans in warrior-blood,
Neck-deep in the gore of soldiers,

Until sated with fighting in the house,
With battling between the tables.

Based on banquet scenes in other myths, we might next expect the postbattle communion and reconciliation of a feast in a divine palace.[13] Instead, in a macabre twist anticipated by the ominous adjective, "unsated," Anat begins the battle anew. Finally satisfied, the next lines describe the Maid cleaning her palace, washing her hands, and reapplying her cosmetics;[14] the benign domestic rites that mark the transition of a war goddess from storm to calm.

The features from this episode that introduce our discussion of heroic motifs in biblical literature are: the depiction of supreme battle performance; the taking of grisly trophies, here heads and "hands";[15] the implied metaphor, seen in the verb "gleaning," $\sqrt{gll}$, of plunder as the harvest of war; and the motif of the satiation of a bloodthirsty, flesh-hungry divine warrior.[16] The Babylonian goddess of war, Ishtar, whose "feast is the melée, the dancing about of (grim) reaping . . . the harvest song," is also described in terms which link the themes of human slaughter and divine consumption elsewhere in Western Asia.[17]

Regarding these latter themes, Mark Smith, the translator of the above lines, draws attention to lines from the Mesha Inscription.[18] On a basalt monument, now in the Louvre and dating to the mid-ninth century B.C.E., King Mesha of Moab recounts his victories over Israel in the days of the Omride dynasty.[19] Lines 11–12 and 15–17 contain echoes of the theme of a divine warrior being satiated with the repast of slain enemies.

Mesha, or his royal speechwriter, says:

> I fought against the [Israelite] city [of Atarot] and took it,
> and I killed the entire population of the city—a satiation
> for Kemosh [the Moabite deity] and for Moab.[20]

Of a later battle against the Israelite city of Nebo, Mesha says,

> So I went at night and fought against it from the break of
> dawn until noon. I seized it and killed everyone of [it]—
> seven thousand native men, foreign men, native women,

for[eign] women, and concubines—for I devoted it to Ashtar-Kemosh.[21]

The final verb in the above lines, "devoted," is a form of the root *ḥrm,* a cognate of Hebrew *ḥerem,* "ban," and is best understood in martial contexts, confirmed by its usage in the Mesha Inscription, as "ritual slaughter."[22] Its Ugaritic cognate also appears in another text about Anat, where she is urged to "devote to destruction [*ḥrm*] . . . , kill . . . , harvest hand(s), pour out [blood?], to your belt attach heads."[23] Smith contends that we here have a mythological rationale, a theological sanction, for a mean reality of warfare in the ancient Levant: the belief that divine warriors, whether Ugaritic Anat or Moabite Kemosh, received satisfaction from human slaughter.

Did Israelite warriors practice the *ḥerem* sacrifice? Did they ritually slaughter the vanquished? Did they believe that YHWH desired this form of human sacrifice? Many of the biblical scenes which use the word *ḥerem* in reference to the annihilation of foes, the formulaic references in Joshua which provide few specifics and make it appear as if an entire regional population was erased from the earth ("Joshua . . . defeated the whole land, . . . left no survivors, . . . utterly destroyed all that breathed," Josh 10:40), have an air of unreality (e.g., Josh 10:28, 30, 32, 33, 35, 37, 39).[24] Such texts, especially prominent in the early portions of the Deuteronomistic History (e.g., Dt 2:30–35; 7:2–6; Josh 6:17, 21; 8:24–29; 10:28–40), probably say less about late Bronze and early Iron Age military practices than about the radical call of later, seventh and sixth century, Deuteronomic reformers for the most extreme expression of religious purity.[25] Still, as Susan Niditch suggests, the references to *ḥerem* occur in so many different biblical contexts—poetry, prose; early texts, late texts—that is it hard to imagine that the *ḥerem* sacrifice was not a reality in Iron Age Israel.[26] Beyond the texts that employ some form of the term *ḥerem* itself, there are battle scenes which describe the ceremonial slaughter of enemy captives (e.g.,

Josh 8:29; 10:26; Judg 8:21; 1 Sam 15:32–33), and there are these lines, as noted by Smith, from an old poem embedded in the scroll of Deuteronomy where the speaker is YHWH.[27]

> I will make my arrows drunk with blood
> And my sword will eat flesh,
> The blood of the slain and the captives,
> The chief (*rō'š*) of the long-haired enemy. (Dt 32:42)

The question at hand, however, is to what extent did these mythological narratives from Ugarit, set in the divine realm, mirror social values and serve as charters for martial behavior in a region just north of and in an era just prior to Israel? Did Anat, the "tomboy goddess" in Wall's phrase, who apparently never gave birth to gods, nevertheless have sons; not semidivine hybrids as in Greek heroic tradition but human devotees?[28]

The Sons of Anat

In fact, the personal name "Son of Anat," *bn 'nt,* appears in Ugaritic and Egyptian records dated to the fourteenth through the twelfth centuries.[29] One Ugaritic ritual text concerning a banquet hosted by El for the dead ancestors, an active and potent group in Ugaritic religion, does contain the phrase "soldiers of Anat," *mhr 'nt,* though it is unclear whether these are humans participating in a funerary ritual or deceased heroes summoned from the underworld.[30] The most important evidence linking the mythological character of Anat to warrior culture has emerged not from the literature unearthed by Middle Eastern and Western excavators and linguists, the official faces of archaeology, but from unofficial sources, the antiquities market.[31]

Beginning in 1926 and continuing virtually to this day, a series of inscribed bronze "arrowheads" dated roughly between 1200–1000 B.C.E. have surfaced. Almost fifty are known, only one of which is the product of an excavation; the vast majority have emerged through the network of farmers, goatherds, antiquity dealers, and collectors.[32] Presumably most originated in Lebanon with an important set of five from the vicinity of Bethlehem in Israel.

The inscriptions follow a similar pattern. On one side of the blade is the phrase, "Arrow of So-and-So"; on the reverse, the owner's title (e.g., "Man of So-and-So," "Commander," "the Sidonian") or patronymic ("Son of So-and-So").[33] Though it would be half a millennium before stamped coinage was introduced in the eastern Mediterranean world, the style of representation on the arrowheads, an obverse and reverse with complementary inscriptions, anticipates the two sides of a coin.[34]

An analysis of the names and titles provides clear evidence for warrior groups in the Levant during the early Iron Age, the putative historical horizon of the book of Judges. The names and titles are fitting for warriors. The names include 'abdlabi'at, "Servant of the Lion-Lady" (the latter could be an epithet for either Ishtar or Anat); maharān, "Soldier"; bin ("Son of") Ishtar; and bin ("Son of") Anat. The titles include "Commander" (rb), "Commander of a unit" (rb 'lp), and "Man of So-and-So," i.e., warrior in the service of a certain commander.

Remarkably, several of the names and titles indicate that their owners were related to each other in a social network. Of the forty-three arrowheads analyzed by Robert Deutsch and Michael Heltzer as of 1995, a total of seven belonged to the same two owners; one subset of names of owners and fathers yields evidence for three generations of the same family; in some cases, the titles reveal that some of the owners served the same commanders.[35] Given that the vast amount of realia discovered from the ancient world is anonymous and epiphenomenal, the catalogue of arrowheads stands out for representing the artifacts of a specific subculture: a social group of warriors in early Iron Age Syria, Phoenicia, and Israel, a guild with ties of kinship, whether hereditary (like the biblical slinger clan mentioned in Judges 20, the "Sons of the South," the Benjaminites) or fictive, in the sense that men allied themselves to each other with oaths of fidelity and mutual protection (like, to use another biblical example, David and Jonathan in 1 Sam 18:1–4).[36]

As mentioned above, the phrase "son of Anat" occurs among the names on the arrowheads and we can surmise that this war goddess was among the divine matrons and patrons (along with Ishtar, Baal, and others) of such martial groups. There are three men with the name "Son of Anat" in the collection, and the name *'abdlabi'at,* "servant of the Lioness," an epithet of Anat or another Canaanite goddess, appears on five arrowheads.[37] Beyond the general association of military men with a war goddess, Anat probably had special associations with archers. The same name, *'bd lb't,* appears in a list of archers from Ugarit and one of the central themes of the Ugaritic narrative poem "Aqhat" is the goddess's acquisition of a bow with special powers.[38]

But why did archers in early Iron Age Syria and Palestine incise their names on bronze arrowheads? Did they do so to identify kills, so that archers received their due honors and plunder?[39] Were they used to track placement in competitive archery contests?[40] One problem with proposals for martial or competitive uses of the inscribed arrowheads is their size. Most of the bronze blades are 3 to 4 inches long, double the size of arrowheads (albeit made of iron) from the Iron 2 period, the subject of a recent analysis by Allan Emery.[41] Perhaps, then, they were not arrowheads but the points of light spears.[42] An older proposal by Samuel Iwry that the arrowheads were used for oracular purposes has not received much support.[43] Iwry's suggestion of belomancy, in which arrows with the names of projected victims are cast, is unlikely; surely these names, proudly indicating lineage and rank, belonged to members of the guild rather than to their victims.[44]

A different oracular practice, cleromancy, the casting of lots to determine the divine will, is conceivable. Would soldiers have drawn arrowheads, not straws, to select persons for dangerous assignments? There is evidence for the use of arrows, the whole arrow not just the blade, in divinatory practices.[45] In biblical narratives in which men at war cast lots to select a leader or to assign blame for some misadventure, the process was a long series of binary discriminations akin to the parlor game "Twenty Questions," paring the field from large group to small group to an individual, probably with dice-like objects.[46] On a few occasions in biblical passages about warfare, the question arises, "Who will go first?"[47] Who will initiate combat, who will draw first blood? Special, extra-large, arrowheads, conceivably the emblems of initiates into an archer group, could have served as personal tokens in martial divination rites.

Whatever their function, the evidence of the arrowheads provides a connection between Anat and warrior groups in the early Iron Age. We still do not know how or whether the late Bronze Age myths known from Ugarit, or similar ones, functioned for these or other warriors. Did these archers, or other warriors in areas where Anat was venerated, seek her support, see themselves in her divine image, engage in combat in her name, and take gruesome trophies in imitation of her? Did they imagine their victims to be sacrifices to satisfy Anat, in the same way that Mesha did for Kemosh? We do not know. Still, the analysis of these Syrian myths and Lebanese arrowheads, some of which bear her name and epithet, provides useful background for our analysis of biblical heroic materials.

The best known Son of Anat from the ancient Levant remains the biblical "Shamgar son of Anath," *šamgar ben-ʿănāt*, a legendary warrior mentioned in the Song of Deborah (Judg 5:6) and credited in a peculiar notice with slaying six hundred Philistines with an oxgoad (Judg 3:31).[48] As far as we know, Shamgar son of Anath was the exception among biblical warriors in his affiliation, in name if nothing else, with Anat. The warriors in Joshua, Judges, and Samuel sought guidance from Yhwh, they fought and gleaned trophies from the fields of combat in the name of YHWH, and they killed and incinerated enemies in *herem* sacrifices to YHWH.

David's Heroes

Near the end of what we know as "Second" Samuel but what was for most of its literary existence a single scroll, a set of variegated materials (2 Sam 21–24) interrupts the biographical narrative flow, separating the account of David's final internal crisis, weathering another revolt (2 Sam 20), from the account of the aged king in decline and the machinations of Solomon's succession that begin the next scroll, Kings (1 Kgs 1–2). Other biblical scrolls include, near their end, poems (Gen 49; Dt 33); so does Samuel (2 Sam 22:1–51; 23:1–7). The end of Samuel also includes a pair of stories (2 Sam 21:1–14; 2 Sam 24:1–25) and, the focus of our attention, two separate texts that honor and name heroes, 2 Samuel 21:15–22 and 23:8–39.

The first text, 2 Samuel 21:15–22, recounts three anecdotes about the heroics of certain of "David's servants" (2 Sam 21:15, 22) or "David's men" (2 Sam 21:17). The second, 2 Samuel 23:8–39, contains anecdotes and a long list of the *gibbôrîm*, the heroes or champions, who "belonged to David" (2 Sam 23:8). Apart from this list, David's men are referred to in several places in 1 and 2 Samuel[49] and seem to represent the corps of men, conventionally numbered as six hundred,[50] who came up, the hard way, with David as he moved from an officer in Saul's army to freelancing warlord working both sides of the Israelite-Philistine conflict to king, first over the tribe of Judah and then the tribes from the North.[51] Even after David assumed kingship and leadership over some form of nascent army drawn from the militias of Judahite, Benjaminite, and Ephraimite tribes, there is often a distinction drawn between this larger army and David's *gibbôrîm* (2 Sam 10:7; 20:7), which suggests that they maintained an identity apart from the regular army even after their warlord went legitimate. The men described in the anecdotes and listed in the catalogue of 2 Samuel 23:8–39 represent some elite set of this larger group. McKenzie calls them "David's honor guard."[52]

The list in 2 Samuel 23:8–39 has an uneven texture. Its beginning, vv. 8–23, is very similar to the anecdotes in 2 Samuel 21:15–22, containing brief accounts of solo heroics against beasts or over-sized, over-armed, outfitted opponents. Its ending, vv. 24–39, is a curious list, found in expanded form in 1 Chronicles 11 (see also 1 Chr 27), giving only names and epithets of warriors. Most of the discussion about the date of the list in 2 Samuel 23:8–39 has been finely tuned, whether it, or some direct antecedent, stems from a particular era of David's career.[53] This could place the creation of the list near, if not in, the era of the arrowheads. McCarter notes Elliger's analysis that many of the warriors named early in the list (from Elhanan to Heleb, vv. 24b–29a, NRSV) are from the region of Bethlehem, where—though millennia later—a cache of the arrowheads surfaced.[54] Though it may go too far to suggest, as Benjamin Mazar does, that some of the arrowheads found near Bethlehem actually belonged to David's men listed here, the roster of David's gibbôrîm in 2 Samuel 23 may provide a window into premonarchical Israelite martial groups, comparable to the corpus of epithets on the arrowheads.[55]

There are problems of interpretation with the list. The list appears to be organized by a distinction between "the Three" (2 Sam 23:8–17) and "the Thirty" (2 Sam 23:18–39). The Three, named and credentialed through heroic anecdotes (2 Sam 23:8–12), apparently constitute the most elite circle of David's gibbôrîm. Their exploits are directly followed by a brief account of three anonymous warriors (2 Sam 23:13–17), which appears to represent a wholly independent tradition placed here because it refers to "three" warriors, though there is nothing to suggest they should be identified with "the Three."[56] The second major section of the list, 2 Samuel 23:18–39, concerns "the Thirty," presumably another elite subset of the gibbôrîm, a notch below the Three in the martial pecking order.

This second section continues in the style of the first, naming and anecdotally attesting the heroics of two leaders of the Thirty, Abishai and Benaiah (2 Sam 23:18–23), and then shifting to a roster of mere names and identifying phrases, about lineage or clan, for the remainder (2 Sam 23:24–39).

The first problem with the list is that the numbers do not add up. It is possible to identify thirty separate individual names among the Thirty but it is also possible, in this thicket of names and patronyms (e.g., "son of X") to read as many as thirty-two or more.[57] At the end of the entire list, in a note that seeks to bring numerical and editorial closure but only further confuses matters, a scribe notes that the number of *gibbôrîm* is thirty-seven, even though, if one adds the Three to the anonymous trio of warriors in vv. 13–17 to the Thirty, we are still missing someone.[58] Then there is the question of the correct spelling and interpretation of the terms "three" (*šālōš/šĕlōšâ*) and "thirty" (*šĕlōšîm*). Though these spellings dominate, there is evidence, both in the MT of 2 Samuel 23 and *1* Chronicles *11*, as well as in other versions of this text, for reading *šālîšîm* ("officers") instead of *šĕlōšîm* ("Thirty").[59] Do we have a list of David's "thirty" or of David's "officers"?

The names themselves of the *gibbôrîm* deserve brief mention, though many have various spellings in the versions and parallel texts so that we cannot always be sure of their original spelling. There is *mahray* (2 Sam 23:28b), a shorter version of *maharān*, a name inscribed on one of the arrowheads. There is an entire array of colorful Runyonesque names that invite us to imagine the stories that the Bible did not tell. There are two men named "Donkey," *'ira*, (2 Sam 23:26b; 23:38a). There is a "Blackie," *ṣalmon*, (2 Sam 23:28a); a "Reed[-thin]," *ḥeṣray*, (2 Sam 23:35a); a "Scabby," *gareb* (2 Sam 23:38b); maybe a "Sleepy," *yašen*, (2 Sam 23:32b), though the reading is not secure;[60] and a character whose name means either "Fats," if we accept the MT *ḥeleb* for 2 Samuel 23:29a, or "Mole" if we read it as *ḥeled* (1 Chr 11:30) or *ḥelday* (1 Chr 27:15).[61] The observation about the names which is most salient for this study is that the form of this biblical roster of warriors, consisting of names and epithets, roughly approximates the form of the inscriptions on the arrowheads. In both the list from 2 Samuel and a handful of the arrowheads from Lebanon, the contents are roughly the same though the media are not.

Whatever their precise number, and whether we vocalize the Hebrew consonantal sequence šlšm as "thirty" or "officers," the list certainly has a hierarchical arrangement. Indirectly, the evidence of the arrowheads suggested that warrior groups were hierarchical, with terms such as rb, chief or commander; rb 'lp, commander of a unit; and "man of So-and-so," expressing social stratification and rank, even if such terms were not formal military titles. Issues of hierarchy and rank also emerge in 2 Samuel 23. The entire roster of men "belong to David," lĕdāvid (2 Sam 23:8a), to whom, presumably, they have sworn loyalty. The list itself separates men into two classes: an elite subset (2 Sam 23:8b–12), and a larger corps (2 Sam 23:18–39). However, a broader understanding of these gibbôrîm and any specific martial subculture in early Israel is dependent upon our understanding of their larger host culture.

Military functions in early Israel, like all other aspects of its culture, were kinship based. In the initial section of this chapter, we discussed the textual evidence for Syrian and Lebanese warrior groups whose divine matron was Anat. In this section, we have sketched the archaeological evidence for martial clans, a couple of centuries later, in roughly the same geographic area, and have coordinated this biblical lists of warriors. If the assumption of the existence of warrior groups in the early Iron Age, based on isolated pieces of evidence—epithets in extra-biblical texts, names inscribed on arrowheads—is correct, we must ask whether the biblical materials that purport to describe this period, Judges and Samuel, refer to a similar phenomenon.

TERMS

Let us first briefly analyze four important terms in biblical heroic texts: *gibbôr, gibbôr ḥayil, 'elep,* and *'ănāšîm rêqîm. Gibbôr* (pl. *gibbôrîm*) means something like "hero" or "champion."[62] Etymologically, with its doubled middle consonant, *gibbôr* is an intensive form of *geber,* "man."[63] In this regard, as masculinity squared, *gibbôr* roughly compares to the English compound "he-man."[64]

Gibbôr ḥayil literally means something akin to "warrior (or man) of means," but its second element, *ḥayil,* is difficult to define precisely, ranging from "capable" to "powerful," since *ḥayil* refers to both wealth and strength.[65] Most often translators take the second element as adjectival and render the phrase as "valiant man," "brave warrior," (de Vaux) "hero of might" (Bal); even simply "knight" (Boling).[66] The main question is whether there is an economic element to *ḥayil* since, in 2 Kings 15:20, *gibbôrê ḥayil* refers to landowners subject to royal taxation. If this element is present in usages in Judges and Samuel (Judg 6:12; 11:1; 1 Sam 9:1), it could mark a class of *gibbôrîm* who possessed land and who were firmly entrenched, with concomitant honors and responsibilities, in the traditional kinship networks, with the means to outfit themselves or others, in contrast to the small farmers and artisans who hastily beat plowpoints into swords, mustering into units under a leader.[67] The best known use of *ḥayil* in the Hebrew Bible is in the phrase, "a capable woman," from Proverbs 31:10; in this light, a *gibbôr ḥayil* is best understood as a "capable warrior."

Units of men organized for warfare constituted an *'elep* (e.g., Judg 4:10). Though *'elep* can mean and often means "a thousand," many scholars now adopt George Mendenhall's observation that *'elep* in some contexts refers simply to a military unit.[68] An *'elep* probably had a kinship basis, representing the unit mustered from the village, the *mišpāḥâ.*[69] How large was an *'elep*? Hobbs estimates from nine to fourteen men; McCarter ten to twelve; in either case a far cry from the melée of thousands depicted in most translations, though, to be fair, often "a thousand" must mean "a thousand" ("Saul has slain his thousands, but David his myriads," 1 Sam 18:7) and it is exegesis, not philology, which must wrestle with the issue of realism versus heroic exaggeration.[70] Individuals in an *'elep*, then, frequently would have been related to each other through kinship, not unlike some of the men named on the arrowheads. It is also possible that units could be differentiated by martial specialization—for example, facility with a sling (Judg 20:16; 1 Chr 12:2; cf. 1 Chr 12:9 [12:8 ET])—based on common training and material resources. In the book of Judges alone, clan units bound by kinship and a variety of local customs were mustered by leaders such as Deborah and Barak (Judg 4:10), and Gideon (6:34–35).

There were also men who fell between the cracks of kinship groups. By analogy, groups of men alienated from or alien to traditional structures, outlaws or outlanders, misfits or mercenaries, could bind themselves to each other and to leaders through covenants of mutual protection and loyalty, i.e., through fictive kinship. In Judges, such men are called *'ănāšîm rêqîm*, "men with nothing," "empty men" (Judg 9:4; 11:3; cf. 2 Sam 6:20; 2 Chr 13:7; for a phrase equivalent to "empty men" with respect to David, see 1 Sam 22:2).[71] "Empty men" is not how *'ănāšîm rêqîm* is usually understood; rather these men are "worthless men" (NRSV) or "unprincipled."[72] The question is what it is that "men with nothing" lack.

There are two possibilities, which could be related: kinship affiliation and land. "Empty men" may have lacked sturdy kinship attachments, based on the instances in Judges and Samuel where Abimelech (Judg 9:4), Jephthah (Judg 11:3), and David (1 Sam 22:2) all, for one reason or another, are alienated from society and form gangs or pseudofamilies. Robert Boling translates the phrase as "mercenaries."[73] The other possibility is that empty men lacked land, or, more specifically, a portion of the family estate, the *naḥalâ*. Moore refers to them as "portionless."[74]

A contrast with comparable phrases that employ the adjective "full," *mālē'*, in reference to persons might help us focus our view of "empty men." The tribe of Naphtali is "full" of YHWH's blessing (Dt 33:23); Moses' successor Joshua (Dt 34:9), the gifted Phoenician artisan Hiram (1 Kgs 7:13–14), and an unnamed king of Tyre (Ezek 28:12) are all "full" of wisdom; the blessed man, according to Psalm 127:5, has a quiver "full" of sons. So we might say that "full men" possessed good fortune, wisdom, a trade, high birth or commission, and a large family.

I know of one "empty woman" in the Hebrew Bible, Naomi in the book of Ruth. Naomi, who years before had left her village of Bethlehem in Judah with her husband and two sons, laments her condition when she returns home widowed and childless.

> I was full (*mĕlē'â*) when I walked away [from Bethlehem]
> but YHWH has returned me empty (*rêqām*). (Ruth 1:21)

This empty woman is economically and socially marginal, though in the subsequent story her fortunes will be restored and her identity fulfilled.

What did empty men have? These *worth*-less and un-*principal*-ed men, without a stake, who were not vested in the economy of primogeniture, had each other. Based on the research of Lawrence Stager, McKenzie suggests that the growing population in the highland areas that were home to early Israel increasingly may have created a class of men, often younger sons such as David, without inherited land who either attached themselves to wealthy landowners or to warlords.[75] Abimelech hires a group of empty men in order to kill his cohort of kinship peers and gain the holdings of his *bêt 'āb* (Judg 9:4–5). Jephthah and his empty men, and David

and his, operate both as raiders (Judg 11:3; 1 Sam 27:8) and mercenaries (Judg 11:4–11; 1 Sam 28:1), hiring themselves and their gangs
to local potentates in exchange for territorial holdings, acquiring
their patrimony (which traditional society could or would not grant
them) through brigandage and brutality. The arrowheads that contained the epithet "man of So-and-so" may refer to a similar phenomenon, to members of such gangs of "empty men."[76] Although no
biblical text uses gibbôr ḥayil, the "warrior of means," and 'îš rêq, the
"man with nothing," as contrasting terms, they may be just that.

When juxtaposed, the abstracted list of warriors from the
arrowheads and the information about David's gibbôrîm indirectly
give evidence for social groups of warriors in early Iron Age Syro-
Palestine, at times working as clan militias within the boundaries
of kinship structures, and at times working as empty men outside
of consanguinity. The anecdotes about some of David's heroes in
2 Samuel may name other groups, though scholars disagree about
the meaning of certain terms for the opponents of the Judahite
champions. Notices in 2 Samuel 21:16, 18, and 20 describe the
gigantic opponents of Israelite warriors as the yĕlidê hārāpâ, which
has traditionally been read, as in the NRSV, as "descendants of the
giants," but which many now understand as, in McCarter's phrase,
"the votaries of Rapha," referring to members of a Philistine warrior
group whose group name honors their divine patron.[77] It is possible too that "sons of Ariel" (LXX; MT omits "sons"), the Moabite
opponents of Benaiah in 2 Samuel 23:20, is the epithet for a Transjordanian warrior group whose patron was a warrior or mythological figure, though the definition of "Ariel"—"El's Lion"? "altar
hearth"?—remains elusive.[78] This is as far as the analysis of mere
names and epithets can take us. I now turn to the isolation of literary motifs in the biblical anecdotes about the gibbôrîm and about
other warriors in Judges and Samuel, hoping to shed light both on
the character of these men and on the flavor of Israelite heroic
storytelling.

NOTES

1. For recent answers to this question, see S. McKenzie, *King David*; and B. Halpern, *David's Secret Demons*.

2. The most promising methods for dating biblical texts are those based on a linguistic typology related to the historical evolution of the Hebrew language. The research of Cross and Freedman developed diagnostics for identifying "early" texts through their relationship to late Bronze Age, West Semitic languages (first described in F. M. Cross and D. Freedman, *Studies in Ancient Yahwistic Poetry*; and, more recently, F. Cross, "Toward A History of Hebrew Prosody," pp. 135–47 in *From Epic to Canon*). A. Hurvitz identifies "late" texts on the basis of their relationship to Aramaic (e.g., Hurvitz, "The Date of the Prose-Tale of Job Linguistically Reconsidered."

3. For a survey of the diversity of contemporary methods in biblical interpretation, noting both the limits exposed in and possibilities remaining for historically focused methods, alongside ahistorical approaches, see S. McKenzie and S. Haynes, *To Each Its Own Meaning*.

4. S. McKenzie, *King David*, 44.

5. See 1 Sam 13:19–22. For the Philistine superiority in military organization and technology over early Israel, see L. Stager, "Forging an Identity."

6. S. Niditch has explored the underdog theme in the folklore of the Hebrew Bible in *Underdogs and Tricksters*.

7. For "votaries of Rapha," see P. McCarter, *2 Samuel*, 447–51. Building on the research of F. Willesen ("The Philistine Corps of the Scimitar from Gath"), and C. L'Heureux ("The *yᵉlîdê hārāpā'*—A Cultic Association of Warriors"), McCarter argues that the opponents of the Israelite heroes in 2 Sam 21:15–22 should not be understood in the traditional sense ("descendants of the giants," NRSV) but as members of a Philistine martial group whose patron was Rapha, a divine name or epithet found in Ugaritic texts. See also N. Tidwell ("The Philistine Incursions into the Valley of

Rephaim") who describes the votaries of Rapha as "a guild of warriors, experts in single combat" (p. 204).

8. P. Day, "Why Is Anat a Warrior and Hunter?"; "Anat: Ugarit's 'Mistress of Animals' "; N. Walls, *The Goddess Anat in Ugaritic Myth*.

9. P. Day, "Why Is Anat a Warrior," 145.

10. For Anat's home at Mt. Inbubu, see "The Ba'lu Myth" (trans. D. Pardee), 243, n. 9.

11. M. Smith, "The Baal Cycle."

12. N. Walls, *Goddess Anat*, 54. For a comparison of Anat with the Hindu goddess Kali, see further, pp. 54–61.

13. S. Niditch lists some ancient Near Eastern examples of such victory banquets, as well as biblical allusions to the kind of violent banquet scene depicted in this Ugaritic text, in *War in the Hebrew Bible*, 38–40.

14. Anat's cosmetic was some sort of by-product of murex (M. Smith, "Baal Cycle," 109), the indigo dye ("royal purple") based on a mollusk extract (C. Bier, "Textile Arts in Ancient Western Asia," 1575). In Egypt, a different ointment, *kohl*, served as an eye liner and was often stored in stone and alabaster containers with elaborately carved ivory tops (M. Dayagi-Mendels, "Cosmetics").

15. Ugaritic *kp* here is equivalent to English "hand(s)," in contrast to *yd*, often translated as "hand" but actually, in Semitic languages, "forearm."

16. M. Smith, "Anat's Warfare Cannibalism and the West Semitic Ban," 371, 383.

17. For the Ishtar text, see B. Foster, *Before the Muses*, 1:80.

18. M. Smith, "Anat's Warfare Cannibalism," 379.

19. Moab was the Iron Age kingdom in what is now western Jordan. The biblical account of the Moabite war is in 2 Kgs 3.

20. K. Jackson, "The Language of the Mesha Inscription," 97–98. The martial character of Kemosh may lie behind the Roman name for a town in central Moab: Areopolis, "City of Ares" (G. Mattingly, "Moabite Religion and the Mesha' Inscription," 222).

21. "Ashtar-Kemosh" refers to Ishtar as consort of Kemosh, i.e., "Kemosh's Ashtar" (G. Mattingly, "Moabite Religion," 219–21). The term is functionally equivalent to the expression "Yahweh and his Asherah" from the Kuntillet 'Ajrud inscription; see D. Freedman, "Yahweh of Samaria and His Asherah."

22. A. Dearman, "Historical Reconstruction and the Mesha Inscription," 206.

23. CAT 1.13.

24. For a summary of the issues, see S. Niditch, War in the Hebrew Bible, 28–77.

25. S. Niditch, War in the Hebrew Bible, 56–57. If 2 Kgs 23:19–20 is to be believed, then the Deuteronomic reformers in Jerusalem themselves practiced the herem sacrifice against rival, provincial priests (see also, below, n. 27).

26. S. Niditch, War in the Hebrew Bible, 28–77. M. Smith ("Anat's Warfare Cannibalism," 379) suggests the following pattern for the herem sacrifice, based on the episode with Anat: (1) battle; (2) presentation of captives at a divine palace; and (3) "divine consumption of the captive warriors," i.e., ceremonial slaughter.

27. M. Smith, "Anat's Warfare Cannibalism," 383. See also 2 Kgs 23:20 where King Josiah "sacrifices" ("slaughtered" NRSV), √zbh, i.e., ritually butchers, the priests of shrines from outside Jerusalem.

28. N. Walls, *Goddess Anat*, 218.

29. J. Milik, "An Unpublished Arrow-head with Phoenician Inscription of the 11th–10th Century B.C.," 5; N. Shupak, "New Light on Shamgar ben 'Anath," 518–19; P. Day, "Anat," 37.

30. T. Lewis, "The Rapiuma," 203.

31. N. Silberman's comments about how often the finds made by residents of the region have out-trumped the professional archaeologists is apt. In reference to the Dead Sea Scrolls, Silberman (*The Hidden Scrolls*, 32) writes,

> Over the years the Taamireh had proved far more skillful, thorough, and daring in finding ancient artifacts in the ravines and caves of the Dead Sea region than the Western archaeologists who lived (and still live) with the conceit that their motives are somehow more idealistic and less self-serving than those of the bedouin.

32. J. Milik and F. M. Cross, "Inscribed Arrowheads from the Period of the Judges"; J. Milik, "Unpublished Arrowhead"; F. M. Cross, "Newly Found Inscriptions in Old Canaanite and Early Phoenician Scripts"; R. Deutsch and M. Heltzer, *Forty New Ancient West Semitic Inscriptions*, 11–21; *New Epigraphic Evidence from the Biblical Period*, 11–38; P. McCarter, "Pieces of the Puzzle"; "Over the Transom: Three New Arrowheads."

33. R. Deutsch and M. Heltzer, *New Epigraphic Evidence*, 24–27.

34. For the origins of coins, see J. Betlyon, "Coinage." For the observation of stylistic similarities between the inscribed arrowheads and coins, I am indebted to Marsha White (private communication).

35. R. Deutsch and M. Heltzer, *New Epigraphic Evidence*, 28–31; P. McCarter, "Pieces of the Puzzle," 40.

36. On the use of 'îš, "man," in the arrowhead inscriptions to refer to members of "gangs," see R. Deutsch and M. Heltzer, *New Epigraphic Evidence*, 30. On fictive kinship (kinship-in-law as opposed to kinship-in-blood) in

the account of David and Jonathan, see F. M. Cross, "Kinship and Covenant," in *Epic and Canon*, 8–9.

37. E. Puech, "Lioness."

38. J. Milik and F. M. Cross, "Inscribed Arrowheads," 6; A. Mazar, "The Iron Age I," 300. For English translations of "Aqhat," see S. Parker, *Ugaritic Narrative Poetry*; and M. Coogan, *Stories from Ancient Canaan*, 27–47.

39. P. McCarter, "Pieces of the Puzzle," 41; R. Deutsch and M. Heltzer, *New Epigraphic Evidence*, 36.

40. R. Deutsch and M. Heltzer (*New Epigraphic Evidence*, 36), citing the view of T. C. Mitchell.

41. A. Emery, "Weapons of the Israelite Monarchy." Commenting on the extra-large size of the these Iron ɪ artifacts, Emery (private communication) called them "superarrowheads" and wondered if they served symbolic or ritual purposes.

42. "Darts" according to J. Naveh, *Early History of the Alphabet*, 37.

43. S. Iwry, "New Evidence for Belomancy in Ancient Palestine and Phoenicia."

44. For the practice of belomancy, see Ezek 21:26 (21:21 ET).

45. S. Iwry, "New Evidence"; M. Greenberg, *Ezekiel 21–37*, 428–29.

46. For a summary of biblical lot casting, see J. Sasson, *Jonah*, 188–201. The biblical passages are Josh 7:16–18; 1 Sam 10:19–21; 14:41–42.

47. Judg 1:1–2; 10:18; 13:5; 20:18; 1 Kgs 20:13–14; 1 Chr 11:6. The question is answered through unspecified oracular means in Judg 1:1–2 and 20:18. In Judg 10:17–11:10 (with Jephthah) and 1 Chr 11:6 (with Joab), warriors volunteer to initiate combat in exchange for elevated status.

48. See N. Shupak, "New Light on Shamgar" and F. M. Cross, *Leaves from an Epigrapher's Notebook,* 219.

49. 1 Sam 23:13, 24b; 25:13; 27:2, 8; 28:1; 29:2, 11; 30:1, 3, 9; 2 Sam 2:3, 17, 31; 10:7; 11:11, 16–17, 24; 16:6; 20:6.

50. 1 Sam 23:13; 25:13; 27:2; 30:9; cf. 1 Sam 13:15 where Saul's force numbers "about" six hundred.

51. On David's men and the *gibbôrîm* materials in 2 Sam 21 and 23, see R. de Vaux, *Ancient Israel,* 219–20; B. Mazar, "The Military Elite of King David"; N. Na'aman, "The List of David's Officers (*šālîšîm*)"; D. Schley, "David's Champions."

52. S. McKenzie, *King David,* 143.

53. B. Mazar, "Military Elite," 312; P. McCarter, *2 Samuel,* 501; N. Na'aman, "List of David's Officers," 79; D. Schley, "David's Champions," 51.

54. P. McCarter, *2 Samuel,* 500–501; see his map that identifies each hero with a village (map 9, p. 529).

55. B. Mazar, "Military Elite," 312; 315, n. 4; but see S. McKenzie's dissent (*King David,* 18).

56. P. McCarter, *2 Samuel,* 499.

57. For instance, though P. McCarter (*2 Samuel,* 500) finds thirty names in the original list, by assuming that the names in vv. 36–39 represent a later expansion, D. Schley ("David's Champions," 51) finds a minimum of thirty-two.

58. The most common way interpreters have resolved this problem (e.g., P. McCarter, *2 Samuel,* 499) is to assume that the inclusion of Joab, David's chief of command, was taken for granted, even though he is not named in 2 Sam 23. Joab is named in the Chronicler's version, in 1 Chr 11:6–8.

59. There is increased support for reading "officers" instead of "the Thirty;" see B. Mastin, "Was the šālîš the Third Man in the Chariot?"; N. Na'aman, "List of David's Officers," 71–79; D. Schley, "The šālîšîm"; "David's Champions." The word šālîš ("officer") is etymologically related to the word for "three" and could refer to officers "of the third rank," i.e., those who occupy a place in the military hierarchy after the king and the commander of the army (B. Mastin), or to the origins of this military elite in special three-man commando units (Schley).

60. P. McCarter (2 *Samuel*, 492) retains *yāšēn* among the group but others (e.g., S. Driver, *Notes on the Hebrew Text and Topography of the Books of Samuel*, 371; B. Mazar, "Military Elite," 316) do not.

61. Not only are the names of the warriors colorful, but their epithets are too. B. Halpern (*David's Secret Demons*, 65) notes that one of the *gibbôrîm*, Shamma (2 Sam 23:11, 33), bears the epithet "Hararite," "the mountain man."

62. *HALOT* 1:175.

63. *HALOT* 1:175; H. Kosmala, "גבר *gābhar*."

64. Etymologies can be deceptive, as J. Barr has demonstrated, in elucidating the meaning of a word in context (*The Semantics of Biblical Language*, esp. 107–60). Drawing a distinction between *gibbôr* and *geber* in some contexts can be artificial since "man," i.e., *geber*, can also be used in martial or competitive contexts ("Gird up your loins like a man [*geber*]," Job 40:7). Nevertheless, the distinction was sometimes made in classical Hebrew usage, as is clear from Ps 52 where, as M. Dahood (*Psalms II*, 13) points out, the boastful *gibbôr* (52:3; 52:1 ET) is "cut down to size," to a mere *geber* (52:9; 52:7 ET), by the divine nemesis, Elohim.

Incidentally, basketball fans will recognize a cognate of *gibbôr*: the Arabic word for "giant," *jabbār* (H. Wehr, *Arabic-English Dictionary*, 111.)

65. P. McCarter, *1 Samuel*, 173.

66. R. de Vaux, Ancient Israel, 66; M. Bal, *Death and Dissymmetry*, 22; R. Boling, *Judges*, 196.

67. R. Albertz describes the *gibbôrê ḥayil* of the era of Judges as landowners with implicit or explicit responsibilities to serve in the militia (*A History of Israelite Religion in the Old Testament Period*, 75). C. Gordon considers the *gibbôrê ḥayil* to be landed nobles, who were granted their holdings in exchange for military service (*Before the Bible*, 295) though it is hard to see how an outlaw like Jephthah, a *gibbôr ḥayil* according to Judg 11:1, fits such a category. On the translation "plowpoints," instead of the traditional "plowshares," see P. King, *Amos, Hosea, Micah*, 113.

68. G. Mendenhall, "The Census Lists of Numbers 1 and 26."

69. R. de Vaux, *Ancient Israel*, 216; N. Gottwald, *The Tribes of Yahweh*, 270–76.

70. T. Hobbs, *A Time for War*, 76–79; P. McCarter, *2 Samuel*, 168, 249.

71. "Outlaws" according to R. Albertz, *History of Israelite Religion*, 1:75. In Scottish traditions from the first half of the second millennium C.E., men who lacked affiliation with a clan were known as "broken men," a functional equivalent of the biblical term "empty men." For the "broken men," see G. Fraser, *The Steel Bonnets*, e.g., 395 and the pages listed on 397.

72. *HALOT* 3:1229.

73. R. Boling, *Judges*, 165, 171, 196.

74. G. Moore, *A Critical and Exegetical Commentary on Judges*, 244.

75. L. Stager, "The Archaeology of the Family in Ancient Israel," 25–27; S. McKenzie, *King David*, 59–60.

76. R. Deutsch and M. Heltzer, *New Epigraphic Evidence*, 30.

77. P. McCarter, 2 *Samuel*, 447–51; D. Schley disagrees ("David's Champions," 49).

78. S. Münger, "Ariel"; K. Jackson, "Language of the Mesha Inscription," 112–13.

3

HEROIC

CONVENTIONS

HONORS

What determined status in the martial groups analyzed in the previous chapter? Consider, for instance, this literary refrain in the roster of David's *gibbôrîm*, where of Benaiah it says, "Among the Thirty [officers] he was honored *(nikbād)*."[1] In 2 Samuel 23, two warriors are described with this same phrase: Abishai for slaying three hundred men with a spear; and Benaiah for several feats, including slaying a lion and an Egyptian giant.[2] As we might expect, it seems clear that honor was granted and, subsequently, status determined on the basis of heroic performance. But what constituted heroic performance? In the biblical idiom, how did men gain "a name," *šēm*, a reputation (e.g., 2 Sam 23:18)?

Keeping Score

One measure of heroic performance was the number of kills. In the *gibbôrîm* list, single warriors trade in wholesale slaughter: eight hundred for Josheb-bashebbeth (or according to McCarter "Yesh-baal") (2 Sam 23:8); three hundred for Abishai (v. 18).[3] Similarly grim statistics are tallied throughout Judges and Samuel: Shamgar his six hundred (Judg 3:31); Samson his thirty at Ashkelon, his *'elep* at Lehi, his innumerable victims at Dagon's temple in Gaza (Judg 14:19; 15:15; 16:30); and Jonathan and his armor-bearer their twenty at Michmash (1 Sam 14:14). David's myriad victims, the basis for his great reputation, for his *šēm*, are tallied in several distinct traditions (e.g., 1 Sam 18:27; 2 Sam 8:5, 13). Clearly, status in the martial sub-culture and, furthermore, leadership in the larger community, were based to some extent on this measure, as demonstrated by Saul's anxious statement in 1 Sam 18:8, "They have ascribed to David myr-iads and to me [mere] thousands. What more can he have but the kingdom?"

The inflated numbers in literary accounts based on oral tra-ditions are not the only quantitative measure of heroism. In addi-tion, there are gruesome trophies, veritable scalps: heads, hands, and phalli (Judg 7:25; 8:6; 1 Sam 17:51, 54; 18:27; 2 Sam 3:14; 4:8). In-deed, the image of Anat comes to mind when one reads some of these biblical accounts.[4] The word for the "hands" of the Midianite captains possessed by Gideon is not *yād*, "forearm," but *kap*, just like those dangling from the goddess' belt in the Ugaritic tablet (Judg 8:6).[5] The heads of slain opponents that the Ephraimites brought to Gideon earlier in the same story (Judg 7:25) represent their share of the martial harvest, their "gleaning," though the men of Ephraim complain that their pickings, *'ōlēlôt*, were slim (Judg 8:1–3).[6] Though the specifics of some of these accounts may be, like the numbers of kills, incredible (e.g., the one hundred foreskins David presented to Saul according to 1 Sam 18:27, reading with

LXX; cf. 2 Sam 3:14), there is enough extrabiblical literary evidence of battlefield mutilation and trophy-taking to consider the historicity of the practice credible.[7] Booty, whether weapons and armor for the warriors (1 Sam 17:54), jewelry and finery for their wives (Judg 5:30; cf. Isa 9:2 [9:3 ET]), or icons for their patron and matron deities (1 Sam 4:22–5:1; 2 Sam 5:21), was also harvested from fields of battle.

Killing an Elite Adversary

The *gibbôrîm* list contains a single example of this, the note that Benaiah, among other feats, slew "an Egyptian man who was of [notable] appearance" (2 Sam 23:21). In the Chronicler's version, his opponent's description is more specific: "an Egyptian man of [some] stature, five cubits" (seven feet three inches?) (1 Chr 11:23). An Egyptian text from the thirteenth century B.C.E. offers this motif from the other perspective, warning its audience about gigantic Canaanites, "four or five cubits (from) their noses to the heel."[8] In other texts in Judges and Samuel, defeating a beast (Judg 14:5–6; 1 Sam 17:36; 2 Sam 23:20) or an opponent with monstrous proportions, such as the votaries of Rapha (2 Sam 21:16–22)—some of whom, measured by their extra large armature, must have been gigantic; one was a polydactyl—or Goliath (1 Samuel 17), is also worthy of special note. Killing an enemy leader, as when the Kenite woman Jael slew the Canaanite warlord Sisera in her tent, brings "honor" (*tip'eret*; Judg 4:9). Indeed, battle descriptions in Joshua, Judges, and Samuel often devote special attention to this secondary stage, the pursuit, capture, and ritual execution (Keegan, "ceremonial slaughter") of enemy leaders (Josh 8:29; 10:26; Judg 8:21; 1 Sam 17:54; 1 Sam 31:8–10).[9]

The opposite case—the shame of falling to an inferior—is also a feature of many narratives and probably reflects early Iron Age martial culture. Though the narrative in Judges 4 does not emphasize the shamefulness of Sisera's falling to a woman, it does emphasize that the Israelite warlord, Barak, Sisera's opposite, lost face too.

Jael actually bests two men in the story: from Sisera, she steals life, from Barak, martial honors (Judg 4:9).[10] Abimelech's death at the hands of the anonymous woman of Thebez, who dropped a stone from a tower (Judg 9:53–54), became a proverbial symbol of disgrace (2 Sam 11:21).

Often this dynamic is expressed through the contrast between a *gibbôr*, in this context an experienced warrior, and a *na'ar*, which can mean many things—"boy," "servant," "assistant," "infantryman"— but in every case is less than a *gibbôr*.[11] To the superior party, a veteran warrior, there was no glory in fighting below his station. Goliath disdains the *na'ar*, David, who emerges from the Israelite camp to face him (1 Sam 17:42). When Asahel, the baby brother of David's warlord Joab, shadows Abner, provoking him to fight, Saul's warlord initially refuses, resisting the idea of engaging a junior, and urges his too eager rival to "seize one of the *nĕ'ārîm*," an opponent from Asahel's own weight class (2 Sam 2:21). To the inferior party, the young warrior, combat offered opportunities for advancement, to win a name like David did against Goliath in 1 Samuel 17. Outside of combat, however, a *na'ar* might shrink from violating codes of station, as if these masculine codes transcended ethnic allegiance. Gideon offers his son Yether the honor of ceremonially slaughtering the Midianite princes Zebah and Zalmunna, satisfying a blood feud. But Yether balks: "[H]e was afraid since he was still a *na'ar*."[12] Even his Midianite victims urge Gideon, the *gibbôr ḥayil* (Judg 6:12), their peer, to finish them (Judg 8:21).

Fighting Solo

The anecdotes in the *gibbôrîm* list place individual performance in the foreground. Two in particular, regarding Eleazar (2 Sam 23:9–10) and Benaiah (2 Sam 23:20–23), add something else: individual heroism contrasted with group cowardice. The Israelites withdraw, leaving Eleazar alone against a mass of Philistines, but he "stood firm," *qām*, fighting until "his hand grew weary and stuck to his sword."[13] The larger force returns after the work is done, merely to plunder. Benaiah prevails under similar circumstances: the larger army flees before the Philistines but the *gibbôr* digs in—literally, takes a stand, *yityaṣṣēb*—and defeats the enemy single-handedly. Both of these encounters are described with the same phrase: *tĕšû'â gĕdōlâ*, "a great victory" (2 Sam 23:10, 12).

This narrative isolation of a *gibbôr* from the group is a telling arrangement, especially when it is juxtaposed with accounts of duels, whether between singles or twelves; all of these scenes freeze the chaotic flow of combat into single frames. The question is, to what degree does this reflect martial practice and to what degree does this reflect narrative convention?

Judges and Samuel recount other great victories. Samson boasts of his *tĕšû'â gĕdōlâ* when, after three clan militia units from Judah had surrendered him to a Philistine raiding party, he slew the "foreskinneds" by himself (Judg 15:9–18). Jonathan is credited with "the great victory," *haššû'â haggĕdōlâ*, for, aided by his squire, routing a Philistine garrison while the main Israelite force remained at their camp (1 Sam 14:45). Jonathan later refers to David's defeat of Goliath—in which David's solo heroics emerge in the wake of his comrades' cowardice (1 Sam 17:24)—as a *tĕšû'â gĕdōlâ* (1 Sam 19:5). In all the above accounts, both the hero's courage and his comrades' cowardice are emphasized; furthermore, whether cast as one-on-one duels, such as David versus Goliath, or individual triumphs against hosts, they profile "cameo" portraits, in Niditch's term, of solo heroics.[14]

Were duels, such as between David and Goliath, an element of Iron Age warfare in Syro-Palestine? The evidence cited in favor of the practice of duels (Yadin) or single combat (de Vaux) or the contest of champions (Hoffner) has been sketched by an earlier generation of scholars.[15] De Vaux's analysis of 1 Samuel 17 delineates the structure of such duels: the arrangement of rival forces; the issue of a challenge by one side (Goliath: "Select your man," 1 Sam 17:8); the mutual taunts (ḥărāpôt, 1 Sam 17:43–47; cf. 17:10, 25, 26) as each combatant warms up to the challenge; and, finally, the contest.[16] One of the combatants in this scene, Goliath, is referred to by a rare term, 'îš habbênayim, literally "the man in between," which de Vaux contends refers precisely to men who enter such arenas.[17]

An Egyptian text from a millennium before the narrative horizon of 1 Samuel 17, "Sinuhe," depicts a similar contest somewhere in Syria.[18] Sinuhe, an Egyptian courtier who had fled his homeland, fearing for his life after a change in administration, wrote of his odyssey through greater Syria. The result—part travelogue, part an account of Life among the Savage Tribes of Syria—included an episode in which "a hero of Retenu," somewhere in highland Syro-Palestine, issued a challenge to him. The next morning, the tribes of Retenu and of Sinuhe's Syrian hosts assembled—"every heart burned for me, the women jabbered"—to witness the spectacle in which Egyptian urban prejudices both about the savagery of the "Asiatics" and the superiority of a "Delta-man" were confirmed.[19] A small but perhaps crucial detail of Sinuhe's victory is that, after felling his opponent, the Delta-man used the Asiatic's own weapon, an ax, to finish him.[20] David too, in 1 Samuel 17, used the Philistine's own sword to finish his rival (1 Sam 17:51). Harry Hoffner adduces evidence of a Hittite contest of champions from the fourteenth century B.C.E. in which King Ḥattušiliš III, claims, as Hoffner understands it, to have personally slain a rival champion, in the name of his matron, Ishtar.[21]

Homeric scenes are often cited as evidence for the practice of single combat in the ancient eastern Mediterranean and Levant, such as, in Robert Fagles' translation, Paris "str[i]d[ing] forth, challenging all the Argive best / to fight him face-to-face in mortal combat," and sparring with Menelaus (Iliad 3: 21–22); or Hector's challenge, "[L]et one whose nerve impels him to fight with me / come striding from your lines, a lone champion / pitted against Prince Hector," a challenge taken up by Ajax (Iliad 7: 86–88).[22] The victor in these contests ceremoniously strips the gear from his victim and donates it to a temple (*Iliad* 7: 96–97), just as David takes the Philistine's sword, apparently, to the shrine at Nob (1 Sam 22:10).

The contest of the Twelves in 2 Sam 2:12–17 recounts what Kyle McCarter calls a "gladiatorial" competition between twelve *něʿārîm* from the house of Saul and twelve from the house of David.[23] McCarter cites other examples of this phenomenon of "battle by representative" and, following Yigael Yadin, refers to an almost contemporaneous Mesopotamian stone relief (tenth century B.C.E.) which could have been commissioned by the narrator of 2 Sam 2:16: "Each grabbed his opponent by the head, his sword in the side of his opponent."[24] In this passage there is a special use of the verb *śḥq*, "to play," which probably (in the *piʿel* form) refers to "representative fighting" or dueling.[25] Abner, Saul's warlord, issues the challenge to Joab, David's warlord, "Let the *něʿārîm* rise and play (*yiśaḥăqû*) before us" (2 Sam 2:14). The verb has the same meaning in the final scene of the Samson story (Judg 16:25).[26] One can imagine there, as in the tale of Sinuhe, every Philistine heart burning, men and women jabbering before the spectacle, a kind of Iron Age prize fight, as Samson "plays" in Dagon's Temple.[27]

This small but precise body of evidence from biblical and extrabiblical sources suggests that dueling, whether by designated individuals or by groups, was part of Iron Age martial culture. We might even wonder if less deadly competitions were, on a fraternal level, an aspect of the training of a *naʿar*. Beyond these speculations, there is the clear ethos of martial culture among Israel's Mesopotamian neighbors, where warfare is "the festival of men at arms," which suggests that the biblical sense of *śḥq* as gladiatorial "play," rests on a deeper ancient Near Eastern foundation of idioms for war as manly sport.[28]

To summarize: the biblical accounts of individual performance suggest that this was a prominent component of warrior groups. The *gibbôr* most distinguished himself by accomplishing (with YHWH's aid) the "great victory" through solo combat, whether in a ritualized duel or solitary encounter with an enemy. To a great extent, this must have been true since, in the end, as the military historian John Keegan notes, "all infantry actions, even those fought in the closest of close order, are not, in the last resort, combats of mass against mass, but the sum of many combats of individuals."[29]

Having said that, however, the clear tendency of biblical heroic narrative (or Homeric, for that matter), best seen in the examples where group combat is portrayed as a mere background for individual heroism, is to isolate the *gibbôr* against the single opponent or an entire *'elep,* and must be a mixture of artistry and history. Like gunfights in cowboy movies, the depiction of the solo combatant was surely a far more prominent narrative convention than historical occurrence. How else could prose narrative, just emerging from and still largely limited to the conventions of oral narrative— as in Olrik's observation of how northern European oral tales prefer scenes with two and only two characters—render the chaotic melée of Iron Age warfare except as a series of one-on-one, or one-against-a-group encounters?[30]

By contrast, in ancient Oriental art, and I am thinking here especially of Egyptian and Assyrian reliefs of battle scenes, the canvas was broad enough to capture, albeit with its own conventions, a more representative display.[31] Biblical heroic narratives, in artistic terms, then, provide something more like the cameos on cylinder seals than the birds-eye-views on palace wall reliefs.[32] Still, the focus on individual heroics in battle accounts did not simply result from the limitations of ancient narrative media. It is far more effective dramatically to personalize the story; even contemporary cinema, with its wide canvas, invariably tracks the fortunes of a single soldier or unit.

INFERIOR WEAPONS

In Judges and 1 Samuel, the relative inferiority of the weapons of the biblical heroes is emphasized. Shamgar ben Anat is lauded for killing six hundred Philistines with a *malmad habbāqār,* probably a wooden pole with a nail on the end, a cattle prod (Judg 3:31).[33] In the prose version of the battle in the Jezreel Valley, the militia units of Naphtali and Zebulun, inspired in a sacred grove by the prophet Deborah and led on the field by the warrior Barak, must contend against Canaanite infantry and, as constantly underlined through repetition, a huge chariot corps (Judg 4:3, 7, 13, 15, 16). Both the prose and poetic versions of this battle reach their climax when Jael, a Kenite woman in league with the Israelite clans, dispatches the Canaanite general Sisera with a hammer and tent peg (Judg 4:21; 5:26).[34] A line from the Song of Deborah, composed and preserved through performance at pilgrimage festivals, proudly encapsulates this popular motif through a rhetorical question:

[Was] shield (*māgēn*) or spear (*rōmaḥ*) to be seen among the forty *'elep* in Israel? (Judg 5:8)

In another example, Gideon leads a select group of clansmen from Abiezer, Manasseh, Asher, Zebulun, and Naphtali, armed with torches and rams' horns, against an encamped army of Midianites (Judg 7:16). Samson, always the rawest, does not even bother with fashioning a tool at all: he kills an *'elep* of Philistines with the jawbone of an ass (Judg 15:15–16). In the account of the Battle of Michmash (1 Samuel 13–14), the Philistine advantage in numbers and technology, emphasized through exaggeration, is introduced in terms similar to those from the Israelite-Canaanite battle in Judges 4, only with worse odds: Saul's six hundred contends against a chariot corps of thirty thousand (thirty *'elep*), a cavalry unit of six thousand (six *'elep*), and innumerable—"like the sand on the seashore"—infantry (1 Sam 13:5). Meanwhile, "neither sword nor spear could be found" among the Israelite foot soldiers; only Saul and Jonathan were outfitted properly (1 Sam 13:22).

Idiomatically enshrined through the centuries in a number of expressions for the idea of the underdog, this motif is best seen in David versus Goliath. The story in 1 Samuel 17 is a composite of two versions, but the motif of primitive weapons is in both, so it is unnecessary to analyze them separately here.[35] The description of the Philistine champion mixes the precision of a military history with the exaggeration of a tall tale, and its texture and spirit are captured in McCarter's translation, where sober indicative, aiming for verisimilitude, is undone by wide eyed parenthetical interjection.

> And there marched forth from the ranks of the Philistines a certain infantryman from Gath whose name was Goliath. (His height was four cubits and a span!) A helmet was upon his head, and he was dressed in a plated cuirass. (The weight of the cuirass was five thousand bronze shekels!) Bronze greaves were upon his shins, and a bronze scimitar was slung between his shoulder blades. The shaft of his spear was like a weavers' heddle rod. (Its blade weighed six hundred iron shekels!) (1 Sam 17:4–7)[36]

Though the arms and the man are inseparable, this story emphasizes the combatants' contrast in weapons more than their contrast in size or experience. Goliath looms over David: if one follows the received Hebrew text, the Philistine was about nine feet five inches; according to the Greek and Qumranic text tradition, a disappointing, in modern terms, six feet seven inches.[37] Goliath's experience in battle (Saul warns David, "He has been a man of war from his youth") is contrasted with David's inexperience (1 Sam 17:33). But the contrast in weapons, not size, is the main emphasis. Saul outfits David with the warlord's own bronze helmet, armor (in most manuscripts), and sword (1 Sam 17:38–39). All of this, however, weighs David down, and so "armed with" (běyad) only his shepherd's crook, five stones from what is now called the Wadi-es-Sant, and a sling, David answers the challenge (1 Sam 17:40). The contrast in forms of weaponry is then summarized in the combatants' mutual taunts (1 Sam 17:43, 45):

> The Philistine said to David, "Am I a dog that **you come toward me** with sticks?" . . . David said to the Philistine, **"You come toward me** with sword and spear and mace (kidôn),[38] but **I come toward you** in the name of YHWH Ṣĕbā'ôt, god of the ranks of Israel."

Indeed, as illustrated throughout Judges and 1 Samuel, and in terms that have close enough analogues in other texts to suggest that it was a cliché (Judg 5:8; 1 Sam 13:22; cf. a similar idea in 2 Kgs 6:15–17, 22), "YHWH," David boasts to Goliath before felling him with a stone to the forehead, "does not bring victory through sword and spear" (1 Sam 17:47). Again, once Goliath is down, the narrator cannot resist reminding us of this: "David overpowered the Philistine with a sling and a stone. . . . There was no sword in David's hand" (1 Sam 17:50).

It is not, however, that a ḥereb or ḥănît could not be useful. Poetic justice could be rendered to those who lived by the ḥereb and honor could be gained by finishing an opponent with his own weapon. David decapitates the Philistine with his own sword (1 Sam 17:51). Benaiah, one of David's elite gibbôrîm, possesses a šebet, a wooden standard or staff which could be pointed, when he squares off against an Egyptian "armed with" (běyad) a spear, ḥănît (2 Sam 23:21), but Benaiah wrests the superior weapon from his rival and kills him with it.[39]

Agricultural implements, domestic tools, ritual paraphernalia, wadi stones: the biblical heroes in Judges and Samuel are portrayed as artisans and pastoralists who, at best, beat plowpoints into swords, jerry-rigging victory against outfitted, diversified armies through a mixture of divine favor, tactical ingenuity, and resourcefulness. This emphasis on the inferior weaponry of the Israelites—"Were spear or shield to be seen among forty *ʾălāpîm* in Israel?"—might well be based in economic reality; certainly, it was a point of special emphasis, a narrative plea for underdog status and a theological declaration of divine support.

INSPIRATION

Among the elements of the war oracle, the speech offered by religious intermediaries to men entering combat, was an assurance of divine presence: "Yнwн is with you."[40] There were benefits to having this God on one's side.

> One man among you puts to flight an *ʾ[e]lep* because Yнwн your God fights for you. (Josh 23:10)

From comparative and biblical sources, it is clear that the benefits included the intervention of the deity, whether through natural forces, personified intermediaries (demonic or angelic, according to one's perspective) such as the Destroyer (*Mašḥît*),[41] Anger (*Qeṣep*),[42] Stinger (?) (*Qeṭeb*),[43] and Pestilence (*Rešep*),[44] or through the shadowy but often invoked cosmic military unit, the *ṣĕbā'ôt*.[45] But there was something more. Yнwн also inspired heroic, even superhuman, performance in Israel's warriors.

"With my God I can leap a wall."[46] With Yнwн, Caleb drives out the gigantic Anakim (Josh 14:12–15). With Yнwн, David slays a Philistine giant, initiating the flight of an entire army (1 Sam 17:37, 48–50), and, later, along with comrades, kills one hundred Philistines (1 Sam 18:14, 27).[47] Though attributions of success to divine support in any endeavor are universal and, by themselves, unremarkable, there are hints in Judges and Samuel of a more specific idea of "heroic inspiration," expressed in the idiom of "the breath of YHWH."[48]

The breath of YHWH is "upon" Othniel and Jephthah (Judg 3:10; 11:29). The breath of YHWH "clothes [itself with]," √lbš, Gideon (Judg 6:34).[49] The breath of YHWH impels (Judg 13:25) and (in three instances) "rushes over" Samson (Judg 14:6, 19; 15:14), and, elsewhere, Saul (1 Sam 10:10; 11:6) and David (1 Sam 16:13). Rainer Albertz understands these references in Judges and Samuel as descriptions of the "charismatic capacity" of certain leaders "to overcome the notorious group egoisms and convince several tribes of the necessity and possibility of joint military action."[50] But this explanation does not do justice to the usage in the Samson narrative, where the breath of YHWH rushes over him as the prelude to heroic feats: ripping a lion apart barehanded (Judg 14:6), killing thirty men (Judg 14:19), and, later, snapping ropes from his arms and using the jawbone of an ass to kill a Philistine 'elep (Judg 15:14–15). Here we have something closer to what Max Weber described, in florid terms, as "an acute demonic-superhuman power of varying, most frequently frightful, character."[51] In simpler terms, certainly for Samson, the rushing of the breath of YHWH represents the ancient Israelite idiom for divinely inspired martial fury.[52]

This is a common idea in heroic literature. Terms for battle fury in cultures of the ancient eastern Mediterranean include, in Homeric epic, lussa (Bruce Lincoln, "wolfish rage"); in Mesopotamian literature, labābu, "to rage" (often in comparison to a lion, labbu).[53] War deities often inspired these lupine or leonine performances. In the Assyrian Tukulti-Ninurta epic, Ishtar, goddess of war, cracks a jump rope, inspiring a berserk rage in warriors.[54] In Greek religion, Athena was thought to both excite the forces she favored and spread panic among those she did not.[55]

Another example of this kind of martial inspiration is, in Celtic tradition, the ríastarthae, the battle fury or, as Thomas Kinsella puts it, "warp-spasm," of the Ulster hero Cú Chulainn.[56] I cite this distant example because of a coincidence of imagery, namely that Cú Chulainn's martial rage causes him to heat up. In one story, the enraged warrior becomes civilized, literally cools down, only after being forcibly plunged successively in three tubs of water.[57] When the breath of YHWH rushes ($\sqrt{slḥ}$) over Samson (Judg 14:19) and Saul (1 Sam 11:6), they also literally heat up, that is, become angry. The normal idiom for anger in biblical Hebrew, *ḥārâ 'ap*, to have one's "nose become hot," involves the idea of heat which argues against reading the phrase literally. Still, with Samson, the narrator, at the least, plays on this image in Judg 15:14 for there, after the divine breath overcomes Samson, the Philistine rope restraints "melt from his hands," as if the inspired hero is actually on fire.

Again, we must consider the realism of this motif of heroic inspiration. I am discussing it as if it were only an idiom of the heroic dialect, but it can also be seen as a colorful expression for the super- or subhuman aggressiveness exhibited in and necessary for success in close combat. Against a background of comparative data—such as the rope with which Ishtar beat Assyrian warriors into a frenzy; or the panic Pan inspired in the Athenian's opponents—it appears, if we may abstract, that YHWH breathed on the Israelite *gibbôr*, inspiring superhuman performance and, as seen next, "threw" panic into the enemy *gibbôr*—a winning combination.

PANIC

"Panic" is a Greek word that described "a sudden, unforseeable fear" that Pan, patron first of shepherds, then of sentries, eventually of soldiers, inspired in the foes of his worshipers.[58] In Israelite tradition, YHWH, the divine *gibbôr* (Ex 15:3) and patron of Israel's *gibbôrîm*, was credited with confusing Israel's enemies (e.g., Josh 10:10; Judg 4:15; 1 Sam 7:10).[59] This too is a common motif in ancient literature. In Egypt, Seth was called the "Lord of Confusion"; in Babylon, as seen in the rhetorical overkill of the epilogue to Hammurapi's Code, Inanna (a.k.a., Ishtar), "the lady of battle and conflict," is invoked to "create confusion," not only for enemies in battle but even for civic scofflaws.[60]

In battle descriptions in Joshua, Judges, and Samuel, the decisive moment of an encounter, when one side or the other "fled" or "turned its back" (Josh 7:8), is described in terms functionally equivalent to panic.[61] The verb *hāmam*, "to confuse," describes acts of God, meteorological and mythological, when Yhwh fights on behalf of Israel, utilizing the sort of weapons at the disposal of a West Semitic storm deity: hail (Josh 10:10–11), thunder (1 Sam 7:10), and, probably, a sudden cloudburst (Judg 4:15; cf. Judg 5:4, 20–21).[62] Surprise attacks also cause "confusion," *mĕhûmâ* (√hmm) that can lead an army to turn on itself (1 Sam 14:20; cf. Judg 7:22 where the same phenomenon is described without *mĕhûmâ*). A plague, literally "a stroke [of the hand]" delivered by Yhwh, also causes "deadly confusion" (1 Sam 5:9, 11).[63] This panic can also be expressed by forms of √hrd, whether *hārad*, "to tremble," *hehĕrîd*, "to startle," or the adjective *haradâ*, "trembling," usually caused by surprise attack (Judg 8:12; 1 Sam 14:1–15). On at least one occasion, however, the text implies that divine craft augments human craftiness by the agency of a geological tremor (1 Sam 14:15).

The speech of the royal adviser Ahithophel to the rebel prince Absalom (2 Sam 16:20–17:23) describes the conditions that leave a group of men susceptible to panic: alighting on them suddenly when they are "fatigued" and have, literally, "slack hands," *rĕpēh yādayim*, i.e., they have "let go," or "lost [their] grip" (2 Sam 17:2; cf. 2 Sam 4:1).[64] Panic and flight can also arise from the appearance of an overwhelming force (1 Sam 13:5–7) and, on several occasions, the capture of, mortal injury to, or death of a leader (e.g., 1 Sam 31:7; 2 Sam 4:1; 10:18).

Consistently, then, in battle descriptions there is a moment of truth, described in terms of panic, leading to retreat and rout, expressed in idioms for fear, the latter often involving the heart, *lēb*. Panicked men feel their hearts "fall" (1 Sam 17:32) or liquefy (Josh 5:1; 7:5). The idiom can be turned around for, despite the unmanly shame of flight, proverbially expressed in 2 Sam 19:4 (19:3 ET), there are times when it is the better part of valor to flee. To obstinately, quixotically persist in the face of grave loss is evidence that one's heart, instead of melting, had been hardened, perhaps even supernaturally (Josh 11:20; cf. "the hardening" of Pharaoh's "heart" in Ex 4:21; 7:3; etc.). In the previous section of this chapter, the benefits of a warrior receiving a dose of the deity's "breath," *rûaḥ*, were delineated; its converse, an idiom for martial paralysis, is to have "no breath," no spirit, left (Josh 5:1). Another term for panic, √*bhl* (Judg 20:41; 2 Sam 4:1), may convey this same idea: the passive verb *nibhal*, "to be horrified," can also be understood as meaning "to be breathless."[65]

Battles described in Joshua, Judges, and Samuel often contain two parts: a primary engagement in which one opposing force induces the "flight" (Hebrew √*nûs*) of the other, followed by "pursuit" (√*rādāp* or √*dābāq*), and a secondary engagement in which advantages are pressed, trophies taken, and martial honors gained (e.g., Josh 8:21–29; 10:26; Judg 8:16–27; 1 Sam 17:51b–54; 1 Sam 31:7–10). The sense of battlefield panic, the moment in which engagement gives way to flight and pursuit, is far from literary convention, though the sequence of engagement, panic, flight, and plunder did provide biblical and other ancient narrators with a set of generalizations capable of moving accounts along. Often the panic refers to what is now called "friendly fire," when front lines retreated and armies fell on themselves.[66] The significance of this turning point in ancient battle accounts is encased in the Greek ancestor of the English word "trophy." The precise site of the turning point of a battle was memorialized on Greek battlefields by draping an article taken from or discarded by an enemy on a tree limb or post, and this battlefield marker was called a "trophy," from *tropaion*, "turning [point]."[67]

COURAGE

Martial profit or loss, then, is expressed in the currency of fear. Which side, which combatant, will panic, flee, lose heart? There was much for fighting men to fear. Loss meant, for the warrior, painful injury, torture, enslavement, humiliation; for his kin, rape, enslavement, economic devastation, alienation from home and field; for the community, the plunder and devastation of agricultural land, the loss and exhibition of sacred artifacts, and the larger truth all this implied: divine abandonment. Death too was surely feared but worse was an end that left the corpse severed—corporeally, communally—from a good death in ritual terms, corpse intact, family reunited in the earth.[68]

The opposite of fear is courage and this supreme martial virtue is conveyed with its own set of idioms, often strung together in the war oracle issued by intermediaries—military or religious leaders—to warriors. The formulas can be cast negatively: "Do not fear, '*al tîrā*'; "do not be terrified," '*al taʿărōṣ*; "do not be panicked," '*al tēḥat*. Positively, war oracles could include the exhortations "be strong," whether with forms of √*ḥzq* (literally, "be firm, hard") or √'*mṣ*. All war oracles were based on the speaker's assurance of divine presence, "YHWH is with you."[69]

A similar exhortation, rare in extant war oracles themselves (Ex 14:13) but belonging to the same stock of idioms, is *hityaṣṣēb*; in these contexts, "to take a stand," "to dig in." To assume a position and hold it in the face of an opponent is the supreme test of the mettle of a *gibbôr*, like Shammah in 2 Sam 23:12, or of a *geber*, like Job in Job 38:3 and 40:7. This is the opposite of panicked flight, clearly demonstrated in contexts where these alternatives are contrasted (Dt 7:23–24; 11:25; 2 Sam 23:11–12).

So far we mainly have discussed these matters on a literary level and have said little about the degree to which these narrative conventions relate to the practice of ancient Oriental warfare. The preponderance of the motif of "flight," however, is consistent with the analysis of the contemporary British military historian John Keegan. According to Keegan, it was only in the fifth century B.C.E., among the Greeks, that the "primitive" style of warfare, based on "evasion, delay, and indirectness," on fleeing to fight again another day, gave way to "the practice of face-to-face battle to the death" between massed armies.[70] In this light, these conventional, shorthand descriptions of flight are accurate reflections of the turning point of the battles from the Iron Age Levant.

We have observed that biblical accounts of combat—between tribal militias and warrior bands in Judges, and between the rudely formed armies of nascent Iron Age states and members of elite martial groups in Samuel—greatly exaggerate the casualties and decisiveness of victory. Ritual honor—the capture of sacred trophies, the mutilation and/or execution of enemy elite—often brought satisfaction enough. At the same time, resting uneasily next to our skepticism about the incredibility of biblical battle accounts is the credibility, the psychological verisimilitude, of biblical descriptions of panic. Keegan may be correct that the employment of lines of infantry, controlled by a culture of military discipline, advancing in waves in the style of the Greek phalanx, was unknown in Iron Age Israel, Jordan, Syria, and Philistia. Nevertheless, even if battles were not waged to the death by entire armies, the volleys of light spears, stones, and arrows eventually had to give way to close fighting. Biblical battles were characterized by "deadly clashes of infantry armed with spear, shield and sword."[71]

To win a battle, one line had to force the other to turn at the flank, or to break in the middle, but to do either of these they could not depend on the firepower of sling or bow indefinitely, the lines had to meet.[72]

Then followed the panic, as imagined by the biblical scholar T. R. Hobbs:

> Once the line broke, with men falling back or being killed, the message would be quickly relayed down the line, and only the most resolute would dare stay and continue the fight.[73]

"The most resolute" are those whose actions embodied the exhortations of the war oracle: they overcame their fear and neither panicked nor trembled; they took their stand. Or, if they fled, they engaged again the next day, fortified by ritual, by the war oracle. In Judges 20, after the Israelite tribal coalition had suffered grave losses against the Benjaminite warriors at Gibeah, they "wept before YHWH until evening, and they inquired of YHWH" (Judg 20:23). The means by which the oracle spoke is unstated (prophecy? the manipulation of an oracular device?) but its effect is not: "The Israelites took courage [i.e., 'felt strengthened,' yithazzēq] and reformed the[ir] battle line" (Judg 20:22). When, in a different story, the "mighty shout" or war cry of the Israelites causes fear among the Philistines at Aphek, the narrator reconstructs the Philistine's own war oracle: "Take courage (hithazzĕqû) and be men, O Philistines . . . fight like men" (1 Sam 4:9). Fortified by their own ritual war oracle, the Philistines fight and cause the Israelites to flee (1 Sam 4:10).

The war oracle articulates the ideals of a heroic culture, emphasizing courage in individual combat, and is best captured in scenes of solo combat. The proving grounds for these martial virtues were ritualized duels and the violent scrum of close combat. The elements of the biblical war oracle, originating in the camps and sacred sites of the *gibbôrîm*, have been reused throughout the Bible and in Jewish and Christian history as encouragement for noble and base endeavors. "Do not fear," "Yhwh is with you," "Be strong," "Do not panic": however combined, these phrases were variations on a single theme, epitomizing the virtues of the *gibbôrîm*, and describing the basis for martial success or failure. In the moment of truth, do not flee.

Here and there, biblical texts suggest that much warfare was of a different sort. What was the nature of these so-called "battles" waged by rival groups of *gibbôrîm* in early Iron Age Syro-Palestine? Beyond the ritualized contests, a form of limited warfare according to Keegan, and blood feuds and border wars and sieges, there were, according to N. L. Tidwell, who has paid special attention to details of time and place, raids where bands of men sabotaged or plundered the agricultural resources of rivals.[74] You can hear this in the temporal clauses in these accounts: "Whenever the Israelites put in seed, the Midianites and Amalekites would come up" (Judg 6:3); "at the time of the wheat harvest," Samson descends on Timnah (Judg 15:1); at the threshing floor (1 Sam 23:1) or lentil field (2 Sam 23:11), Philistines "raided," from the root √*nṭš*.[75] In battles against towns, the most prized objects of the martial harvest were sacred objects, as rivals looted each other's shrines and temples, a violent version of collegiate fraternity pranks. The Philistines, for instance, steal the Ark of the Covenant from the Israelites in 1 Samuel 4–7; David and his men return the favor, capturing Philistine sacred objects, in 2 Samuel 5:21.[76] It is no wonder that dueling and "great victories" inspired more anecdotes than the looting, agricultural mayhem, and malicious pranksterism of raiding, but the latter may have been the more common practice for the militias, armies, and gangs of early Israel and Philistia.

Against this backdrop of culture and convention, of grim realities and romantic idealizations, we now turn to hear the individual stories of the *gibbôrîm*.

NOTES

1. 2 Sam 23:23. I refer to this line as a refrain because it can be reconstructed earlier in the list (with Abishai, in 2 Sam 23:19, based on the Syriac version); see P. McCarter, 2 *Samuel*, 491.

2. Assuming with P. McCarter (2 *Samuel*, 491) that some text similar to the Chronicler's version ("a man of [great] stature," 1 Chr 11:23) was the original form of the extant Hebrew text ("an Egyptian who was a sight [to see]") of 2 Sam 23:21.

3. P. McCarter, 2 *Samuel*, 489.

4. See pp. 23–26.

5. *CAT* 1.3.II:13.

6. See p. 25, n. 16.

7. For examples of Egyptian practices, see Y. Yadin, *The Art of Warfare in Biblical Lands*, 2:258, 260; S.-M. Kang, *Divine War in the Old Testament and the Ancient Near East*, 107. As an example of Mesopotamian practice, consider this boast of a Neo-Assyrian provincial governor of the eighth century B.C.E. "I removed the hands and lower lips of eighty of their troops" ("Ninurta-Kudurrī-Uṣur" [trans. K. Younger], 280).

8. The Egyptian document is Papyrus Anastasi I, as seen in "An Egyptian Letter" (trans. J. Wilson), 477.

9. J. Keegan, *A History of Warfare*, 132.

10. The structure of Judg 4:17–22, the account of Jael's slaying of Sisera, emphasizes that Jael bests two men. Twice (4:18, 22) "Jael comes out to meet," *wattēṣē' yā'ēl liqra't*, a man; Sisera and Barak, respectively.

11. J. MacDonald, "The Status and Role of the Na'ar in Israelite Society."

12. Judg 8:20. J. MacDonald, "Status and Role of the Na'ar," 154.

13. P. McCarter, 2 *Samuel*, 487.

14. S. Niditch, *War in the Hebrew Bible*, 91.

15. Y. Yadin, *Art of Warfare* 2:265–67; R. de Vaux, "Single Combat in the Old Testament"; H. Hoffner, "A Hittite Analogue to the David and Goliath Contest of Champions?"; C. Gordon, "Homer and Bible," 87.

16. R. de Vaux, "Single Combat"; C. Gordon, "Homer and Bible," 87.

17. R. de Vaux, "Single Combat," 124; P. McCarter, *1 Samuel*, 290–91.

18. "Sinuhe (1.38)" (trans. M. Lichtheim).

19. "Sinuhe," 79.

20. "Sinuhe," 79.

21. H. Hoffner, "Hittite Analogue," 222.

22. Homer, *The Iliad* (trans. R. Fagles), 129, 217.

23. P. McCarter, 2 *Samuel*, 96.

24. P. McCarter, 2 *Samuel*, 95–96; Y. Yadin, *Art of Warfare*, 2:267.

25. N. Tidwell, "The Philistine Incursions into the Valley of Rephaim," 202–03.

26. P. McCarter, 2 *Samuel*, 96.

27. Although the Samson narrative, whatever its literary horizon (sixth century B.C.E. at the latest), predates Roman gladiator culture (ca. third

century B.C.E.) by centuries, the scene in which the captive Samson "plays" before the crowd in the Philistine temple at Dagon has features, such as the drafting of prisoners of war as combatants and the public display (J. Balsdon and A. Lintott, "Gladiators, Combatants at Games"), evocative of gladiatorial practice.

28. "The festival of arms": see J. Westenholz, *Legends of the Kings of Akkade,* 63.

29. J. Keegan, *The Face of Battle,* 100.

30. A. Olrik, "Epic Laws of Folk Narrative."

31. E.g., the illustrations in Y. Yadin, *Art of Warfare,* 2:333–37, 382–93, 406, 416–47.

32. For cylinder seals depicting martial scenes, see D. Collon, *First Impressions,* 162–63.

33. *HALOT* 2:594. If Shamgar were a *ben 'Anat,* we might expect him to have been an archer, like the men whose names are on the arrowheads (see p. 29). The fact that, in this brief editorial footnote that clarifies the otherwise enigmatic allusion to him in the subsequent song of Judg 5, Shamgar uses a cattle prod rather than a bow underscores again the theme of primitive weapons in the heroic traditions of Israel.

34. S. Ackerman imagines a smith's hammer because the Kenites were metallurgists (*Warrior, Dancer, Seductress, Queen,* 101).

35. On the two versions of the story of David and Goliath in 1 Sam 17, see P. McCarter, *1 Samuel,* 284–309.

36. P. McCarter, *1 Samuel,* 284. The description of Goliath's armor is probably artificial, improbably listing various pieces from a wide range of cultures and eras (McCarter, *1 Samuel,* 292–93; S. McKenzie, *King David,* 74).

37. See the account of the humorous exchange between F. M. Cross and P. Skehan, Dead Sea Scroll researchers, on the implications of the Hebrew scroll from Cave 4 at Qumran listing Goliath's height as 4 cubits and a span, confirming the antiquity of the LXX reading (Cross, "Problems of Method in the Textual Criticism of the Hebrew Bible," 53–54. Skehan grudgingly agrees with Cross that the earliest textual tradition listed Goliath's height as 6 feet 6 inches and laments that "now the villain couldn't even play basketball," at least not in the frontcourt of the N.B.A. (p. 54).

38. "Mace": Hebrew *kidôn* is often translated as "javelin" or "scimitar" (*HALOT* 2:472). Here I follow the suggestion of A. Emery, who seeks a meaning that differentiates it from the other weapons, "sword" and "spear," in the series (Emery, "Weapons of the Israelite Monarchy," 131).

39. A. Emery ("Weapons," 164) also notes that a *šebet* is used as a weapon in 2 Sam 18:14.

40. For the war oracle in the Hebrew Bible, see E. Conrad, *Fear Not Warrior*.

41. Ex 12:23; 2 Sam 24:16; 1 Chr 21:15–16. See S. Meier, "Destroyer."

42. Num 17:11 (16:46 ET). See J. Milgrom, *Numbers*, 142; cf. Dt. 29:27 (29:28 ET); Jer 21:5; 32:37.

43. Dt 32:24; Ps 91:6, Isa 28:2; Hos 13:14. See N. Wyatt, "Qeteb."
Incidentally, the idea expressed in texts such as Dt 7:20, that after YHWH leads the Israelites to victory over the enemies, "YHWH will [then] dispatch the Hornet [*haṣṣirʿâ*] against them," is a description of the all-too-real horrors that follow in the wake of warfare, though here formulated in the ancient mythological, personifying style. Consider it this way: a divine warrior, whether YHWH in Judah or Erra in Babylonia, marches out to war. In Mesopotamian myth, Erra is trailed by his divine entourage of personified weapons, the Sibitti. In Israelite myth, YHWH's entourage include *Mašhît* ("Destroyer"), *Rešep* ("Plague") and *Ṣirʿâ* ("Hornet"), i.e., in modern terms, something akin to "Cholera," "Dysentery," and "Starvation." For

English translations of "Erra," see B. Foster, *Before the Muses*, 2:771–805; and S. Dalley, *Myths from Mesopotamia*, 282–315.

44. Dt 32:24. See P. Xella, "Resheph."

45. 1 Sam 17:45. The cosmic army motif is especially prominent in the Elisha legends (2 Kgs 2:12; 6:17; 7:6).

46. 2 Sam 22:30 = Ps 18:30 (18:29 ET).

47. Reading with LXX (100 foreskins) rather than MT (200).

48. For this motif with Saul, see P. McCarter, *1 Samuel*, 65, 203.

49. Cf. with the images in 2 Sam 22:33–46 of YHWH, according to P. McCarter (*2 Samuel*, 469–70), creating the warrior from head to toe.

50. R. Albertz, *A History of Israelite Religion in the Old Testament Period*, 1:81.

51. M. Weber, *Ancient Judaism*, 128.

52. G. Moore, *A Critical and Exegetical Commentary on Judges*, 290.

53. B. Lincoln, *Priests, Warriors, and Cattle*, 127, n. 104; *CAD* 9:7; 24–25.

54. P. Machinist, "The Epic of Tukulti-Ninurta I," 121, 357; B. Foster, *Before the Muses*, 1:225; G. Mobley, "The Wild Man in the Bible and the Ancient Near East," 226. For the possibility of a relationship between the playful dancing of a war goddess and the reference in Song 7:1 (6:13 ET) to a female character, Shulammit, "dancing between the two armies," see M. Pope, *Song of Songs*, 601–14.

55. W. Burkert, *Greek Religion*, 140.

56. T. Kinsella, *The Tain*, 29, 77.

57. T. Kinsella, *The Táin*, 92. See also M. Eliade, *Rites and Symbols of Initiation*, 84–85. For a comparison of Samson and Cú Chulainn, see J. Fontenrose, *Orion*, 221–22; and G. Mobley, "Wild Man," 230.

58. Madeleine Jost, "Pan."

59. G. von Rad, *Holy War in Ancient Israel*, 46–49.

60. S.-M. Kang, *Divine War*, 35, 104. N. Walls, *The Goddess Anat in Ugaritic Myth*, 44. For the reference to Inanna, see "The Code of Hammurabi" (trans. T. Meek), 179.

61. Beyond the Former Prophets, idioms for panic are especially prominent in the Psalms (e.g., Ps 55:2–6 [55:1–5 ET]) and Latter Prophets, including several which compare battlefield panic to labor pain: Ps 48:6–7 (48:5–6 ET); Isa 13:7–8; 21:3–4; Jer 6:24; 13:21; 30:5–6 (T. Hobbs, *A Time for War*, 100).

62. Such a view of divine meteorological aid is not unique to Israel. For an Assyrian example see, A. Millard, "How Reliable is Exodus?," 57.

63. In the book of Exodus, the "plagues" are "strokes [delivered by the hand]" (√nkh) (Ex 3:20; 9:15; 12:12); see J. Conrad, "נכה *nkh*," 420–22.

64. The idiom of "slack hands," of releasing one's grip, can be used positively, however, as in Ps 46:11 (46:10 ET) where the audience is exhorted to relinquish human attempts to defend Jerusalem and trust in YHWH, commander of the heavenly armies, to defend the city. E. Conrad notes an entire set of biblical war oracles that emphasize passivity, trusting in divine intervention in battle, rather than martial activity (*Fear Not Warrior*, 52–62).

65. *HALOT* 1:111; B. Otzen, "בהל *bhl*."

66. E.g., Judg 7:22; 1 Sam 14:20–23; see T. Hobbs, *A Time for War*, 175–76.

67. J. Anderson, "Wars and Military Science: Greece," 689; W. Burkert, *Greek Religion*, 128.

68. H. Brichto, "Kin, Cult, Land and Afterlife."

69. Examples of war oracles include Dt 31:6; Josh 1:9; 10:25. For the entire topic, see E. Conrad, *Fear Not Warrior*. For *'al tēḥat* as "do not be panicked," see W. Holladay, *Jeremiah 1*, 44.

70. J. Keegan, *A History of Warfare*, 332, 389. The contrast between Greek and Asian styles of warfare is best seen in Herodotus, where the Persian general Mardonius expresses his amazement at Greek tactics (as seen in J. Anderson, "Wars and Military Science," 685).

> When [the Greeks] declare war on each other, they go off together to the smoothest and levellest bit of ground they can find, and have their battle on it—with the result that even the victors never get off without heavy losses, and as for the losers—well, they're wiped out. Now surely, as they all talk the same language, they ought to be able to find a better way of settling their differences: by negotiation, for instance, or an interchange of views—indeed by anything rather than fighting. Or if it is really impossible to avoid coming to blows, they might at least employ the elements of strategy and look for a strong position to fight from. In any case, the Greeks, with their absurd notions of warfare. . . . (Herodotus, *Histories*, 7.9.2; *The Histories* (trans. A. de Sélincourt), 376.

71. T. Hobbs, *Time for War*, 167.

72. T. Hobbs, *Time for War*, 167.

73. T. Hobbs, *Time for War*, 175–76.

74. J. Keegan, *History of Warfare*, 387; N. Tidwell, "Philistine Incursions."

75. N. Tidwell, "Philistine Incursions," 195–98.

76. For a survey of ancient Near Eastern literary treatments of the capture of divine images, see P. Miller and J. Roberts, *The Hand of the Lord*, 9–16.

4

E H U D   A N D   T H E

M O N O L I T H S

THE STORY

There is the story itself. With what passed for in Iron Age terms as
diplomatic cover, an agent for the Israelites is dispatched to deliver
tribute—protection money, really—on their behalf to an oppressive
regional warlord. But from the privileged view given us by the narrator of Judges 3:12–30, we know that the real mission of Ehud ben-
Gera is something else altogether, that this left handed man is
actually an agent for Yнwн, and that his true mission is to be a de-
liverer, a *môšiaᶜ* (Judg 3:15), for sure, but not of the punitive levy imposed by the occupying rival army.

Ehud fashions a special weapon for this assignment of assassinating the Moabite king Eglon, a sword: two edged for stabbing
in close quarters, not hacking in the open field; a *gōmed* (the short
cubit) in length so it could be concealed more easily.[1] Left handed,

Ehud straps the sword under his clothes onto his right thigh (Judg 3:16). Already Yнwн had fashioned Ehud for this assignment of assassinating Eglon. His "disability"—their idiom for left handedness was "impeded in the right hand"—gives Ehud specific advantages for such a time as this: easing Ehud's passage through the security protocols of guards accustomed to right handers; granting Ehud some margin of time, some measure of surprise, when, in a private audience in the royal apartment, his left arm suddenly reaches toward his right leg, for the cross-draw by the southpaw.[2]

Already you can hear elements of a spy story: the agent who crafts and conceals a secret weapon, then under diplomatic cover infiltrates a foreign court. Indeed, Baruch Halpern has imagined Ehud as an Iron Age James Bond.[3] The Ehud narrative also resembles those stories, whether one thinks of them as adventure stories or spy stories, about solo missions in and out of inaccessible fortresses. The heart of the story, in Judges 3:19–25, begins as Ehud has dispatched the embassy of porters and lackeys who had initially accompanied him to Eglon's palace and has returned by himself, on some pretext, to the Moabite fortress. The narrator describes how Ehud talks his way past the guards into the private royal apartment (Judg 3:19–20), murders Eglon, and then manages to exit this apartment while also locking the door (Judg 3:23), giving Ehud a head start on his escape before the Moabite guards discover their dead king.

Halpern deserves great credit for reconstructing, on the basis of archaeological and philological research, the blueprint of a palace from the (broadly defined) period.[4] Reading along with Halpern, modern readers can imagine what ancient audiences knew, namely, the three-chambered layout of such a palace and know exactly, among all the enterings (Hebrew $\sqrt{bw'}$; 3:20, 24) and exitings (Hebrew $\sqrt{ys'}$; 3:19, 23, 24) of Ehud and the guards, which room each character is in at any narrative moment. Reading along with Halpern, one can imagine each threshold Ehud crosses, and feel the suspense build and release, as the assassin makes his labyrinthine way from zone to zone, and chamber to chamber, until he reaches the inner sanctum of Eglon's apartment, kills him there, and then moves, threshold by threshold, back out of the enemy lair to safety.[5]

THE STORYTELLING

Then there is the storytelling.[6] All the crucial details are arranged in view of readers and hearers within the span of the first half dozen verses (Judg 3:12–17) of the Ehud narrative. One by one, they will be picked up and utilized as the story unfolds. One more detail, transparent in Hebrew from the second sentence of the story (3:12b), is the meaning of the name "Eglon": it is the diminutive of "bull," i.e., "bull calf" or "little calf."[7] Later in the story, this description of Eglon will be modified further: this Baby Bull is 'îš bārî' mĕ'ōd, "a very fat man" (Judg 3:17).

It is all too easy anachronistically to project modern body conceptions onto Eglon. The word bārî', "fat" or, better, "fleshy," is rarely used of humans in the Hebrew Bible; its only other occurrence is in a description of the young Jewish heroes in the book of Daniel who eschew the ritually unclean cuisine of a foreign court and, nonetheless, develop into living testaments to kosher eating and righteous living (Dan 1:15). In Daniel, bārî' is hardly indicative of a "good-natured . . . unsuspicious character";[8] neither is it "an emblem of . . . stupidity," nor "a kind of grotesque feminization."[9] Yet these are some of the associations, themselves verging on the grotesque, that biblical scholars have projected onto Eglon. Most often in the Bible, bārî' is used of animals, like the "fat" cattle that graze in Pharaoh's dreamscape as omens of prosperity (Gen 41:4).[10]

As many have noted, Eglon, then, is described as a young fleshy animal ripe for slaughtering, a graphic narrative encapsulation of the motif of the ceremonial slaughter of enemy leaders.[11]

Considering the detailed description of the assassin's preparations and such a depiction of the victim, Meir Sternberg observes, "Everything so falls into place . . . that Eglon is already as good as dead even before he grants the ambassador a private audience."[12]

This terse gem of an adventure story—its nineteen verses amount to about a single page of Aramaic script in the Hebrew Bible—is dense with repetition of words (e.g., *yāmîn*, "right hand" in Judg 3:15 [twice], 16, 21; *yād*, "hand, forearm" in 3:15, 28, 30)[13] and syntactical structures (cf. vv. 15–17 with vv. 21–22).[14] Words are not wasted; instead they are exhausted: introduced, then seconded (e.g., √*sgr* in 3:22 and 23; *dābār* in 3:19 and 20),[15] sometimes trebled (e.g. √*slh* in 3:15, 18, 21; √*mlt* in 3:26 [twice], 29; *hinnēh* in 3:24 and 25 [twice]),[16] and occasionally bent (e.g., √*tqʿ* means "to [strike a] blow" with a sword in 3:21; it means "to blow" a sound on a *shofar* in 3:27).[17]

Consider the way that the idea of and words for "hand"— *yāmîn*, "right hand"; *yād*, "hand, forearm"; and *śĕmōʾl*, "left hand"— ornament the entire literary structure.[18] Ehud is a "son of the right-hand (region)," i.e., the "south" (3:15); Ehud is "impeded in the right hand" (i.e., left handed) (3:15); Ehud straps the dirk to "the right hand (side)" of his body (3:16) and, later, draws it from the same (3:21). There is also a sequence with *yād*: the Israelites send their tribute to Eglon via Ehud's "hand" (3:15); Ehud initiates the Israelite offensive with the cry, "Yʜᴡʜ has given them into your 'hand'" (3:28); and, at the end of the story, the Moabites are humbled under the "hand" of the Israelites (3:30). The word for "left hand" is used only once (3:21), though the idea of left handedness underlies every sentence.

And all this wordplay rests on a sound platform, a balanced series of repetitions that describe, with parallel words and syntax, Ehud's movements into and out of danger. I will say more about this larger narrative structure below but, here, consider these parallel clauses that function as brackets around the central section of the story.

> But he [i.e., Ehud] turned back at the monoliths
>   (Judg 3:19a)
> He [i.e., Ehud] made it past the monoliths (Judg 3:26b)

> *wĕhû' šāb min-happĕsîlîm*
> *wĕhû' 'ābar 'et-happĕsîlîm*

The syntax is identical (inverted word order which begins with a pronoun + suffix conjugation verb), the language parallel, and the effect is, in essence, to frame a door for Ehud into the dangerous space behind enemy lines and, for readers, the section in which all the details compressed into the initial sentences of the story—Ehud's preparations, the distinctive physical features of Ehud and Eglon—are released.

Then within the bracket of these "monoliths" which, whatever their physical referent, are used here as landmarks to describe the border outside of town where Moabite territory ends and Israelite territory begins, there is another bracket that frames Ehud's movement in and out of the audience chamber of Eglon's palace.

> All of [Eglon's] guards exited (√*yṣ'*) from his presence.
> Then Ehud entered (√*bw'*) (Judg 3:19b–20a)

After the assassination, we have the corresponding bookend.

> Then [Ehud] exited (√*yṣ'*) and [Eglon's] servants entered (√*bw'*). (Judg 3:24)

SCATOLOGY AND SATIRE

There are other such brackets framing the action but before I analyze the literary structure in more depth, there is one more preliminary issue to be discussed. We have here a suspenseful adventure:
the solo mission of an assassin into a heart of darkness where a
warlord's apartment becomes an abattoir. We have here careful nar-
ration: the symmetrical economy of the narrator is equal to the cal-
culated efficiency of the protagonist. With such a story and such
storytelling, why is it that Ehud is an obscure character to many?
Why has Judges 3:12–30 attracted so little attention until recently?

Most likely its graphic violence and scatological humor have
kept pious or casual readers at a distance. It is not simply reported
that Ehud "killed," (i.e., "[mortally] struck," √*nkh*) Eglon. Instead,
the narrator slows down, focuses, and lingers on every detail (Judg
3:21–22a):

> Ehud extended his left arm
> and drew the sword from his right thigh
> and struck a blow into [Eglon's] belly.

> The hilt entered after the blade
> and the fat closed behind[19] the blade
> because [Ehud] did not pull the sword out of [Eglon's]
>   belly.

Given the economy of the storytelling so far, this may appear as
gratuitous violence, the jingoistic dehumanization of the enemy as a
fleshy bovine to be gutted. Certainly the story dehumanizes Eglon,
but the description of the violence is not merely for effect. For, as
Michael Barré points out, the fact that Ehud did not withdraw the
sword makes his escape that much easier: how could he, bearing a
bloody knife, get past the guards?[20]

And the violence is combined with scatology. Though in hindsight the narrative aside in Judges 3:17b, about Eglon's "fleshiness," had already set a tone of physicality, most readers are still unprepared for the clause that completes the above description of Eglon's death and the grotesque location to which it steers the story. The NRSV, adopting an interpretation that first issued in written sources from the early Jewish interpreters who produced the Aramaic Targums and which continued in the Latin Vulgate and the English KJV, has this translation for Judges 3:22.

> [Ehud] did not draw the sword out of [Eglon's] belly; and the dirt came out.

The Hebrew word translated above as "dirt" is *paršĕdōnâ*. What does *paršĕdōnâ* mean? The word occurs only here in the Hebrew Bible. As one standard Hebrew reference book puts it, in the shorthand formulations of dictionaries, "meaning uncertain, text uncertain."[21] Most often, it has been understood as a cognate of a Hebrew word for "feces," *pereš*, but that does not account for the second half of the word, *-dōnâ*.[22] Barré argues convincingly that the traditional interpretation of *paršĕdōnâ* as "excrement" is correct but he thinks this rare Hebrew noun is akin to an Akkadian verb, *naparšudu*, which shares the same basic four consonants, *pršd*, and usually means "to escape" but refers, on at least one occasion, to the "escaping" of feces from the bowels.[23]

But there is a major problem with this reading.

The sentence translated above as "and the dirt came out" is, in Hebrew, *wayyēṣē' happaršĕdōnâ*. The first word, *wayyēṣē'*, consists of a conjunction ("and") plus a masculine singular verb. Since there is a pronominal element encoded into the very form of the verb, we must read the rest of the sentence to discover whether its subject is simply "he" (i.e., "he exited") or some other masculine singular noun (i.e., "it came out"). The following word, *happaršĕdōnâ*, is a noun prefixed by a definite article (i.e., "the [*ha-*] *paršĕdōnâ*). As noted above, the meaning of *paršĕdōnâ* is uncertain. Its grammatical form, however, is not. Its final syllable, *-â*, defines the word either as a feminine noun or as the object of a prepositional phrase (*-â* can function in Hebrew as a directional marker; i.e., "toward the *paršĕdōn*").

That is, if we take the *-â* suffix as a marker of gender, then *paršĕdōnâ*, a feminine noun, cannot be the subject of *wayyēṣē'*, a masculine verb. If we take the *-â* suffix as a marker of syntax (what Hebrew grammarians call the directional *hê*), then *paršĕdōn* cannot be the subject of *wayyēṣē'*, but instead the destination of its implied masculine singular subject, i.e., "He [presumably Ehud] exited toward the *paršĕdōn*."[24] In the latter sentence, *paršĕdōn* must represent some architectural feature of Eglon's palace. In terms of syntax, the latter is the only reading possible.

One could argue that the syntax is not a sure guide here because the text is deficient, but there are no rival witnesses among Hebrew manuscripts to challenge the integrity of the extant text.[25] Thus, syntactically and textually, there is no basis for reading *wayyēṣē' happaršĕdōnâ* as "and the dirt came out." The arguments of those who prefer some variation of the latter, such as Barré and Halpern, strong as they are, would be stronger if they admitted this.[26]

Yet, stylistically and contextually, arguments can be made for an emended reading. Let us view Judges 3:22, assuming the above reading of *happaršĕdōnâ* as Ehud's destination, in tandem with the sentence that follows.

> and he   exited toward the *paršĕdōn*.
> And Ehud exited toward the *misdĕrōn*.

> *wayyēṣē'*   *happaršĕdōnâ*
> *wayyēṣē' 'ēhûd hammisdĕrônâ*

Juxtaposed with the sentence that follows, the first sentence does appear awkward; taken together, the pair of sentences seems unduly repetitive. We would expect an explicit identification of the subject (i.e., "Ehud") in the first position, with the second utilizing a pronoun.[27] Instead, we have the opposite. Furthermore, the sentences are close enough in syntax and diction to raise suspicions of a dittography, that is, that a scribe has erroneously copied some element twice, though this is circumstantial evidence. Contextually, however, there is no ambiguity about the puzzled guards' reaction to Eglon's prolonged absence. They assume he is defecating (Judg 3:24), and the text even focuses our attention on their embarrassment (Judg 3:25).

To review: the bases for understanding *paršĕdōn* as "feces" are: (1) Such a reading prepares us, as the story does in so many other particulars, for a later development; in this case, the guards' assumption that their king was defecating. (2) *Paršĕdōn,* whether from Hebrew *pereš* or Akkadian *pršd* can be etymologically related to words meaning something like "feces."

Barré offers an additional argument: in this central section of the narrative describing the assassination, the verbs for entering ($\sqrt{bw'}$) and exiting ($\sqrt{ys'}$) are arranged in a sequential pattern.[28] In Judges 3:19b, the guards exit the audience chamber; in 3:24a, they enter. In 3:20a, Ehud enters Eglon's apartment; in 3:23a and 3:24a, he exits. At the center of this concentric structure, built from revolutions of entrance and egress, are the sentences in Judges 3:22. In 3:22a, guided by the pattern Barré has observed, Ehud's weapon enters Eglon; in 3:22b, Eglon's *paršĕdōn,* feces, comes out.

In order to read Judges 3:22b as "the feces came out," *happaršĕdōnâ* must be emended to *happaršĕdōn,* a misspelling influenced by the spelling of *misdĕrônâ* in the adjacent, syntactically similar line. I adopt this reading. The alternative is to read the sequence as, "He exited toward the *paršĕdōn.* Ehud exited toward the *misdĕrôn."* If that is the story, then the architectural complexity of Eglon's palace is being emphasized in contrast, implicitly, to the rural homes of Benjaminites such as Ehud, and the motif of the rural underdog making his way, triumphantly, through an urban maze is sounded.[29] But in the end, I find the embarrassed looks on the faces of the palace guards in Judges 3:25 more persuasive than the syntax of the surviving Hebrew text of Judges 3:22.

So Eglon, deprived of life, must be debased too (the great man reduced to a large intestine), and this single detail, though it lowers our standards, raises the rhetoric to a higher level of satiric dehumanization.[30] Moabites are waste to be evacuated from Cisjordan, from west of the Jordan River. While Ehud moves freely across landscapes and through houses, entering (√bw'; Judg 3:20, 27), exiting (√yṣ'; Judg 3:23, 24), and escaping (√mlṭ; Judg 3:26), for the Moabite warriors, there is no escape (√mlṭ; Judg 3:29). For their Baby Bull, locked in his stall, the only entering and exiting is the sword, blade and hilt, going in (√bw'; Judg 3:22a) and the royal effluvium going out (√yṣ'; Judg 3:22b).[31]

And even if the text is uncertain, the meaning uncertain, one thing is certain: the comical manner in which Eglon's guards react to discovering the doors locked to their master's apartment. "Surely," they said, "he is covering his feet," an idiomatic half-truth for defecation which is at the same time accurate (in a squat position, the lower folds of the robe did cover the feet) and yet reticently delicate. We can almost see their uneasiness—and smell Eglon's noxiousness—in the next verse, "They waited until it became embarrassing" (Judg 3:25). "Meanwhile," the next verse tells us, in the words of the NRSV, "Ehud escaped while they delayed," though the translation of the latter verb hardly captures the emphatic mouthful of the Hebrew *hitmahmēah* with its playful doubling of the syllable *mh*. Better: "Ehud escaped while they *dilly-dallied*."[32] So it turns out that these graphic details were neither excessive nor merely rhetorical: "The Almighty has His own purposes."[33] Even Eglon's offal, and its odor, aids Ehud's escape.[34]

What accounts for the intensity of this degrading portrait of Eglon and, by extension, Moab? A number of recent studies have referred to the Ehud narrative as a political satire, a genre that dispenses with small gestures and frequently employs animal appellations (e.g., "Eglon" as "Baby Bull") and scatological and sexual rhetoric to mock the object of the satire.[35] I remain unconvinced about the sexual undertones of this story detected by Robert Alter and Marc Zvi Brettler, who hear connotations of phallic penetration when, behind closed doors, Ehud reveals his "secret word" (Alter, "secret thing") to Eglon.[36] For a degrading portrait of Moab in sexual terms, we should look to Genesis 19:30–38 which smears Israel's neighbor and perennial social and political rival with the charge of incestual origins.

In addition to the scatological details, the Ehud narrative utilizes a number of sacrificial terms. In isolation, "Eglon" ("bull calf"), bārî' ("fleshy," v. 17), minḥâ ("tribute" or "[cereal] offering," vv. 15, 17, 18), haqrēb ("to bring" but also "to offer [a sacrifice], v. 17), and ḥēleb (in v. 22, the "fatty membrane" of Eglon's belly) might have mundane (i.e., nonritual) meanings but, taken together, their sacrificial nuances are unavoidable.[37] As Brettler writes, "The story as a whole plays on the notion of sacrifice. While pretending to bring tribute/offering to Eglon, it is actually Eglon, 'the calf,' who becomes the offering."[38]

The juxtaposition of scatological and sacrificial features in the story has led Gary Anderson to offer a more specific suggestion about the subject of the satire. Certainly a social and political rival, Moab, is dehumanized in the story. But also, Anderson observes, the degrading rhetoric and use of sacrificial terms may reflect Israelite revulsion toward the practice of paying tribute to foreign powers. Anderson calls the story "a satiric description of the symbolic act of periodic tribute delivery."[39] Tribute delivery to a foreign power was not only economically and socially onerous but, for Israelites, blasphemous since YHWH alone was their sovereign and the minḥâ, in its sacerdotal sense of "offering," belonged only to YHWH.[40] Against the background of other narratives in Judges, such as Gideon's destruction of an altar of Baal (Judg 6:25–27) or Samson's destruction of a temple of Dagon (Judg 16:23–30), the theological dimensions of Ehud's heroics come into focus. The heroics of Israel's deliverers and judges, inspired and raised up by YHWH, were understood as directed against rival deities as well as rival warriors.

THE NESTING BOXES

Building on many recent literary analyses of Judg 3:12–30, I will devote additional attention to its narrative structure, articulating the linguistic and syntactic features of the story which are arranged like corresponding brackets throughout the story. The ideas and language of the initial sentences are paralleled in the terminal sentences, those of the next section in the penultimate section, and so on. Such a narrative strategy, an ordered series of inclusions, is fitting for a story that describes a heroic adventure through and back across a series of thresholds. Then, I will devote special attention to one of these thresholds, the *pĕsîlîm*, the "monoliths," at Gilgal.

I will sidestep a detailed discussion of the literary unity of the Ehud narrative.[41] There is much to be said for analyzing the literary development over time of a biblical passage: drawing a cross section of a passage and delineating the shape of its bedrock story and each editorial layer above. Through such an exercise one gets a feel for the dynamics of the community over generations interacting with a biblical story, a dynamic that continues to the present day in synagogue and church. Certainly, the presence of boilerplate editorial formulas found elsewhere in the book of Judges (Judg 3:12, 15a, 30) is evidence of at least one secondary stage of literary activity.[42] Some scholars assume other additions and adjustments to the story, suspecting that the narratives of Judges began as local stories about single tribes. These were later editorially transformed by the addition of a few details to read as larger, regional conflicts that engaged many tribes, creating a unifying national story about the frontier era.[43] Lindars, for instance, argues that the oldest core of the Ehud story ends in v. 25 with the report of Eglon's death, and that the remaining scenes—where Ehud escapes to safety and blows the *shofar* (3:26–27a), prompting "the sons of Israel" to come streaming down from the hills and seize the fords of the Jordan (3:27b–28)— represent, in cinematic terms, leftover footage from countless other Holy War films spliced onto the end of our story.[44]

The Ehud story, however, is best viewed from above, as a single, though uneven, literary landscape. The dramatic heart of the story is Ehud's preparations for and execution of his mission, roughly contained in Judges 3:15b–27, the very section that some critics consider the oldest core of the story.[45] In this respect, the Ehud narrative is a kind of miniature of the book of Judges, consisting of a narrative core to which introductory and concluding additions have been made. We have already mentioned the literary artistry of the Ehud story, which is most dense in this middle, core section. But the same kind of artistry, a variety of types of repetitions in style and content, also appears on the perimeter of the story, in the places where the story seems most formulaic, suggesting either that special redactional care was taken to make the narrative amendments friendly ones or that the impact of the rhetorical devices in the center of the story has sufficient force to affect our reading of the material on the periphery.

Turning then to an analysis of the structure of Judges 3:12–30, I would first observe, again, that the story is framed by two crossings of the Jordan river. The story begins in this way, with the Moabite strike (√*nkh*) into Israelite territory:

> [Eglon and his coalition] went (√*hlk*) [across the Jordan] and struck (√*nkh*) the Israelites and took possession of the City of Palms. (Judg 3:13)

The story ends with the Israelite counterstrike.

> [The Israelites] captured the fords of the Jordan from the
> Moabites and would not let a man get past (√bw'). They
> struck (√nkh) at that [single] time, Moabites, about 10
> units-worth. (Judg 3:28–29a)

According to Judges 3:12–13, Eglon leads a coalition of Moabites,
Ammonites, and Amalekites from Moabite territory, east of the Jor-
dan, to an Israelite town, "the City of Palms," west of the Jordan.[46]
The initial crossing of the Jordan by the Moabites, however, is not
described in straightforward terms. The barrier between Moabite
and Israelite territory, the Jordan, is not explicitly mentioned. The
Israelite town on the western bank of the river occupied by the
Moabites is presumably Jericho but only its epithet, "City of Palms"
(Dt 34:3), is used, probably a secondary editorial choice designed to
avoid an explicit contradiction between this story and the account
in the preceding book of Joshua, where Jericho had been leveled
(Josh 6).[47] Though this initial frame of the story—Moabites crossing
the Jordan to Israelite Jericho—is not described explicitly, its corresponding frame, at the end of the story, is. There, the Israelite militia seizes the fords of the Jordan and the Moabites are prevented
from recrossing the Jordan to return home (Judg 3:28). The contrast
between this initial scenario and the final result, the problem and
the solution, is also emphasized in the use of √nkh, "to strike." Initially, Moabites cross the Jordan and "strike" the Israelites (3:13);
but in the end, Moabites are not permitted to cross the Jordan and
it is the Israelites who "strike" them (3:29).

There is another stylistic feature of the initial section which is
paralleled in the final section. Early in the story (Judg 3:15aβ), the
Israelite hero Ehud is described with a triple epithet, in diction that
itself crosses a generic threshold, from prose to poetry.

Ehud: son of Gera,	'ēhûd ben gērā'
son of the Right-hand [region],	ben haymînî
a man impeded in his right hand.	'îš 'iṭṭēr yad-yĕmînô

This kind of poetic expression can be described as stair-stepped as each line repeats a word from the previous line, progressively extending the trope:[48] *ben* from lines *a* and *b*, i.e.,

> *'ēhûd **ben** gērā'*
> ***ben** haymînî,*

and *yāmîn* from lines *b* and *c*, i.e.,

> *ben haymînî*
> *'îš 'iṭṭēr yad-yĕmînô.*

A similar triple epithet, now for the Moabite victims, employing the same kind of parallelism, appears in the final section of the story. Judges 3:29 describes an ironic reversal but also, perhaps, a heroic salute when it says that the Moabites, killed as they attempted to flee back home across the Jordan, had been

to a man, stout,	'îš kōl-šāmēn
and **every man,** a battler;	wĕkōl-'îš ḥāyil
but escaped no **man**	wĕlō' nimlaṭ 'îš

with the words *'îš,* "man," and *kōl,* "each, every," and combinations of both, spilling down over successive lines.

So far we have seen that the initial (3:12–15b) and terminal sections (3:28–30) of the story employ corresponding expressions of content and style to frame the story. The narrative bracketing continues in the next stage. The style of Judges 3:15b, "The sons of

Israel sent by [Ehud's] *hand* tribute to Eglon, king of Moab," is echoed, with its terms reversed, in 3:28a where Ehud issues his battle cry, "Pursue [the Moabites] for YHWH has given them into your *hand.*" The pause to detail Ehud's preparation of equipment for his solo mission (the fashioning and secreting of his sword) in 3:16 is matched, in the corresponding place on the other side of the narrative architecture, by 3:27, where Ehud blows the *shofar* and the Israelite soldiers come streaming down the hills to mass behind him, the means for accomplishing the group mission.

This narrative structure resembles a series of nesting boxes, and its most clearly crafted piece is next: the corresponding references to the *pĕsîlîm* in, first, 3:19 and, then, in 3:26.

But [Ehud] turned back at the monoliths (Judg 3:19a)
[Ehud] made it past the monoliths (Judg 3:26b)

In the physical landscape of the story, the *pĕsîlîm* mark Ehud's entrance and exit from a deadly arena where he must work solo behind enemy lines. In the narrative landscape of the story, the twin references to the *pĕsîlîm* articulate the decisive and dramatic core of the adventure. Everything that precedes 3:19–26 is preliminary; everything which follows is anticlimactic. The *pĕsîlîm* deserve further attention and I will return to them and to a discussion of sacred architecture and of mythic thresholds in other ancient Near Eastern adventure stories. But first, let us complete the description of narrative structure, aided by Halpern's reconstruction of what Eglon's palace may have looked like.

Even without information external to the story, such as a putative blueprint of a certain type of Iron Age palace, the story itself clearly articulates spatial zones in its middle section. Within the section bounded by 3:19a–26, we are inside the zone defined by the *pĕsîlîm*. Then within 3:19b–25, we are in the architectural zone of

Eglon's audience chamber, clearly bounded verbally by the parallel terms at the beginning and end of this subsection.

> All of [Eglon's] guards exited (√yṣʾ) from his presence. Then Ehud entered (√bwʾ) (Judg 3:19b–20a)

> Then [Ehud] exited (√yṣʾ) and [Eglon's] servants entered (√bwʾ). (Judg 3:24)

Then, within this section there is a smaller—the story's most interior—zone, that of Eglon's royal apartment, Judg 3:20–23, into which Ehud enters (√bwʾ) in 3:20, whose doors Ehud locks, and from which Ehud exits (√yṣʾ) in 3:23. This box in the center of our series, the most private architecturally and most critical narratively, has room for only two characters, hero and villain.

Still, our appreciation for the labyrinthine storytelling is heightened by knowledge of the palace's multichambered layout. Halpern employs the model of contemporary Assyrian and Syrian palaces, often referred to as the *bīt ḫilāni* type, as a model for Eglon's palace.[49] In broad strokes, such buildings had three main areas, not unlike the tripartite architecture of Solomon's temple: (a) an antechamber, (b) a central hall, and (c) a small, most private or most holy, inner chamber; in a temple, the holy of holies; in a palace, the private quarters of the highest official.

Our story does not describe Ehud's initial passage through the antechamber (a). The narrator notes only that Ehud turns back at the *pĕsîlîm* near Gilgal (3:19) and then hurries to usher us directly, presumably, to (b), the audience chamber of Eglon's palace where, according to 3:19, Ehud announces that he has "a secret message" for Eglon. Eglon restrains him from speaking further in this semi-public space (the Hebrew imperative placed on the lips of Eglon, "*hās*," is onomatopoeic and functionally and phonetically analogous to "Sssh!")[50] and the guards leave the royal audience court, presumably to wait in the antechamber (a). Then, in v. 20, Ehud enters the deeper privacy of (c), the royal apartment, an "elevated room," adjacent to and just behind the public throne, where Eglon sits "by himself."

After the assassination, Ehud somehow locks the doors to (c), the apartment, and exits ($\sqrt{y s'}$) (Judg 3:23). The note at the beginning of the next verse (Judg 3:24), that Ehud again "exits" ($\sqrt{y s'}$), is not redundant but describes him leaving the next chamber, the audience hall (b). When Ehud passes the guards, they take this as their cue to leave the antechamber (a), enter the court (b), and wait, puzzled, for their lord to emerge from his quarters (c).

Within the palace itself, then, Ehud crosses three thresholds, each chamber another architectural box. Two of these boxes are explicitly described; one, the antechamber, is not but nevertheless materializes through the narrative context and through knowledge of what this type of palace looked like. The palace scenes are contained within another narrative box, the space delimited by the pĕsîlîm, and this box is nestled in the largest zone on our narrative horizon, the geographic sphere that, from the point of view of the narrator, rightfully belongs to the Israelite tribes: Cisjordan.

In the end, this is a story in which form and content coalesce.[51] A heroic adventure in and out of an inaccessible fortress is itself structured as a series of portals that the hero alone crosses and doors to which he alone holds the key. If we change the focus from these larger rhetorical elements and look again at the verbal repetitions that embroider these columns of structure, we can see that the verbs in the central section of the story (Judg 3:19–26) augment this spatial emphasis. Here in the Moabite stronghold, in the place where Ehud should be in danger and Eglon invulnerable, Ehud escapes safely and Eglon does not. Note all the language in reference to Eglon being closed in and shut in: the "fat," ḥēleb, of Eglon's belly "closes" ($\sqrt{sgr}$) over the sword in v. 22; Ehud "shuts" ($\sqrt{sgr}$) the door of Eglon's apartment in v. 23. Contrast this with the verbs used with Ehud in this section: v. 23, Ehud "exits," √yṣ', the apartment; v. 24 Ehud "exits" the audience hall; v. 26a, Ehud "escapes," √mlṭ, the palace; v. 26b, Ehud "crosses," √'br, the landmark of the pĕsîlîm, and, again, "escapes." While Ehud exits, escapes, crosses, and lives to fight another day, Eglon is locked in a box; the only thing about him that "exits" is feces.

Between these references to the pĕsîlîm (vv. 19, 26), our entire story has been told in miniature. Ehud, the Israelite, locks Eglon, the Moabite, in a box. The final act (vv. 27–29) is a repeat of the first (vv. 12–18), only in reverse. Ehud leads the Israelites in a military campaign, as Eglon had led the Moabite coalition (3:13). Moabites attempt to cross the Jordan from the west, hoping to return to their homeland but they are locked in, just as their king had been locked in, because Ehud and company have seized the fords of the Jordan. Through the medium of a series of parallel narrative brackets, the nesting boxes, that describe entrance and exit through several thresholds, a message is conveyed of Moabites locked in boxes: the royal apartment for Eglon, Cisjordan for his warriors. The tokens of Moabite physical and political superiority—the upper hand, the imposing edifice, the stout belly—become boxes from which there is no escape.

THE MONOLITHS

According to the analysis here, three spatial horizons are articulated in the Ehud narrative: an undefined area of Cisjordan clearly bounded to the east by the Jordan River, vaguely bounded to the west by the zone where Ehud and his fellow Israelites live just beyond Moabite reach; inside of that, the sphere of Moabite occupation in the City of Palms and its perimeter, a zone entered in our story through the gate of the pĕsîlîm; and inside of that, Eglon's three-chambered palace. The story is most explicit about the middle zone, articulating its importance through emphatic diction and syntax. The twin references to the *pĕsîlîm* are contained in parallel sentences (3:19a: *wĕhû' šāb min-happĕsîlîm*; 3:26bα: *wĕhû' 'ābar 'et-happĕsîlîm*), underscoring their significance. The syntax of each sentence, the nominal constructions that invert typical word order, and the use of simple conjunctions and suffix-conjugation verbs which break from normal prose patterns, structurally cue the audience to give special attention.[52] Boling notes that these references (vv. 19, 26) "form an inclusio and indicat[e] that the referent is of pivotal importance."[53]

But what were the *pĕsîlîm?* This text which is all about secrecy and stealth has had its share of secrets—the use of obscure words, its reluctance to mention Jericho—but the reference to the *pĕsîlîm* is perhaps the most enigmatic. The word *pĕsîlîm* occurs about twenty times in the Hebrew Bible, and except for here (Judg 3:19, 26) it refers to divine statues or carved icons that are the object of prophetic renunciation and derision, i.e., "idols."[54] While a pejorative connotation for *pĕsîlîm* in Judges 3 is possible, it seems unlikely given that the context treats them simply as a well-known feature in the vicinity of Jericho. In Judges 3:19, the *pĕsîlîm* are explicitly associated with Gilgal, the site near Jericho of an Israelite shrine. According to biblical sources, the shrine of "Gilgal," which means "circle," in the sense of "[stone] circle," was founded by Joshua (Josh 4:8–9, 20–24); visited by pilgrims in the books of Joshua and Judges (Josh 14:6; Judg 2:1); associated with Samuel, Saul, and David (1 Sam 7:16; 10:8; 11:14–15; 13:4, 7–15; 15:12–13); and in the eighth century B.C.E. condemned by Amos and Hosea.[55]

Whether the Israelites actually erected the stones of Gilgal (Josh 4:20) or adopted a preexisting sacred stone assemblage and provided it with their own foundation legend, the most prominent feature of the shrine, based on the account of Joshua 4 and on the meaning of Gilgal ("stone circle"), was its monoliths, described in Joshua 4:20 as *'ăbānîm*, "stones." The text of Judges 3:19, 26, however, refers to the pĕsîlîm, not the 'ăbānîm, of Gilgal. Some scholars assume by this that the stones of Gilgal are not the referent of pĕsîlîm in Judges 3; rather the pĕsîlîm are a stone landmark outside of town (quarries? a boundary stone erected by the Moabites?)[56] or some other shrine (where the treaty documents defining the terms of the Moabite occupation had been deposited?).[57] I am among those who assume, to the contrary, that the shrine of Gilgal is intended here.[58] The context of Judges 3 suggests that the use of pĕsîlîm in Judges 3:19, 26 is free of negative connotations, reflecting a neutral use of the word prior or in addition to its widespread use in polemics against impure religion.[59]

What is the significance of the pĕsîlîm in our story? Certainly they function as a landmark. On a deeper level, it has been suggested that Ehud's passage at the sacred site is one more detail crucial to plot development, that Ehud paused there to seek (or to be seen seeking) the divine message that he later delivers to Eglon.[60] But could the pĕsîlîm have symbolic significance as well? Robert Polzin and Dennis Olson understand pĕsîlîm as meaning "idols" and see theological significance: when Ehud "passes by," √ʿbr (which can also mean "transgress"), the pĕsîlîm after killing Eglon, he liberates Israel from bondage to Moabite deities.[61] Such an understanding by ancient redactors may have made the reference to "stones/idols" more palatable, but there is no hint in the story itself that these stones are "the evil thing" (Judg 3:12) for which the Israelites are being visited with the Moabite occupation.

THE MONOLITHS AS SACRED SPACE

Ancient Israelites, as well as their neighbors, recognized the presence of sacred spaces. Certain features in the natural landscape, whether mountains (Ex 3:1; 19:18; Dt 34:1; Judg 5:4–5; 9:37; 1 Kgs 19:8), rocks (Gen 28:10–12), springs (Gen 16:7, 13–14), rivers (2 Kgs 5:12), or trees (Gen 12:6–8; 18:1; Judg 4:5; 6:11, 24; 1 Sam 10:3; 14:2),

served as focal points for religious activity. In secondary transformations, such pristine sacred spaces were domesticated and translated
into architecture.[62] On a large scale, temples symbolically represented Sinaitic divine mountains; on a smaller scale, carved stones,
maṣṣēbôt, stylized sacred rocks, did. On a large scale, botanical
gardens, such as the Hanging Gardens of Babylon or the royal ar-
boretum of the kings of Judah in the Kidron Valley of Jerusalem represented Edenic sacred groves; on a small scale, carved wooden
poles, *'ăšērîm*, stylized sacred trees, did.[63]

Sacred spaces served as thresholds between cosmic zones,
marking places where, through appropriate rites and intermediaries, humans could make contact with—according to the tripartite
cosmology of the ancient Near East—the heavenly realm above
and the realm of the dead below.[64] In some Akkadian texts, the
word *nēberu*, "crossing, ford," is used to describe such *limina* (the
plural of the Latin *limen*, "threshold").[65] The Bible refers not to
fords or thresholds but to "gates," the rock at Bethel which serves
as "Heaven's Gate," *ša'ar haššāmayim* (Gen 28:17); the unspecified location mentioned in the book of Job where earth meets
underworld, "the Gates of Death" (or "the Gates of [the deity whose
name is] Death"), *ša'ărê māwet* (Job 38:17). Gary Anderson describes the sacred spaces in Israelite religion as "apertures."[66] Let
us consider the significance of the standing stones in our story as
sacred apertures, sketching first the ways that sacred thresholds
function in some other biblical and ancient Near Eastern narratives.

Many biblical stories contain accounts of adventures at liminal places. The Eden narrative mentions two sacred trees, the tree
of life and the tree of the knowledge of good and evil (Gen 2:9, 17;
3:24), which define the boundary between mortality and immortality, and monstrous sentries, the cherubim, who guard the threshold
to the garden where they stand (Gen 3:24).[67] Jacob, in one story,
lays his head on a sacred rock and dreams of a ramp to the divine

realm (Gen 28:10–22); in another, he encounters a demonic adversary at a river crossing (Gen 32:22–31). Moses, while herding goats, finds himself on a sacred mountain ("the Mount of Elohim") where a divine messenger "appears in a flame of fire out of the bush" (Ex 3:1–2). Joshua is "in" or "by" Jericho—perhaps then, it is Gilgal—when he encounters an officer of the cosmic army (Josh 5:13–15). Elijah and Elisha frequent one sacred place after another: Mt. Carmel,[68] Mt. Horeb,[69] Gilgal,[70] and the Jordan River, which in 2 Kings 2:9–12, represents, as in the Christian songbook, the *limen* separating mortal from immortal life.

The Mesopotamian classic, the Gilgamesh Epic, is punctuated with heroic crossings of cosmic thresholds guarded by monsters, hybrids, or semi-divine figures.[71] Gilgamesh raids the Forest of Enlil, guarded by the monster Humbaba.[72] Unimpressed and unintimidated by this monstrous border sentry, Gilgamesh and his hirsute sidekick Enkidu defeat Humbaba and loot timber from the divine garden. Later, Gilgamesh passes through the morning portal of Sun, the twin mountains of Mashu, guarded by scorpion-men.[73] Reaching this *limen* at night, Gilgamesh, in Andrew George's description, "races against time to complete the path of the Sun."[74] This tunnel deposits Gilgamesh, in George's phrase, "at the edge of the world," an isolated shoreline where a goddess, Siduri, operates a tavern at a cosmic crossroads.[75]

There is another set of adventure stories antecedent to the Hebrew Bible which offer further background for understanding the symbolic function of the *pĕsîlîm* in the Ehud narrative, i.e., stories of underworld journeys.[76] These include, in Babylonian literature, the *Descent of Ishtar to the Netherworld* and, in Ugaritic literature, in the *Baal Cycle*, the journey of Anat to rescue her brother Baal from the subterranean realm of Môt ("Death"), in his town, "the Pit," in his land of "Filth."[77] The former work provides one example of a conventional Mesopotamian description of the underworld as

the house which those who enter cannot leave,
on the road where travelling is one-way only[78]

The realm of the underworld was accessible through its own thresholds. As mentioned previously, the supreme sacred spaces in the ancient Near East were divine mountains and on their peaks, humans gained access to the divine realm (e.g., Ex 3; Dt 34; 1 Kgs 19). Their bases, where subterranean springs issued or caves opened, were portals to the underworld (Sheol in Israelite thought). As Frank Cross writes,

> The mythic pattern which couples the cosmic river(s) with the Mount of God, the place where the gates of heaven and the watery passage into hell are found, may be applied to any great mountain with springs at its foot or side where a [divine] sanctuary . . . exists.[79]

Temples and shrines were conceived of as stylized divine mountains that offered to worshipers the same access to other realms.[80] In official Israelite religion, as reflected in the Hebrew Bible, contact with the underworld was forbidden (e.g., Dt 18:11; 1 Sam 28), and as a corollary, biblical texts about shrines, such as Solomon's Temple, do not exploit the possibility that access to the underworld could be gained at holy places. Postbiblical legends about Mount Zion as the capstone plugging the waters of the cosmic abyss, may, however, provide indirect evidence for such a belief.[81]

In Judges 3:12–30, the Ehud narrative, the world of the story remains *terra firma* throughout. The monuments at Gilgal function as landmarks; if they are doors to other realms—mythological manholes—Ehud, or the storyteller, does not pry them open. In Judges 2:1, a mere chapter earlier, the stones of Gilgal do, however, function as a *limen*. The note there that a divine messenger "ascended from Gilgal" suggests that the same shrine that figures in our story served as a portal for traffic between the divine and earthly realms in some stories.

Still, I would argue that the emphatic underscoring of Ehud's passage at the site of the *pĕsîlîm* provides this adventure with mythic potential. Though it never quite breaks through, this mythic background presses up against the surface of the narrative, giving the story an energy and tension that, if not obvious to modern readers, must have been felt by ancient audiences accustomed to stories about heavenly ramps and fiery bushes and gates leading straight to the center of the earth. The monoliths at Gilgal clearly serve in the Ehud narrative as a threshold, between "home" and "away," between safety and danger, between working with comrades and working solo.[82] But the monoliths, which in ritual life served as thresholds between cosmic realms, deepen and heighten and broaden the stakes of the adventure. For when Ehud's journey takes him past the monoliths, past the security of comrades, and into the heart of the enemy stronghold, is he not "on the road where the traveling is one-way only" and bound for "the house where those who enter cannot leave"? Through the *limen* of the *pĕsîlîm*, Ehud enters a kind of underworld whose ruler lies, it will be revealed, like a chthonic deity in his mud.

HEROIC MOTIFS

As for the features of heroic culture and conventions analyzed in previous chapters, we view in Ehud the emphasis on solo heroics. Though the triumph of Israelites over Moabites is its goal, the group encounter is secondary and anticlimactic, relegated to a few verses at the conclusion of the story (Judg 3:27–29) which rely on the conventions of flight and pursuit. In contrast, the principal of narrative detail is spent on introducing, arranging, and isolating the two rivals, Ehud and Eglon. It is not a fair fight, however, as satiric values have trumped heroic values in this story. Though Ehud is heroic, his opponent, the Baby Bull, is caricatured, not valorized.

Furthermore, there are ritual undertones in the description here of the killing of an enemy king. The transparent meaning of Eglon's name suggests that he is a sacrificial candidate. In addition, the use of sacrificial terms—i.e., *minḥâ*, "tribute" or "offering" (Judg 3:15, 17), especially in combination with *hip'il* √*qrb*, "to present" (Judg 3:17; cf. Lev 2:14; Num 15:4; 28:26); and *ḥēleb* (Judg 3:22)—prepares the audience for the ceremonial slaughter of a victim.[83]

The motif of the underdog using inferior weapons is also a part of the story. As Michael Patrick O'Connor writes of Ehud (and of Jael, in Judg 4–5),

> [I]n both cases a clever Israelite sympathizer (Ehud, Jael) is able to assassinate an enemy leader (Eglon, Sisera) who has enormous material resources (Eglon's palace, Sisera's chariotry); the Israelite uses simple instruments (Ehud's dagger, Jael's tent peg) and "natural" qualities (Ehud's left-handedness, Jael's confinement as a woman).[84]

The story encapsulates this motif so common to heroic Israel narrative. "Neither sword nor spear" (Judg 5:8) are seen, "neither sword [of typical length for warriors] nor spear" (1 Sam 13:22) are found in Ehud's hand.

THE GATES OF RIGHTEOUSNESS

Before allowing Ehud to return to the procession of heroes in the book of Judges, I want to pause, a final time, at the place in the story where he emerges from the *pĕsîlîm* after completing the solo part of his mission (Judg 3:26). Psalm 118, a liturgy celebrating a military victory, contains a reference to "the Gates of Righteousness"

(Ps 118:19), either an architectural feature of Solomon's Temple or a gate to Jerusalem itself.[85] As for the former, the temple gates represented an important *limen* in the religious and cultural life of ancient Israel. The Bible contains special liturgies for entrance, ethical interrogatories, which, whether self-directed or intoned by a priest, assured that those entering the temple were ethically and ritually free of guilt (i.e., *ṣaddîq*, "righteous") and thus worthy, or even capable, of benefiting from the blessings mediated by the temple and its rites (Ps 15; 24:3–6; cf. Mic 6:6–8). The term "righteous" also occurs in martial contexts in the Bible (Isa 41:2, 10; 49:24; Jer 23:6), where, as with similar ideas in other cultures, its background is that of warfare as an ethical ordeal (i.e., "May the *best* man win").[86] It was believed that the Powers-that-Be—in the world of the Hebrew Bible, Yнwн—judged between combatants, awarding victory to the righteous and meting out defeat to the guilty (Judg 11:27; 1 Sam 24:16 [24:15 ET]; 2 Sam 10:12; cf. Prov 14:19). As Jephthah declares on the eve of battle with Ammonites, "May the Judge Yнwн judge between [us]" (Judg 11:27), or Joab, on the eve of battle with Arameans, "May Yнwн do what is pleasing in his eyes" (2 Sam 10:12).

We do not know whether there was a specific victory arch in Jerusalem, but the entrance to a temple or to a town surely functioned as "gates of [those found] righteous" in battle by virtue of their victory. Through such gates, victorious warriors brought gifts of booty, gave thanks, and celebrated their acquittal in the cosmic martial court. The first time Ehud passed through the threshold of the *pĕsîlîm* and entered, alone, a deadly arena, the monoliths of Gilgal represented "the Gates of Death." On the other side of his mission, when Ehud passed through those monoliths—after forming his plan, fashioning his weapon, talking his way past the guards and into Eglon's most private space, assassinating the Moabite king, locking the doors, and escaping the palace—they represented a different kind of *limen*, a victory arch, "the Gates of Righteousness."

NOTES

1. Though *gōmed* occurs only here in the Hebrew Bible, it probably refers to a shorter linear measure (i.e., from elbow to knuckles—Mandaean *gurmaiza* means "fist"—or wrist) than the standard (and expected) *'ammâ*, "cubit" (by comparison, only here, "long cubit") which measures from the elbow to the fingertips (*HALOT* 1:196; 61–62; J. Slotki, "Judges," 180). For the tactical advantages of Ehud's two-edged, short sword, see, among others, B. Lindars, *Judges 1–5*, 142.

2. A phrase, *'îš 'iṭṭēr yad-yěmînô*, "a man impeded in his right hand," is used here (and in Judg 20:16) to describe left handedness, rather than a form of the word for "left hand or side," *šěmō'l*. The form (*qiṭṭēl*) of the adjective *'iṭṭēr* is typical for Hebrew descriptions of disabilities, e.g., *'iwwēr*, "blind," or *pissēaḥ*, "lame." J. Soggin thus contends that Ehud was disabled, and is contrasted here with his physically imposing rival Eglon, described in Judg 3:17 as "fat" or "stout" (J. Soggin, *Judges*, 50). This is unlikely since, as B. Lindars writes, "a visible handicap to [Ehud's] right hand would have ruined the stratagem" and have negated the element of surprise that left handedness brings to the adventure (B. Lindars, *Judges 1–5*, 141).

That still leaves the possibility that Ehud's preference for the left hand is not congenital but, rather, the result of special training (J. Gray, *Joshua, Judges and Ruth*, 250; J. Martin, *The Book of Judges*, 46; B. Halpern, *The First Historians*, 40–41). Gray and Martin cite the Kerr of Scotland, and Halpern the Maori of New Zealand as examples of ethnic groups who trained warriors to use the left hand in order to gain a strategic advantage. Roman gladiators also cultivated "sinister," i.e., left-handed, deliveries (T. Wiedemann, *Emperors and Gladiators*, 30). Whether by nature or nurture, Ehud is left handed (B. Lindars, *Judges 1–5*, 141), and I favor the former interpretation (see B. Waltke and M. O'Connor, *An Introduction to Biblical Hebrew Syntax*, 173). As in many cultures, this deviation from the norm may well have been understood as a disability in Israelite culture. The portrayal of left-handed Ehud as an underdog, emphasized by Soggin, pertains, but Ehud is not maimed.

3. B. Halpern, *First Historians*, 43.

4. B. Halpern, *First Historians,* esp. 46–54.

5. For similarities between Ehud's adventure and the description of Judith's mission, see p. 242.

6. On the economy of the storytelling, the remarks of B. Lindars (the story supplies "[all] the necessary details," [*Judges 1–5,* 142] and B. Halpern ("not a detail in the story is superfluous," [*The First Historians,* 44] are typical. The recent spate of literary treatments of the Ehud story began with L. Alonso Schökel ("Erzählkunst im Buche der Richter") and include later contributions by R. Alter (*The Art of Biblical Narrative,* 38–41), D. Gunn ("Joshua and Judges," 115–16); and M. Sternberg (*The Poetics of Biblical Narrative,* 328–37).

7. *HALOT* 2:784–85. M. O'Connor ("Judges," 133) notes "the linguistically transparent" names of many characters in Judges; here we have Eglon ("little calf") and Ehud ("splendor"), respectively. The diminutive element in "Eglon" is the suffix -*ôn.*

Here, and below, I am reading a pejorative connotation into the name of Ehud's antagonist Eglon ("Baby Bull"). This suggests that the name is an invention of the storyteller. I cannot know this. In fact, the use of animal designations and appellations for men is quite common; in the book of Judges alone we find "Caleb," i.e., "Dog" (Judg 1:11–15, 20; 3:9); "Oreb," i.e., "Raven" (Judg 7:25; 8:3); and "Zeeb," i.e., "Wolf" (Judg 7:25; 8:3). On the other hand, there are other instances in Judges in which the names ascribed to Israelite opponents seem explicitly rhetorical: "Cushan-rishathaim" (Judg 3:8, 10) means something like "Cushan, the Doubly Evil" (cf. *HALOT* 2:467); and the name of the Midianite king whom Gideon captures and ritually slaughters in Judg 8:5–21 is "Zebah," i.e., "Sacrifice" or "Victim." I attach rhetorical significance to the meaning of Eglon's name, not on its meaning alone, but on the combination of its meaning "(Bull") and on the motif of sacrifice that runs throughout the Ehud narrative.

8. J. Soggin, *Judges,* 50.

9. R. Alter, *Art of Biblical Narrative,* 39.

10. D. Gunn, "Joshua and Judges," 115; G. Anderson, *Sacrifices and Offerings in Ancient Israel*, 67.

11. Cf. R. Alter (*Art of Biblical Narrative*, 39) "Eglon turns out to be a fatted calf readied for slaughter" and B. Lindars (*Judges 1–5*, 138) "[Eglon] is a fatted calf ready for slaughter." See also pp. 25–27.

12. M. Sternberg, *Poetics of Biblical Narrative*, 333–34.

13. Other significant verbal repetitions include √*nkh*, "to strike," in Judg 3:13, 29; √*šlḥ*, "to send," in 3:15, 18, 21; √*bw'*, "to enter," in 3:20, 22, 24, 27, 28; √*yṣ'*, "to exit," in 3:19, 22, 23, 24; *pĕsîlîm*, "[standing] stone monuments," in 3:19, 26; √*tq'*, "to blow," in 3:21, 27; √*sgr*, "to close," in 3:22, 23; √*mlṭ*, "to escape," in 3:26, 29; and *hinnēh* in 3:24, 25 (bis).

For these repetitions and others, see the studies in n. 6; esp. A. Schökel, "Erzählkunst," 157; and, in addition, M. Barré, "The Meaning of *pršdn* in Judges III 22," 8–10.

14. Y. Amit ("The Story of Ehud") has delineated the syntactical parallels between Judg 3:15–17, on the one hand, and vv. 21–22, on the other, as shown below.

vv. 15–17	vv. 21–22
The sons of Israel **sent** by **his hand**	Ehud **sent** forth **his left hand**
Ehud made for himself a **sword**	and he took the **sword**
[girding it] on **his right thigh**	from **his right thigh**
[Now Eglon was] a very **fat** man	[and struck him] in his belly ... the **fat**
wyšlḥw bny yśr'l bydw	*wyšlḥw 'hwd 't yd śm'lw*
wy'ś lw 'hwd ḥrb	*wyqḥ 't hḥrb*
'l yrk ymynw	*m'l yrk ymynw*
'yš bry' m'd	*bbṭnw ... hḥlb*

This "shows," as Amit puts it, "the tight connection between the plan and its execution" (p. 114).

15. In Judg 3:22 the folds of Eglon's belly "close" over the hilt of the sword; in 3:23, Ehud "closes" the doors to the royal apartment, now a mausoleum, cumulatively terminating the Moabite king.

Consider the twofold repetition of *dābār*, "word": Ehud says to Eglon in 3:19, "I have a *secret* word for you;" then in 3:20, one step deeper in plot, another degree more intense and precise in modification, "I have a *divine* word for you." R. Alter (*Art of Biblical Narrative*, 40) sees a *double entendre* here: the secret *dābār* that Ehud has for Eglon turns out to be the concealed sword, with *dābār* as both "word" and "thing." This might be possible in lexical Hebrew, where *dābār* is defined as "word," "matter," or "thing" (e.g. *HALOT* I:211) but in actual classical Hebrew usage, *dābār* only means "thing" in the abstract sense of "matter of concern" (J. Bergman, et al., "דבר *dābhar*," 3: 104–06) but never an unspecified concrete material object, for which *kĕlî* would be used.

16. The three instances of √*šlḥ*, "to send," abstracted, track the stages of Ehud's mission: the Israelites "dispatch" Ehud to deliver tribute to Eglon (Judg 3:15); Ehud "dismisses" his entourage and reenters the Moabite palace (3:18); Ehud "extends" his left hand to draw his sword and strike Eglon (3:21).

The three instances of √*mlṭ*, (*nip'al*, "to escape") abstracted, contrast Israelite and Moabite fortunes: Ehud "escapes" from the Moabite palace (3:26a); Ehud "escapes" to "Seirah," a safer place for him, further removed from the Moabites (3:26b); but, at the fords of the Jordan, no Moabite "escapes" (3:29).

Three instances of *hinnēh* (translated below as an interjection, "there!") focus on the progressive nature of the Moabite guards' discovery of their predicament (3:24–25):

> [Eglon's servants] saw—**there!**—that the doors of the room were locked. . . . They waited until it became embarrassing. And—**there!**—he was not opening the doors of the room. So they took the key and opened and—**there!**—their master had fallen to the ground, dead.

17. On the use of √*tq'* in Judg 3:21, 27, see G. Anderson, *Sacrifices and Offerings*, 71–74.

18. On repetitions of "hand," see L. Schökel, "Erzählkunst," 157; M. Sternberg, *Poetics of Biblical Narrative*, 337; D. Olson, "The Book of Judges," 771; Y. Amit, "Story of Ehud," 106; J. Soggin, *Judges*, 50; and M. Brettler, *The Creation of History in Ancient Israel*, 80.

19. On *bĕʿad* in Judges 3:21 (and 3:22) as "behind," see M. Barré, "Meaning of *pršdn*," 6, n. 22.

20. M. Barré, "Meaning of *pršdn*," 7.

21. *HALOT* 3:978.

22. B. Lindars, *Judges 1–5*, 147.

23. M. Barré, "Meaning of *pršdn*," 2–6; *CAD* 11/1: 283.

24. For a thorough review of the possible interpretations of Judg 3:22, including views not discussed here, see B. Lindars, *Judges 1–5*, 146–48.

25. The Aramaic Targum and the Latin Vulgate do provide rival witnesses, but in the absence of any collaborating evidence in Hebrew or Old Greek manuscripts (the entire sentence is missing in LXX[B]), it is difficult to ignore the received Hebrew text.

26. M. Barré ("Meaning of *pršdn*," 10) never directly owns up to the syntactical difficulty of taking *happaršĕdōnâ* as the subject of the sentence but he does admit that his rendering is dependent on an emendation of *hpršdnh*. B. Halpern marginalizes the issue by dealing with it in a footnote and giving it little attention: "It is difficult to see what other rendering could be appropriate" (*First Historians*, 69, n. 3). In the recent treatments of the Ehud story by M. Sternberg (*Poetics of Biblical Narrative*, 336) and M. Brettler (*Creation of History*, 82), respectively, the former hedges his bets (*"if* the concluding *va'yetse ha'parshedona* means, 'the filth came out,' *then* it carries the . . . wordplay to new lengths") [italics mine], while the latter ignores the problem ("The text explicitly refers to Eglon's excrement").

27. G. Moore comments that "no author is negligent enough to write, *and he went out to the* parshedon, *and Ehud went out to the* misderon" (*An Exegetical and Critical Commentary on Judges,* 98).

28. M. Barré, "Meaning of *pršdn,*" 8–9.

29. As suggested by David Noel Freedman (personal communication).

30. On the satiric tone of the story, see R. Alter, *Art of Biblical Narrative,* 39; B. Webb, *The Book of the Judges,* 129–30; M. Brettler, *Creation of History,* 79–90; and G. Anderson, *Sacrifices and Offerings,* 59.

31. M. Barré observes a pattern in the use of √*bwʾ* and √*yṣʾ,* "entering" and "exiting," respectively ("The Meaning of *pršdn,*" 8–9).

32. Perhaps B. Halpern had this in mind when he wrote that "the Moabites dallied" (*First Historians,* 60). In Gen 19:16, *hitmahmēah* also describes dangerously foolish delay. Biblical Hebrew had a simpler verb for "to hesitate, delay," i.e., *ʾēḥār, piʿel* of √*ʾḥr.*

33. Y. Amit does not invoke the epic diction of Lincoln's second inaugural address but observes in plainer style how the delay of the guards ("Story of Ehud," 116) is just one more link in a chain of coincidences and near misses which suggests, between the lines, that Providence is with Ehud throughout his adventure, despite the emphasis on human ingenuity (pp. 120–21).

34. For another scatological feature in the story, see B. Halpern (*First Historians,* 54–58). He describes Ehud escaping Eglon's palace through a privy hole, which is how Halpern understands the obscure *misdĕrôn* (Judg 3:23), a word found only here in the Hebrew Bible. Unfortunately, questions about the state of the text of this portion of the story (vv. 22–23), along with uncertainty about the meaning of the obscure words *paršĕdōnâ* and *misdĕrônâ,* make any interpretation insecure (B. Lindars, *Judges 1–5,* 146–49). Halpern's ingenious and entertaining discussion solves several problems but, at the same time, creates a new one: how could Ehud pass

through the bowels of the palace plumbing unsoiled, in a condition that would not alert the Moabite sentries to suspicions of foul play?

35. For a detailed discussion of the Ehud story as a "political satire," see M. Brettler, *Creation of History*, 79–90. Other studies which analyze satiric elements in the story include R. Alter (*Art of Biblical Narrative*, 38–41) and G. Anderson (*Sacrifices and Offerings*, 57–75). For the topic in general, see Z. Weisman, *Political Satire in the Bible*.

36. R. Alter, *Art of Biblical Narrative*, 39; M. Brettler, *Creation of History*, 82–83.

37. M. Brettler, *Creation of History*, 81; G. Anderson, *Sacrifices and Offerings*, 57–75; Y. Amit, "Story of Ehud," 109–11.

38. M. Brettler, *Creation of History*, 81.

39. G. Anderson, *Sacrifices and Offerings*, 59.

40. G. Anderson, *Sacrifices and Offerings*, 57–58, 75.

41. For this, see G. Moore, *Judges*, 91–104; and B. Lindars, *Judges 1–5*, 135–36.

42. See A. Mayes, *Judges*, 18–19, for a succinct description of editorial formulas characteristic of the central section (chs. 3–16) of Judges.

43. For instance, in our story the reference in the introductory section to the Ammonites and the Amalekites (Judg 3:13) seems superfluous to the story; only Moabites are mentioned in what follows. In the Gideon material (Judg 6–8), where the enemy throughout is the Midianites, there are two references to "the Amalekites and the people of the East" (Judg 6:3, 33). In both cases, it is likely that the stage of an older story has been expanded to accommodate a larger cast of villains.

Some scholars have doubted that the personal name "Ehud" was original to the story since, as a personal name, it is apparently unique before the Common Era (though that could change with the next inscription discovered). It does appear as the name for a Benjaminite family in 1 Chr 7:10 and 8:6. J. Gray once referred to this as "the personification in saga of clan history" (*Joshua, Judges and Ruth*, [Century Bible], 263) although the comment is omitted in the corresponding section of his revised edition of the commentary, *Joshua, Judges, Ruth* [New Century Bible], 250).

44. B. Lindars, *Judges 1–5*, 152. For Judg 3:27, see Judg 4:14; for 3:28a, see 4:14a, 7:15; for 3:28b, see the almost identical formulation in 12:5 (cf. also 7:24); for 3:27–28, taken as a whole, see Josh 6:16, 20.

45. G. Moore, *Judges*, 90; B. Lindars, *Judges 1–5*, 152.

46. See B. Lindars (*Judges 1–5*) for commentary on the many historical and geographic problems in the narrative, such as its apparent setting in Jericho (p. 139), the location of Gilgal (pp. 143, 153), and the political history of Moab and of its relations with Israel (p. 137). If we allow the story some historical basis, it could reflect a conflict between a local Transjordanian warlord from the region known in the Bible as "the plains of Moab" (Num 22:1), northeast of the Dead Sea, and Benjaminite and Ephraimite tribal militias from the vicinity of Jericho (M. Miller, "Moab and the Moabites," 34–35).

47. J. Soggin, *Judges*, 54; L. Hoppe, *Joshua, Judges*, 122.

48. "Stair-stepped" is a term used by some to describe a certain technique in poetic parallelism, usually involving triple-line units where each successive line preserves some elements with its predecessor while also introducing a novel element. W. Holladay, for instance, uses "stair-step" parallelism to describe lines with an $A + B + C \parallel A + B + D \parallel A + D + E$ pattern (*The Psalms through Three Thousand Years*, 20).

49. B. Halpern, *First Historians*, 46–60.

50. C. Burney, *The Book of Judges and Notes on the Hebrew Text of the Book of Kings*, 71; R. Alter, *Art of Biblical Narrative*, 40.

51. As B. Halpern notes, "Form and content correspond" (*First Historians*, 44).

52. J. Slotki, "Judges," 181.

53. R. Boling, *Judges*, 86.

54. E.g., Dt 7:25; Isa 21:9; Jer 8:19; Hos 11:2.

55. *HALOT* 1:191.

56. *HALOT* 3:948; J. Martin, *Book of Judges*, 48.

57. R. Boling, *Judges*, 86; J. Gray, *Joshua, Judges, Ruth*, NCB, 251.

58. Hos 12:12 (12:11 ET); Am 4:4. G. Moore, *Judges*, 95; J. Soggin, *Judges*, 51.

59. *HALOT* 3:948–49.

60. E. Kraeling, "Difficulties in the Story of Ehud," 206.

61. R. Polzin, *Moses and the Deuteronomist*, 160; D. Olson, "Judges," 771. R. O'Connell says the choice of *pĕsîlîm* here reflects a later critique of the impure religion of the entire era (*The Rhetoric of the Book of Judges*, 84).

62. F. M. Cross, *Canaanite Myth and Hebrew Epic*, 36–39; R. Clifford, *The Cosmic Mountain in Canaan and the Old Testament*; J. Levenson, *Sinai and Zion*, 111–45; G. Anderson, "Introduction to Israelite Religion," 278–79; L. Stager, "Jerusalem and the Garden of Eden."

63. L. Stager, "Jerusalem and the Garden of Eden."

64. For a single biblical verse that refers to all three zones, see Ex 20:4, given here in the translation of E. Fox, *The Five Books of Moses*, 369 (emphasis mine):

You are not to make yourself a carved-image or any figure
that is in **the heavens above,** that is on **the earth beneath,**
that is in **the waters beneath the earth.**

65. T. Abusch, "The Socio-Religious Framework of the Babylonian Witch-craft Ceremony *Maqlû*; *CAD* 11/2:145–47. The concept of liminality is best associated with A. van Gennep, *The Rites of Passage*; and V. Turner, *The Ritual Process*.

66. G. Anderson, "Israelite Religion," 277.

67. For a recent interpretation of this story, see N. Gillman, *The Death of Death*, 38–44.

68. Elijah in 1 Kgs 18; Elisha in 2 Kgs 2:25, 4:25.

69. Elijah in 1 Kgs 19:8–18.

70. Elijah and Elisha in 2 Kgs 2:2; Elisha in 2 Kgs 4:38.

71. For an English translation, see A. George, *The Epic of Gilgamesh*.

72. Gilgamesh Epic, Tablet V; A. George, *Epic of Gilgamesh*, 39–47.

73. Gilgamesh Epic, Tablet IX; A. George, *Epic of Gilgamesh*, 71–75.

74. A. George, *Epic of Gilgamesh*, 70.

75. Gilgamesh Epic, Tablet X; A. George, *Epic of Gilgamesh*, 75–79, 123–25.

76. For a survey of the genre, which includes accounts in Jewish and Christian apocalyptic writings, see R. Bauckham, "Descent to the Underworld."

77. For "The Descent of Ishtar," see B. Foster, *Before the Muses*, 1:403–09; and "The Descent of Ishtar to the Underworld (1.108)" (trans. S. Dalley). For the Baal myth, see M. Coogan, *Stories from Ancient Canaan*, 75–115,

esp. 106–15; M. Smith, "The Baal Cycle," esp. 141–64; and "The Baʿlu Myth (1.86)," (trans. D. Pardee), esp. 265–73. For the above description of Death's (i.e., Mot's) abode, see M. Smith, "Baal Cycle," 144.

78. S. Dalley, "Descent of Ishtar," 381.

79. F. M. Cross, *Canaanite Myth and Hebrew Epic,* 38.

80. See p. 110, n. 62.

81. J. Levenson, *Sinai and Zion,* 133–34. A New Testament example of a sacred natural precinct that combines, at its apex, access to heaven and, at its base, a portal to the underworld, is Mt. Hermon, site of numerous shrines throughout the centuries. In the text of Matthew, Jesus refers to the "Gates of Hades" while situated at the base of Mt. Hermon, at the cave from which the springs at Banyas (in the area known in the Roman period as Caesarea Philippi) emerge (Mt 16:13–18).

Another indication that the base of Mount Zion has been understood as an aperture between earth and the underworld is the Palestinian tradition that refers to a cave beneath the Dome of the Rock as *bir al-arwah,* "the well of souls," as seen in the notes to K. Makiya's novel, *The Rock,* 292.

82. For the motif of thresholds in the book of Judges, see M. O'Connor, "Judges," 132.

83. M. Brettler, *Creation of History,* 81; Y. Amit, "Story of Ehud," 110.

84. M. O'Connor, "Judges," 137.

85. M. Dahood, *Psalms III,* 155, 159.

86. For the use of ṣaddîq to mean "victorious," see Dahood, *Psalms III,* 158–59; for warfare as divine judgment between participants, see Sa-Moon Kang, *Divine War in the Old Testament and in the Ancient Near East,* 14, 50, 194.

5

GIDEON AND THE WINEPRESS

CATHEDRAL

The story of Ehud moved in straight lines through a landscape marked by monoliths and a palace defined by thresholds. Characterization was sketched in bold lines through picturesque details: the hero's left-handedness, the villain's corpulence. A single detail, the *pěsîlîm*, "monoliths," introduced early in the narrative and right on its surface, served as a kind of homing device to which the storyteller returned. This type of patterning provided an outline for the storyteller, leaving a trail to follow out of the forest on the other side of the rhetorical adventure. This type of storytelling, with hardly a word wasted, beguilingly invited its audience to mentally plot its own progress along the sphere of rising action and anticipate and then recognize its parallel egress, step-by-step, through the falling action. Protagonist, narrator, audience: everyone arrived home together.

Such a narrative style is more than engaging and useful. It expresses a worldview. The economy of the story suggests that reality does not include loose ends. Its edges have been squared, like those of the four-cornered world alluded to in some biblical texts.[1] Stories that end at the beginning, like Ehud and the Monoliths, confirm that the drama of reality has been scripted. You *can* get home again. Underdogs rise, tyrants fall; a moral gravity prevails. Furthermore, the Invisible Hand has a deft touch, imbuing the science of cause and effect with a poetic quality: the despot greedy for tribute becomes a sacrificial victim himself; the grand palace with its defensive perimeters a mausoleum from which there is no escape; the portals of the Gates of Death, the monoliths that mark Ehud's solo mission behind enemy lines, are transformed into an *Arc de Triomphe* when the hero, against all odds, emerges to blow the *shofar* after his solo adventure.

In contrast to Ehud and Monoliths, the Gideon material contains confusing repetitions, a meandering plot, and multiple endings. Four full chapters in the book of Judges (Judg 6–9), 157 verses compared with the nineteen verses of the Ehud narrative, concern Gideon and Gideon's putative son, Abimelech; and this large block of literature is complicated.[2] If the Ehud narrative in Judges 3:12–30 resembled a set of nesting boxes, the material about Gideon and Abimelech in Judges 6–9 resembles a cathedral: sprawling, constructed over the course of centuries, containing many finely built chapel-like individual scenes and numerous vividly drawn features, but lacking in overall structural coherence.

Judges 6–9 presents three major literary complications: the conflation of contradictory and redundant details in the account of Gideon in chapters 6–8, the uneasy literary juxtaposition of the story of Gideon in chapters 6–8 with that of Abimelech in chapter 9, and the story's long history of literary development, as suggested by new evidence from Qumran.

BROKERED DESIGN IN JUDGES 6–8

The first major section, concerning the adventures of Gideon (essentially Judg 6–8), moves in fits and starts and contains numerous doublets. The overall picture sketched in this section is clear, that of a small, select band of warriors triumphing over an enemy of uncountable, entomological proportions through a daring, unorthodox, and spectacular raid on a sleeping enemy camp. But elements from two competing designs have been incorporated into the cathedral of the realized project.

The First Design: Gideon and Abiezer

In one version, Gideon, who is introduced as standing beside the upper apparatus of a winepress, a *gat*, musters and leads the militia from his clan of Abiezer to stem the seasonal raids of Midianites who had been plundering Israelite farms at harvest time. Gideon and the Abiezer militia visually startle a large slumbering Midianite encampment by shattering clay jars to reveal kindled torches.[3] This design seems complete when one of the Midianite leaders is slain at the site of the lower apparatus of a winepress, a *yeqeb*. The decapitated heads of Zeeb, killed at the winepress, and his fellow Midianite captain, Oreb, are then presented to Gideon.

> They brought **the heads** of Oreb and Zeeb to Gideon.
> (Judg 7:25)

Narratives in the middle part of the book of Judges begin and end with conventional editorial structures. Entrances are marked by one formula, "the Israelites did the evil thing in the eyes of Yhwh," and exits by another formula, "and the land had rest." One enters Judges 6–8, the central chamber of the narrative, through such a door in Judges 6:1. The exit from this section appears in

Judges 8:28 and it seems specially tailored to fit with this design, ending with a grim reaping of Midianite scalps.

> So Midian was subdued before the Israelites, and **they never again raised their heads.** The land had rest for forty years in the days of Gideon. (Judg 8:28)

We have here three verbal structures that mark resolution: military resolution through the defeat of the Midianites (Judg 7:22–23), rhetorical resolution through the initial and terminal images of the parts of a winepress (Judg 6:11; 7:25), and editorial resolution through the note that the land had rest (Judg 8:28). There is only one problem. There is a long episode (Judg 8:4–27) between the scene where the Midianite heads are presented to Gideon (Judg 7:25–8:3) and the terminal formula with its reference to the heads of the Midianites (Judg 8:28).

The Second Design: Gideon and the 300 Manassites

The episode between the ceremonial slaughter of the Midianite leaders Oreb and Zeeb and the terminal editorial formula that invokes their decapitation details a blood feud. The account of the blood feud is part of a different design for telling the story of Gideon. In this version, the warriors that Gideon musters are described not as from the clan of Abiezer but as from the tribe of Manasseh.

Abiezer was a kinship subset, a clan, of the larger group of Manasseh. The terms, Abiezer and Manasseh, thus, might be seen as functionally synonymous were it not for the fact that each term is developed in specific ways in different sections to further a common theme. That common theme is the triumph of a select group of warriors over a vast enemy. In the design noted above, Gideon fights with the Abiezer militia, the "thinnest" (Judg 6:15) clan of the tribe of Manasseh. In the design noted here, Gideon gathers his troops from the tribe of Manasseh; the clan of Abiezer is not mentioned. The total number of troops given in Judges 7:3, the second design, is thirty-two *'elep* units. But thirty-two *'elep* units "are too many" (Judg 8:2, 4) to suit the guerrilla tactics in and theological purposes of the story. The thirty-two *'elep* units of Manasseh must be sifted by ordeal to a mere three hundred men. From this point on (Judg 7:8), this version of the story, the Manassite version, uses the image of Gideon and the Three Hundred, not of Gideon and the Abiezer clan militia, to express the theme of the triumph of a small band.

In this version, Gideon and his three hundred raid the camp but they startle the Midianites aurally—not visually—by breaking the nocturnal silence with the unison cacophony of trumpet blasts. In this version, the hostilities spill over into Transjordan—the arena of the other design is confined to Cisjordan—where Gideon tracks down two Midianite leaders and executes them. In this version, the names of the Midianite leaders are not Oreb and Zeeb, as in Judges 7:25–8:3, but Zebah and Zalmunna (Judg 8:5).

So this central chamber of the cathedral, the account of Gideon's campaign against Midian, conflates elements from two designs. This conflation of elements has so complicated the plot of Judges 6–8 that in its extant form parts are more memorable than the whole. Individual scenes, such as Gideon's reluctant protestations at his call (Judg 6:11–16), the test of the divine will involving the fleece (Judg 6:36–40), and the war party raiding with torches flaring and horns blaring (Judg 7:19–23), or vivid images, such as a crafty hero threshing wheat in a winepress (Judg 6:11), men lapping water from a spring (Judg 7:4–6), and a leader blowing a trumpet (Judg 6:34; 7:18), have arrested the attention of audiences for centuries. But the complexity of the story itself frustrates our apprehension of the way these discrete scenes and images combine into a single story. Our meandering narrative moves as clumsily as the Israelite warriors who, in its brokered climax, raid the enemy camp at midnight improbably balancing clay jugs containing lit torches in one hand and bone trumpets in the other.

Multiple Endings

This conflation of design also obscures our apprehension of the profile of the narrative's rise and fall. Every time we think the story is about to end, there is another twist. The story of Gideon begins in Judges 6:1 but it could have at least seven endings.

1. The problem that launches the story—seminomadic Midianites from Transjordan raiding Israelite territory and plundering its agricultural resources—is fully resolved by Judges 8:3, at the end of which Gideon and company have repulsed the invaders and executed their leaders.[4]

2. But the warfare continues as Gideon, whose name means "Slasher," crosses the Jordan in order to satisfy a blood feud (Judg 8:4–21).[5] Slasher slays the sheiks who had killed his brothers during the course of the earlier hostilities (Judg 8:21). The blood feud satisfied and Gideon's name justified, the story also seems to find a resolution in Judges 8:21. The *gibbôr* has defended both his tribal turf and his family's honor.

3. Gideon retakes the stage for a final bow in Judges 8:22–23, meeting the high standards of Israelite prophets such as Samuel (1 Sam 8:4–22) and Hosea (Hos 8:4) by refusing his people's request to rule over them (Judg 8:22). Only Yʜᴡʜ will rule over Israel, according to Gideon (Judg 8:23). Gideon does not want to be a warrior king; he is content to be a warrior priest and asks only for a measure of the campaign plunder in order to outfit his village shrine (Judg 8:24–27a).

4. But in the subsequent verses (Judg 8:24–27), the judge whose initial call from and dialogue with God (Judg 6:11–24) has invited comparisons with Moses,[6] and whose words in Judges 8:23 have echoes of Samuel and Hosea, prophetic figures in the Mosaic

tradition,[7] abruptly turns into Aaron.[8] Gideon constructs an *ephod*, an oracular device, from the campaign's plunder.[9]

The mere mention of an *ephod* in stories set in the era of the Judges and early monarchy is not a surprise and, by itself, carries no connotations of illicit religious practice.[10] Here, however, Gideon's *ephod* is described as if it were Aaron's golden calf, both constructed from melted "gold earrings" (Ex 32:2–4; Judg 8:24). "All Israel prostituted themselves" to the *ephod* in Gideon's shrine in Ophrah," the text intones, "and it became a snare to Gideon and his family" (Judg 8:27b)."[11]

5. Then, unexpectedly—given that Gideon had just been accused of violating the second commandment—we abruptly move without a single measure's rest from this note of discord in Judges 8:27 to the harmony of the editorial formula typical of Judges in the next verse, Judg 8:28: "So Midian was subdued before the Israelites. . . . The land had rest forty years in the days of Gideon." This is the happy ending on which the preceding stories of Othniel, Ehud, and Deborah and Barak, had closed. But even this does not end our story.

6. A section follows (Judg 8:29–32) with details—Gideon had seventy sons, one of his secondary wives resided in the ethnically mixed town of Shechem, her son by Gideon was named Abimelech— that prepare us for the next, troubling, long story of Abimelech in Judges 9, while, at the same time—finally—finishing the story of Gideon and fixing his legacy, in the wake of so many ambiguities, as honorable. He dies at the end of a long life, literally, at a good "gray-beardedness" (Judg 8:32), and is interred in his family tomb to sleep, as he had fought, with his clan.

Gray hair, proverbially, was the crown worn by a man whose righteousness had been rewarded by a full life span (Prov 16:31, 20:29). This note is an unlikely epitaph for an idolater. The final sentence of this section, "He was buried in the tomb of his father Joash at Ophrah of the Abiezrites," can hardly be from the same writer who told us, a paragraph before, of Gideon's apostasy. This narrator directs pilgrims to the very location, the burial site of a great ancestor, Ophrah, that the preceding narrator condemned as ritually contaminating.

7. Then the story of Abimelech, Gideon's putative son, immediately follows. This story peopled with fratricidal opportunists, arsonists, ambushers, and gangs vying for turf control of the Shechem region, has its own emphases. It is largely a morality tale about thieves falling out and just deserts. But juxtaposed to the preceding stories about Gideon, the Abimelech narrative affects our view of the former. In combination, the entire complex of Judges 6–9 serves as a cautionary tale about the dangers of dynastic kingship.

These multiple endings frustrate our apprehension of the plot of Judges 6–9, obscuring the profile of the narrative's rise and fall. These multiple endings also obscure our image of the story's hero: one minute, he is Moses the reluctant leader (Judg 6:11–18; cf. Ex 3:13; 4:1, 10); the next, he is Lamech the blood feuder (Judg 8:4–19; cf. Gen 4:23–24);[12] the next, he is Aaron the idolater (Judg 8:24–27; cf. Ex 32:2–4); the next, he is Othniel the model judge (Judg 8:28; cf. Judg 3:7–11). Ultimately, in light of the Abimelech narrative, Gideon is comparable to an Eli, Solomon, or Josiah, great men whose respective sons failed to measure up to the standard of their fathers (1 Sam 2:12; 1 Kgs 12:1–19; 2 Kgs 23:28–33).

Doublets

In addition to its multiple endings and confusing character development, the story is further complicated by the fact that there are two of everything.[13] Two names, Gideon and Jerubbaal, are used for its hero; two names, YHWH and Elohim, for the deity (the name "YHWH" is predominant, but one entire episode, Gideon's divinatory test with the fleece, Judg 6:36–40, uses Elohim exclusively). Two intermediaries, a prophet in Judges 6:7–10 and a celestial messenger in Judges 6:11–22, appear in separate scenes near the beginning. There are two accounts of the building of an altar to YHWH in Ophrah (Judg 6:24; 6:25–32), two pairs of Midianite officers executed (Judg 7:25; 8:21), two tests by which Gideon confirms the deity's support for his warfare (Judg 6:36–38; 39–40), and two tests by which YHWH confirms the competence of Gideon's men for warfare (Judg 7:2–3; 7:4–8). Then in the climactic scene, the nocturnal raid on the Midianite camp (Judg 7:19–23), Gideon and his men are described charging into the Midianite camp with two hands full, kindled torches balancing improbably inside jars in their left hands, ram's horns in their right hands (Judg 7:19–20).

How does one account for a narrative (Judges 6–8) that so takes its time, so mixes its motives, and so complicates its plot that its parts are more memorable than its whole? The extant text may very well be composite, as an earlier generation of biblical scholars suggested.[14] The description of the raid on the Midianite camp with torches flaring and horns blaring is a telling blow. The mechanics are impossible.[15] It takes two hands to balance a lit torch inside a clay jar. It takes at least another to lift and sound a *shofar*. This blending of two versions of comparably unorthodox tactics into a single juggling act is the clearest evidence of a composite text. Many, but not all, of the doublets in Judges 6–8 can be explained as belonging to respective versions of Gideon's heroics.[16]

THE BROKERED SAGA

The second major section of Judges 6–9, concerning Abimelech, *"son of Jerubbaal"* (Judg 9:1, 16, 19, 28), is of one piece but its literary relationship to the preceding materials about Gideon—whom the text twice parenthetically insists was also known as "Jerubbaal" (Judg 6:32; 7:1)—is dubious. The entire complex of Judges 6–9 probably combines two independent blocks of material about unrelated characters, a conflated or blended narrative about Gideon and a single-textured narrative about Abimelech, in order to create a multigenerational story about the rise and fall of a family, a blended saga about the dangers of dynasties.

Gideon, Jerubbaal, and Abimelech

The protagonist of Judges 6:1–8:28 bears two names, "Gideon" and "Jerubbaal." This portion of Judges 6–9 is clearly bounded as a narrative unit by the initial and terminal elements of the Judges editorial formula: "And the Israelites did the evil thing in the eyes of YHWH" (Judg 6:1); "And the land had rest" (Judg 8:28). In this portion, which blends two sources, the name "Gideon" dominates (thirty-seven usages) while "Jerubbaal" occurs only twice (Judg 6:32; 7:1). By contrast, in the story of Abimelech (Judg 8:29–9:57), the name of Abimelech's father is given as "Jerubbaal" nine times and as "Gideon" only four. All of the latter are confined to the initial verses of the Abimelech story (Judg 8:29–35), the bridging paragraph between the Gideon and Abimelech traditions.

Neither reference to Gideon as "Jerubbaal" in Judg 6:1–8:28 is convincing. The reference in Judges 6:32 explains how Gideon, i.e., "Slasher," acquired a second name, Jerubbaal, after he destroyed the altar of Baal in Ophrah. Earlier in this episode (Judg 6:25–32), the men of Ophrah had learned that Gideon was responsible for the desecration of their local shrine and were preparing to execute him for this sacrilege. But Gideon's father spoke up, arguing that Baal, if potent, was fully capable of defending his house without their help.

> "If [Baal] is divine, let him contend (*yāreb*) for himself. It was his altar that [Gideon] demolished." (Judg 6:31)

That is why, the narrator explains, Gideon received a new name.

> They (re-)named [Gideon] on that day "Jerubbaal (*yērûbba'al*)," saying, "Let Baal (*ba'al*) defend (*yāreb*) himself against [Gideon]." (Judg 6:32)

"Jerubbaal," according to this etymology, means, "Let Baal contend [against him]," but the syntax is impossible. Names that have the pattern of verb (i.e., "may he contend," *yāreb*) + divine name or epithet (i.e., *ba'al*) are common in the Hebrew and other Semitic onamastica but in every case they express solidarity between a deity and the mortal bearer of the name, not enmity. "Jerubbaal" must mean, "May Baal [or 'the Lord'] contend" *on behalf of* him," not *against* him."¹⁷ The other reference to Gideon as Jerubbaal in Judges 6:1–8:28 is a parenthetical aside in Judges 7:1, "Then Jerubbaal, *that is Gideon*, and the entire army with him camped alongside the Spring of Trembling." The identification with the name Jerubbaal is only loosely connected to the character Gideon in Judges 6:1–8:28.

By contrast, in the narrative of Abimelech in Judges 8:29–9:57, it is the name "Gideon" that seems out of context and "Jerubbaal" dominates as the name of Abimelech's father (Judg 9:1, 2, 5, 16, 19, 24, 28, 57). Only in a transitional paragraph that bridges the stories about Gideon (Judg 6:1–8:28) and Abimelech (Judg 9:1–57), do both names appear (Judg 8:29–35): "Jerubbaal ben Joash" in Judges 8:29 uneasily close to "Gideon ben Joash" in Judges 8:32; "Gideon" alone in Judges 8:30, 33; and in a mediating editorial aside in the final verse of the section, "Jerubbaal, that is Gideon," in Judges 8:35 (cf. Judg 7:1).

It is unlikely that the double names can be assigned to the respective designs we observed in the conflated text of Judges 6–8. The overwhelming prevalence of the name Gideon and the thematic ways that its meaning, "Slasher," functions in that material about a warrior who cuts down foes, shrines, and towers, suggest that the hero's name was known as "Gideon" in both designs. It is likely, however, that there were Israelite oral traditions about a warrior named Jerubbaal who fought against the Midianites in the premonarchical era. There is a reference in 1 Samuel 12:11 to "Jerubbaal" as one of the heroes of the period, alongside Barak, Jephthah—both known from Judges—and Bedan, another hero whose exploits were not recorded in the Bible. Furthermore, a back story about how a warrior named Jerubbaal rescued the region of Shechem from Midianite control (Judg 9:16–17) is essential for the plot of the Abimelech narrative, with its tale of sons vying for the legacy of a great father. But these traditions about the heroics of Jerubbaal, father of Abimelech, against Midian, remain lost for now. Judges preserves only the heroics of Gideon. The *ad hoc*, unconvincing explanation for how Gideon acquired the name Jerubbaal, and the parenthetical clauses in Judges 7:1 and 8:35 that emphasize the equivalence, are most likely mechanisms engineered to bridge two originally independent bodies of tradition about warriors from the era of Judges.[18]

In Judges 6–9, the equation of Gideon with Jerubbaal combines two independent traditions, one about a warrior named Gideon ben Joash, and another about a warrior named Abimelech ben Jerubbaal. The juxtaposition of these warriors, Gideon who eschews kingship and honorably (by their standards) satisfies the killing of his brothers, on one hand, and Abimelech who ruthlessly seeks political power and murders his brothers, on the other hand, augments the themes of each story through the implicit contrast of Gideon and Abimelech's respective virtue and villainy. Furthermore, through the secondary linkage of these two stories, a third story is created as the whole of Judges 6–9 now serves as a cautionary tale about the dangers of dynastic kingship, a topic perennially attractive to biblical writers and audiences.

THE MISSING PROPHET

Something is missing from the fragment of the Gideon story discovered in 1952 among the Dead Sea Scrolls. One entire scene, an account of a prophet delivering a speech, corresponding to Judges 6:7–10, is missing in 4QJudg[a], which for now represents our earliest manuscript of the book of Judges.[19] Scholars sifting through the textual remains of the extant Hebrew text of Judges, trying to understand its literary development, have suspected for over a century that this prophetic speech was a late addition to the story.[20] The find confirms that suspicion.[21]

The pattern for narratives in the middle section of Judges begins with brief descriptions of the oppressive situation (Judg 3:8; 3:13–14; 4:2–3; 6:2–6) and of the Israelites' prayer for deliverance (3:9; 3:15; 4:3; 6:6–7). Except for the Gideon story, the next detail in each of these narratives is another element from this pattern: the introduction of the rescuer selected by YHWH to lead the military campaign against the oppressor. The line, "the Israelites cried out," marks the cue for the hero's entrance.

But in Judges 6:1–8:28, right after the note that the Israelites cried out to YHWH for help (Judg 6:6), Gideon's introduction is delayed by the appearance and speech of a prophet. The content of this speech by an unnamed prophet is unremarkable in itself and is a variant of one given many other times in the Deuteronomistic History.[22] As noted above, the speech interrupts the expected sequence of introductory elements in the stories in Judges, and scholars have assumed that it was added to the story long after a highly patterned, earlier form of the story had emerged. To these subjective grounds for suspecting Judges 6:7–10 to be a later insertion, we now have objective evidence from Qumran Cave 4. Very few lines from Judges are preserved in the latter, second-century B.C.E., scroll, written in ink on tanned animal skin.[23] But the initial lines of the Gideon story are well preserved and we can clearly see that 4QJudg[a] preserves the conventional pattern. The introduction of Gideon (i.e., Judg 6:11) immediately follows the people's cry (i.e., Judg 6:6). There is no scene with a prophet (i.e., Judg 6:7–10).

Unless or until we find other ancient texts, this fragmentary scroll represents our earliest witness to the text of the Gideon narrative. On one hand, it is possible that the missing lines in 4QJudg[a] are merely an idiosyncratic feature of one ancient version.[24] On the other hand, it could be that as late as the second-century B.C.E. the

Gideon narrative was still under literary construction, and that the speech had not yet been inserted by redactors. The small section containing this speech, four verses in a story taking up four chapters in Judges, is not crucial for interpretation of the story. The Qumran evidence does, however, illustrate the literary complexity of Judges 6–9, which includes stories about Gideon and his putative son Abimelech. The present story did not emerge in a moment. The literary complexity of the Gideon narrative thus involves more than the conflation of elements from different versions of his campaign against Midian and the juxtaposition of originally unrelated stories about Gideon, son of Joash, and Abimelech, son of Jerubbaal. The blended saga of Gideon and Abimelech in Judges 6–9, which includes a blended narrative about Gideon in Judges 6–8, was itself amplified during the course of its transmission.

ARCHITECTURAL HISTORY

The cathedral of Judges 6–9 remained under construction for centuries. Some added details were ornamental. The expansion of the parties in the conflict to include, on the Israelite side, warriors from Asher, Zebulun, and Naphtali (Judg 6:35b; 7:23), and on the Midianite side, Amalek and the Easterners (Judg 6:3, 33; 7:12), is common to many stories in Judges.[25] Regional conflicts were editorially expanded into national wars when these accounts became part of a national heroic anthology. Other additions were structural; the speech of the prophet in Judges 6:7–10 added a new scene. A transitional paragraph and a handful of parenthetical asides were constructed to form a bridge between the Gideon narrative and that of Abimelech. The uneasy conflation of two rival versions of the slaying of the Midianite leaders—Oreb and Zeeb in one version, Zebah and Zalmunna in the other—was harmonized by the addition of the note that the latter had slain Gideon's flesh-and-blood brothers during the Cisjordanian hostilities. A later editor, writing when the heroic tales of the frontier era had been recast as one long descent from Mosaic orthodoxy to paganism, seized upon the reference to the *ephod* and editorially carved a didactic inscription above Gideon's shrine in Ophrah (Judg 8:27b).

In addition, the structure of the central chamber, the narrative about Gideon's battle with Midian, was remodeled. The presentation of the heads of Oreb and Zeeb once may have marked the back wall of the story, but in the course of construction, as elements from two designs—Gideon and Abiezer as opposed to Gideon and the Three Hundred—were incorporated into the structure, the terminal formula that alludes to the heads of Oreb and Zeeb (Judg 8:28) was moved to the end of the blood-feud episode.

Though I have sketched the outline of two versions of the Gideon narrative, I will refrain from any further attempts to dissolve this blended narrative into its constitutive elements and to analyze reconstructed, hypothetical precursors to the extant text.[26] Such experiments were conducted in the laboratories of an earlier generation of researchers but did not yield consistent results.[27] The attempts were not misguided but the subjective nature of studies that assign this verse or that to respective sources leaves us without a common space for interpretation. I will stay with this sprawling, busy cathedral of a narrative whose many chambers and details defy reduction to a simple organizing scheme for the entire complex.

Yet, though the acute narrative symmetries of Judges 6–9 may have been blunted in the course of its development, they have not been obliterated. It is true that no single organizing motif, comparable to the *pĕsîlîm* in the Ehud narrative, emerges clearly. But the many chambers of Judges 6–9 contain a surplus of details and narrative symmetries.

In the materials concerning Gideon, one portion of the story (Judg 6:1–8:3) is bracketed by mention of a winepress. It is possible that the terminal repetition of the winepress once represented the back wall of the entire structure. It no longer does, however, as the story barely pauses before following Gideon and the three hundred Manassites into Transjordan on a blood feud. Still, the rhetorical brackets of the winepress, perhaps once a narrative boundary, remain solid enough structurally to define an episodic boundary in the extant text. I will refer to this episode as Gideon and the Winepress (Judg 6:1–8:3).

The rest of the story of Gideon, in Judg 8:4–28, is built around its own symmetrical pattern. In this section, Gideon pursues blood vengeance to atone for the killing of two of his flesh-and-blood brothers during the earlier campaign. He leads his band of three hundred men from the tribe of Manasseh through two villages, accumulating new slights along the way, before apprehending the culprits in a third village. On the way back, Gideon settles the score, one village at a time: a tripartite itinerary of satisfaction dedicated to the mentality of blood feuding. I will refer to this episode as Gideon and the Three Villages (Judg 8:4–28). Originally, this episode may have represented the climax of one version of Gideon's campaign against Midian, a version of the story that emphasized the motif of the three hundred men and that characterized Gideon as a warrior priest who rose to prominence after remodeling the shrine in Ophrah in Yahwistic fashion and ended his adventures by outfitting the same shrine with an *ephod*. Though Gideon and the Three Villages, the blood-feud account, seems anticlimactic in the extant text, it also preserves the symmetrical style of Israelite heroic narrative, even as a secondary episode.

In the Abimelech material (Judg 8:29–9:57) (here, Abimelech and the Stones), two stones serve as its narrative boundary markers: Abimelech begins his quest to be the ruling warlord in his neighborhood by killing his brothers on "a certain stone" (Judg 9:5); "a certain woman" ends it when she drops a stone on his head (Judg 9:53). We will observe these symmetries one section, one narrative chamber, at a time. Its superfluity of detail and design impedes an attempt to find a single or related set of motifs that governs the entire work of Judges 6–9, as we were able to do with the Ehud narrative. But this abundance of patterns, often competing with each other, allows us an opportunity to reflect on the deeper meanings implicit in the ancient style of storytelling.

GIDEON AND THE WINEPRESS

Aristotle, in his *Poetics* (VII: 2–3), describes the structure of a well constructed plot as having a beginning, a middle, and an end, each scene developing organically from seeds planted in what preceded it.[28] Though Aristotle spoke about Greek tragedy, his analysis is applicable to other narrative forms. Our text, as sketched above, has a single beginning in Judges 6:1–6, followed by a bloated middle and several possible endings. Entering this narrative field, its perimeter unclearly marked and so overgrown with competing details and dense with doublets that its primary crop is nearly impossible to identify, we must hold tightly to the plow. We will follow the imprint of the details traced in the one section of the story that is clearly marked: its single beginning in Judges 6:1–6, which details the Midianite incursion into Israelite Cisjordan and plunder of its harvests. The initial details, and the narrative developments that grow directly from them, have left the deepest impression on the story.

From this single beginning, a primary line of plot organically develops in Judges 6–7, reaching fruition when Israelite warriors led by Gideon raid the Midianite camp and chase the raiders toward the Jordan where the locals, the warriors of Ephraim, intercept and cut down the fleeing army, an account whose epilogue ends in Judges 8:3. Furthermore, throughout the story—despite its superfluity of details and scenes, despite its conflated origins, despite its secondary themes and lack of Aristotelian single-mindedness—a single heroic theme appears again and again. If the Ehud narrative represented the improbable triumph of a lone warrior, the narrative about

Gideon in Judges 6:1–8:3 represents, in shorthand, the triumph of a small group over a vast army. In addition to the coherence of its main plot and primary theme, this story about a hero whom we first glimpse standing at a winepress (Judg 6:11) finds a measure of stylistic coherence and closure when, after the climactic battle, one of the Midianite leaders is killed at the site of a winepress (Judg 7:25).[29]

THE INITIAL SITUATION

The descriptions of and contrasts between the combatants Israel and Midian sketched in the introductory verses of "Gideon and the Winepress" (Judg 6:1–8:3) are reutilized and brought to narrative resolution by the end of the section. The elements of the editorial formula common to narratives in Judges have all been utilized by this juncture too, with one exception. Along the way, a number of other issues complicate this initial plot, planting elements to be realized in the subsequent account of Gideon's blood feud and of Gideon's putative son, Abimelech.[30]

"Whenever Israel planted," as recounted in Judges 6:3, seminomadic raiders from east of the Jordan River would enter the Samarian highlands and feast on the produce. The Midianites, along with "Amalek and the Easterners," descended with tents "thick as locusts" and livestock "without number" (Judg 6:5).[31] In a later scene, this eastern horde is described as "falling on," blanketing a landscape (Judg 7:12), and here in Judges 6:1–6 the sense is the same: the entire surface of Cisjordan, from the Jordan to as "far [west] as Gaza (Judg 6:4), on the Mediterranean coast, is swarming with them.

In contrast to this teeming swarm of humans and camels, the Israelites are "very weak," *wayyiddal . . . mĕ'ōd* (Judg 6:6). The verb *wayyiddal* (√*dll*) connotes, in this context, "impoverished, thin, emaciated."[32] In the face of this swarm, the Israelites are driven into the margins, "hiding places in the hills, and caves and strongholds" (Judg 6:2).

The initial contrasts are these. The Midianites have the upper hand over the Israelites (Judg 6:1, 2). The Midianites, along with their tents and livestock, blanket the entire surface of Cisjordan whereas the Israelites are squeezed into holes in the landscape. The Midianite presence is as uncountable and ravenous as a locust plague (Judg 6:5) whereas the Israelites are "very weak." The Midianites feast on the produce of what Psalm 83:13 (83:12 ET) refers to as "the pastures of Elohim" whereas the Israelites have nothing "to live [on]" (Judg 6:4).

In addition to sketching these contrasts that will govern "Gideon and the Winepress," this first scene includes three elements of the framing formula common to narratives in Judges:

1. The Israelites have done the "evil thing."
2. YHWH, a demanding suzerain, has given his servants to another master—a rival people or warlord, here Midian—who treats them cruelly.
3. Israel has prayed for rescue.

The fourth element of the formula, the entrance of the rescuer, should be next.

But Gideon's entrance is delayed by the scene missing in 4QJudg^a (Judg 6:7–10). After this secondary scene, the story picks up in Judg 6:11 where it left off in verse 6, with the appearance of a divine messenger at a sacred site, "the Oak at Ophrah" to commission the hero.[33] Gideon, it says, was beating out wheat in a winepress in order to hide it, when the messenger appears to him and delivers a war oracle, "YHWH is with you, O *gibbôr ḥayil*" (Judg 6:12).

The terms by which Midian, Israel, and Gideon are portrayed in these first dozen verses of Judges 6 are the foundation for a series of reversals, in corresponding terms, in the final sections of Judges 7, which must have represented, in at least one stratum of a story that grew over time and was still under construction as late as the time of the Dead Sea Scrolls: a climax and denouement. Several of these details are revisited in a single scene, the account of a dream overheard by Gideon, that directly precedes the climactic battle.

THE DREAM

In Judges 7:9–15, Gideon and his squire, Purah, receive a divine command to sneak up upon the Midianite camp at night. There they overhear a Midianite sentry recount a dream to his mate. The description of the Midianite camp in this scene repeats formulas from the introductory scene in Judges 6:1–6. "Midian and Amalek and all the Easterners," "as thick as locusts," camels "without number": all these phrases in Judges 7:12 are borrowed, almost word for word, from Judges 6:3, 5.

In the story, the Midianites' "tents" (Judg 6:4; 7:13) seem to represent more than the encampments of soldiers.[34] The Midianite tents and camels (Judg 6:5; 7:12) are tokens of a nonsedentary lifestyle, of an entomological Otherness that is subhuman and repulsive from the Israelite perspective. The description of these tents and their inhabitants, "fallen ($\sqrt{npl}$) in the valley as thick as locusts," sounds like the description of the frogs that "covered" the land of Egypt in the Exodus story (Ex 8:2 [8:6 ET]).

In his dream, the Midianite sentry imagines the falling ($\sqrt{npl}$; twice in Judg 7:13) of those same tents. What causes the tents to collapse? A cake of barley bread tumbles down from the hills to destroy them (Judg 7:13). This is our first reversal: Israel, Midian's meal ticket according to Judges 6:4–5, transmogrifies into a great round of bread that bowls over the Midianite camp.

THE RAID

Then in the battle scene that immediately follows, Gideon, who had once "hidden" wheat (literally "caused [it] to flee," Judg 6:11), forces the Midianites "to flee" (Judg 7:21). The invaders who had once spread out "as far [west] as Gaza," now themselves flee—the verb is used again—"as far [southeast] as Beth-shittah toward Zererah, as far [northeast] as the edge of Abel-meholah near Tabbath" (Judg 7:22; cf. 7:24). Whereas before YHWH had given the Israelites into the hand of the Midianites (Judg 6:1), now the Midianites and their princes have now been given into the hand of the Israelites (Judg 7:7, 9, 15; 8:3). Whereas once the Midianites reaped what the Israelites had sown, as if in fulfillment of the terms of prophetic curse (e.g., Mic 6:15), in the aftermath of the battle, it is the Israelites who reap. Warriors from Ephraim "glean" (Judg 8:2) the heads of the Midianite leaders, Oreb ("Raven") and Zeeb ("Wolf") and present these trophies to Gideon (Judg 7:24–25).[35]

THE WINEPRESS

The details about the raid and its aftermath bring dramatic closure to the entire adventure. Gideon was initially introduced standing at a "winepress," *gat* (Judg 6:11). *Gat* refers to the upper basin of the apparatus, the stone trough where grapes were treaded.[36] The juice from the *gat* flowed down into a collecting trough set on a lower platform, the *yeqeb*.[37] The Midianite captain Zeeb, "Wolf," is slain at the site of a winepress, here referred to as a *yeqeb* (Judg 7:25). The imagery of the two corresponding elements of a winepress structurally marks beginning and ending sections of the story and symbolically summarizes the reversal of fortunes that the intervening episodes charted. The story that began at a winepress (*gat*), with Israel pressed into the hills and its fields treaded upon, ends at a winepress (*yeqeb*), with Midian drained of men and resources. The Midianites, who had once constricted the Israelites, are now squeezed—the work of the *gat*—out of Cisjordan by their pursuers.

The other Midianite prince, Oreb, "Raven," is pursued and

slain at "Raven's Rock" (Judg 7:25). In light of the wordplay between *gat* and *yeqeb*, the site of this killing might also represent an ironic reversal. Raven flees to and receives his just deserts in just the kind of rocky haunts to which the Israelites had retreated in the first scene ("hiding places in the hills, caves"; Judg 6:2). When Isaiah alludes to a tradition of the Israelite defeat of Midian, it is this location, "Raven's Rock," that serves as his focal point (Isa 10:26), which suggests that this image, as well as that of the winepress, had sufficient poetic resonance to live on in popular tradition.[38]

There is a brief episode that immediately follows the raid of the Midianite camp (Judg 8:1–3). In Judges 7:24–25, warriors from Ephraim had been assigned to seize the fords of the Jordan and capture the Midianites desperately fleeing homeward, eastward with, probably, only the robes on their backs (Judg 7:24–25). In this coda to Gideon and the Winepress, the Ephraimites, summoned late to the proceedings, complain that they had missed out on the best plunder, the booty in the camp (Judg 8:1). In an extension of the story's wordplay with *gat* and *yeqeb*, Gideon uses a viticultural metaphor in response to their carping (Judg 8:2). "Is not the gleaning of the grapes of Ephraim," that is, the great martial trophies of the scalps of enemy leaders, "better than the vintage of Abiezer," the small fry caught at the camp, along with their weapons and trinkets? As George Foot Moore put it, "Vintage and gleaning [a]re now complete," as of Judges 8:3.[39] Into the lower receptacle of the winepress, the *yeqeb*, flows the wine red blood of a Midianite captain trampled by the vintagers of a warlord who once stood beside the treading trough, the *gat*.

There is nothing subtle about the political message in Gideon and the Winepress. In Ehud and the Monoliths, the Moabite leader and, by extension, people are nothing more than a pile of something to be evacuated from Cisjordan. In Gideon and the Winepress, the enemy is also dehumanized. The Midianites are vermin driven from Cisjordan.

THE BAND OF GIDEON

The way that the details of the initial dozen or so verses of Judges 6 are reutilized and brought to resolution in the final scenes of Gideon and the Winepress demonstrates the coherence of the story. Between these termini, the story with its confusing doublets and conflated plot moves along in fits and starts. Still, one theme prevails amid the flood, that of a militia defeating a multitude.

Initial Contrasts

We pick up this theme in the opening scene. The entourage of Midianite humans, animals, and tents, "as thick as locusts," with livestock and camels "without number," descend on and blight the cultivated land from the Jordan to the Mediterranean (Judg 6:4–6). In a later scene, on the eve of the final battle, this image of Midian as an uncountable swarm is repeated: the Midianite coalition blanket a valley "like locusts," "their camel without number" (Judg 7:12). Against a foe as innumerable as "the sand on the [Mediterranean] seashore" (Judg 7:12), whose raids extended "as far as Gaza" (Judg 6:4) on that same seashore, stands Israel: thin, emaciated, *dal* (Judg 6:6).

Commissioning

When Gideon is introduced in the commissioning scene (Judg 6:11–24), the comparative disadvantage of the Israelite side sketched in Judges 6:1–6 is underscored by the use of superlatives. In his reluctant protest to the divine messenger, Gideon describes his Abiezer clan militia, his *'elep,* as "the thinnest," *haddal* (again √*dll*) in the larger tribe of Manasseh, and himself as the "least" (smallest? youngest?) of his family (Judg 6:15). Already, the story raises the issue of Gideon's *'elep.* In his two nocturnal adventures, the raid on the shrine at Ophrah (Judg 6:25–32) or the raid on the Midianite camp (Judg 7:1–8:3), Gideon always acts with a group.

The terms used by the divine voice in the commissioning scene are themselves suggestive of the idea of a clan militia. The messenger addresses Gideon with the epithet, "O *gibbôr ḥayil.*" In martial contexts, this could connote that Gideon is a clan warlord, "a warrior of means" capable of mustering and equipping an *'elep.*[40] Gideon, despite his protest that he is the least of his family, seems to have significant social capital: he drafts ten servants for the raid on the shrine, musters the militia of Abiezer to face the Midianites, and takes an attendant, Purah, along with him when he spies on the enemy camp.

Later in the war oracle, the divine voice assures Gideon of success in spite of the odds. "You," that is, Gideon and, presumably, his "thin" *'elep* of Abiezrites, "will slay Midian," this enemy of uncountable, entomological proportions, "as if it were a single man" (Judg 6:16). The accompaniment of YHWH, by whom a single warrior can defeat an *'elep* (Josh 23:10), is the ultimate equalizer, here reducing the Midianite swarm to manageable proportions.

Muster

After the commissioning scene, a series of intervening scenes delay the account of Gideon's battle, complicating the plot, enlarging the cast, and deepening, or muddying, the characterization of Gideon. But among the conflicting details and along the desultory path the story takes between Gideon's commissioning scene in Judges 6:11–24 and the battle scene in Judges 7:16–22, the small size, the "thin" numbers, of Gideon's band of men is emphasized through an exercise of expansion and contraction. Gideon is inspired by the breath of YHWH, and blows on the *shofar* to summon the militia of his clan, Abiezer (Judg 6:34). Readers spoiling for a fight, however, must wait. The very next verse reports that Gideon, at this juncture, mustered warriors a second time, from Manasseh, and then a third, from the neighboring Israelite tribes of Asher, Zebulun, and Naphtali (Judg 6:35).

These verses, Judges 6:34–35, represent a crucial juncture and we must pause here too. The band of men from Abiezer who respond to the blast on the ram's horn in verse 34 represent, despite all subsequent musterings and siftings, Gideon's main force in one of the two designs conflated in Gideon and the Winepress, as confirmed at the end of the story when Gideon refers to those who accompanied him on the raid of the camp as Abiezrites (Judg 8:2). The note, then, in Judges 6:35a, that Gideon mustered troops from the tribe of Manasseh, represents a competing version of the story. The note in Judges 6:35b, that Gideon also summoned troops from Asher, Zebulun, and Naphtali represents a pan-Israelite editorial expansion. The addition of this latter detail works effectively for this redactor eager to include as many ancestors of his Israelite audience in frontier era derring-do. At the same time, ironically, it works against the theme of an older stratum of the story, the triumph of a small group. The involvement of these other tribes, however, because it is confined to the margins of the battle account, in Judges 6:35b and 7:23, ends up having little effect on the story.

The Ordeal at the Spring of Trembling

Meanwhile, among the scenes that occur between this expansion of Gideon's force in Judges 6:35 and the battle scene in Judges 7:16–22, an entire scene is devoted to reducing Gideon's band, recently swollen by the addition of warriors from non-Abiezrite kinship groups. This scene in Judges 7:1–8 is one of the best known, and most confusing, episodes of the Gideon narrative.

As suggested above, the reduction of Gideon's troops in this scene stems from a version of the story that I refer to as Gideon and the Three Hundred. Judges 6–8 conflates two motifs about the composition of Gideon's select group to advance its theme of a small group defeating a multitude. In one source, Gideon fought with the Abiezer militia, the men from a single clan (i.e., Judg 6:34;

8:2). In the other version, Gideon musters men from the relatively larger group of Manasseh. The ordeal at the spring of Harod functions to reduce Gideon's Manassite forces to a size more consistent with the theme of the story.

The episode at the spring of Harod does not explicitly refer to the tribe of Manasseh but it does implicitly. As George Mendenhall points out, the number of men involved in the ordeal number thirty-two *'elep*-units, a figure identical to the number of warriors ascribed to the tribe of Manasseh in the military census of Numbers 1:34–35.[41] In the final form of the story, with Gideon mustering an expanded roster of troops from Abiezer, Manasseh, Asher, Zebulun, and Naphtali, the contraction of his forces in this episode is all the more significant.

The scene begins by arranging the combatants on stage on the eve of battle. Gideon and "the entire army," *kol-hā'ām*, not merely the Abiezer militia, are camped by the spring of Harod, "the Spring of Trembling" (Judg 7:1). Below them, in the valley, Midian is camped near the hill of Moreh, "the Hill of [Oracular] Seeing" (Judg 7:1). Incidentally, these place-names, whether artificial or not, symbolically underscore two motifs that run through the entire narrative, fear and divination.[42]

YHWH then, in two stages, reduces the size of Gideon's army. YHWH says to Gideon "The army with you has too many to give Midian into their hand, lest Israel boast [of itself instead] of me, 'My hand rescued me' " (Judg 7:2).[43] Gideon is instructed then, at the Spring of "Trembling," *ḥărŏd*, to release any men who are fearful and "trembling," *ḥarēd* (Judg 7:3). This reduces the size of Gideon's men by more than two-thirds, from 32 *'elep*-units to 10.

But it is not enough: "The army is still too many," YHWH says to Gideon (Judg 7:4). The second method of sifting the few chosen from the many called has baffled interpreters through the ages. Judges 7:4–5a reads:

YHWH said to Gideon, "The army is still too many. Make them go down to the water and I will sift them for you there. And of whomever I say, 'This one [goes] with you,' that one will go with you. And all of whom I say to you, 'This one will not go with you,' he will not go." So [Gideon] made them go down to the water.

The test follows, in Judg 7:5b–7a.

Then YHWH said to Gideon, "Whoever licks with his tongue from the water, like a dog licks, you should set to [one] side. And whoever crouches on his knees to drink, [you should set to one side]."[44] The number of those who licked with their hand to their mouth was three hundred men. All the rest of the army crouched on their knees to drink water. So YHWH said to Gideon, "With the three hundred men who lapped, I will rescue you and I will give Midian into their hands."

This vague description of men "who licked with their hand to their mouth . . . like a dog licks," without any note about whether they were upright, bent over, or prostrate, has baffled readers for centuries. Josephus in the first century C.E. imagined them trembling as they licked water from cupped hands.[45] According to him, the men who knelt, the eliminated group, were "courageous"—i.e., well-equipped emotionally for battle, *eupsychous*—while the men who lapped, the group selected, were "cowardly," *deilous*.[46] Josephus's interpretation is supported by the motif of fear found elsewhere in the story.[47] A fearful leader is allotted an army of trembling men. But this interpretation has no support in the actual words of the account. "Lapping," or "licking," has no verbal association with "trembling." According to Josephus, the goal of the second test was to produce the most unlikely group possible, so that God might be glorified all the more. The set whose members lick—like dogs, it says; like fools, it implies—are retained. "Lest Israel boast," Yhwh sends Gideon into battle with the hapless.

The surface absurdity of the whole business—in the first test, the fearful are eliminated; in the second, the fearful, according to Josephus, are retained—has led some interpreters to consider the second test itself arbitrary.[48] Its only function is to reduce Gideon's army. The method itself has no apparent meaning.

But the first test at the Spring of Trembling (Judg 7:2–3), in which the fearful were dismissed, was a legitimate barometer of martial readiness (cf. Dt 20:8). We would expect the same of the second. The verb, "to sift," √spr, used to introduce the second test (Judg 7:4), further suggests that men of lower quality material will be eliminated and those of higher retained. Furthermore, the selection of the most unsuitable, Josephus's view, violates the entire spirit of the Israelite heroic tradition. Yhwh triumphs through the underdog—the woman Jael, the left-handed Ehud, the youthful David—whose unexpected victories are evidence of divine support, but Yhwh does not triumph through the comically inept or cowardly.

Theodor Gaster's view must be correct: "The [second] test is one of alertness."[49] We have a clear image of the eliminated group, those that crouched on bent knees, a submissive, unwary posture. The text says nothing about the bodily posture of the three hundred men who were retained, only about the action of their tongues. Moore imagined them as "throw[ing] themselves flat on the ground, with their faces to the water, and lap[ping] it up with their tongues like dogs."[50] But the canine imagery has nothing to do with the posture of a dog when drinking, only with the licking action of its tongue. The three hundred men licked the water from their cupped hands, the way a dog licks with its tongue. What of their posture? Gaster's guess, based on anthropological anecdotes, is the most likely. The three hundred men selected for the battle maintained an alert, upright posture, bending enough "to scoop up [the water] in their hands." Then they lifted the cupped water to their mouths and "lap[ped] it up with their tongues like dogs."[51]

"The militia is too many" was Yhwh's complaint, and so the group had to be pared to a minimum, to three hundred battle-ready, ordeal-sifted men. In Judges 8:10, we are told that the Midianite army numbered more than one hundred twenty 'elep units. The victory of three hundred courageous men over such a group is evidence enough of divine activity, without making them into cowards. Whatever we make of this scene, the result is an emphasis on the small size, not the faint hearts, of Gideon's group. There are no longer "too many" of them (Judg 7:2, 4).

"De Band o' Gideon"

What is the special quality that distinguishes this account of martial heroism from many other biblical accounts where underdogs with Yhwh on their side triumph? Second Samuel 22 (= Ps 18) is a warrior's thanksgiving song that testifies to the certitude of divine companionship which, mixed with measures of desperation, vengeance, unit solidarity, and competitive honor codes, carried men over the threshold of fear and into the arena of war. A line from that poem reads, "By you [i.e., Yhwh], I can crush a troop" (2 Sam 22:30; Ps 18:30 [18:29 ET]). A similar idea appears in an exhortation attributed to Joshua: "One of you puts to flight an [entire] unit [an 'elep] because it is Yhwh your Elohim who fights for you" (Josh 23:10). If one man (or two) can defeat an 'elep, like Jonathan and his armor bearer at Michmash, or fell a giant, or assassinate a king in his very court, then surely, as in this story, three hundred men can defeat a multitude "as if it were a single man" (Judg 6:16).

There is an African-American spiritual that features Gideon, "De Band o' Gideon."[52] The song does not mention the contrasts emphasized here between the swarm of Midianites and Gideon's "thin" band. The song does not mention the Abiezer militia, or the ten men who raid the shrine with Gideon, or the three hundred who accompany him to raid the camp. The song does not refer to the arrangement of scenes that, first, expand and, then, contract Gideon's band. Yet, the spiritual economically makes this very point. The first lines of the song repeat, over and over, "De *band* o' Gideon."

In his analysis of the use of biblical characters and motifs in the spirituals, John Lovell say that this and other spirituals featuring Gideon highlight a single theme, "how a small band can work together to overcome outnumbering forces."[53] In the spiritual, Gideon's band arrives, as in Judges, at the Jordan, but it is a different Jordan. The Jordan in the great double code of the spirituals is both the dividing line between earth and heaven and between slave territory and free land. Once this latter Jordan comes into view, the song quickly abandons Gideon to add its own particulars: twelve milk-white horses hitched to a chariot, bearing a sister "bowed low" and a mourner to a better world. Yet in a single, vivid stroke, the exegesis in the first lines of the spiritual finds the heart of the story: Gideon and his Abiezer clan militia, Gideon and a select group of three hundred Manassite warriors, Gideon and his band.

GIDEON AND THE THREE VILLAGES

The bulk of the second section of Judges 6–9 (Judg 8:4–28) consists of a single, symmetrically-structured episode, Gideon and the Three Villages (Judg 8:4–21). As noted in chapter 3, biblical accounts of battles often depict two stages, a primary encounter pressed until one side turns back, and a secondary stage devoted to flight, pursuit, the capture and execution of enemy leaders, and the retrieval of booty.[54] The primary battle between Israel and Midian is completed in Judges 7, the Midianite camp overrun, its men slain, and its remnant put to flight. The secondary phase seems to be over with the presentation of the heads of two Midianite princes, Raven and Wolf, to Gideon (Judg 7:25).

But as Robert Boling puts it, "the Ephraimites had brought him the wrong heads."[55] It turns out that Gideon's flesh-and-blood brothers, "the sons of [his] mother" (Judg 8:19), had been slain during the battle, and not by Raven and Wolf but by a different pair of Midianite leaders, Zebah and Zalmunna (Judg 7:18–19). Zebah (*zebaḥ*) and Zalmunna (*ṣalmûnnāʿ*) mean, respectively, "Sacrifice" and "Shelter-Withheld."[56] These names can be added to the rogue's gallery of villains in Judges with symbolic names, beside Cushan-rishathaim, "Doubly-Evil Cushan" (Judg 3:8, 10), and Eglon, the "Baby Bull" ripe for slaughter by Ehud's knife (Judg 3:12–22).[57] Slasher pursues Sacrifice and Shelter-Withheld into Transjordan in the role of *gōʾēl*, the "redeemer" of family honor. Bone of his bone, flesh of his flesh; even more, Gideon's brothers were blood of his blood, since the ancient view was that kin shared the same blood and its shedding was an injury felt throughout and requiring satisfaction from the family.[58]

This section, now a secondary episode in the extant Gideon narrative, may have once been the climax of one version of the story, Gideon and the Three Hundred. There is no mention here of the rival expression of the theme of an outnumbered, select band, i.e., Gideon and Abiezer, only of the three hundred (Judg 8:4). The design of the story that emphasized the role of Abiezer ended with the terminal repetition of a word for winepress. This episode ends with a different type of bracket, an allusion to an idea presented near the beginning of the story, namely, Gideon's shrine at Ophrah. There were two accounts in Judges 6 of Gideon's founding of the shrine at Ophrah (each probably stemming from different versions of the story). However we account for the presence of two etiologies for the shrine at Ophrah, the earlier materials make it clear that Gideon was remembered not only as a martial but also a cultic hero.

This episode, Gideon and the Three Villages, ends with a return to that shrine. From the spoils of the Transjordanian campaign, Gideon collects the gold earrings of the Midianite warriors, the caparisons of their horses, and the purple robes and jewelry of their leaders and from them fashions an oracular device which he deposits in the shrine at Ophrah.

Both the arrangement and content of the episode are dedicated to the mentality of blood feuding. In pursuit of Zebah and Zalmunna, Gideon acquires and settles smaller feuds along the way. The itinerary of satisfaction leads through the village of Succoth, whose leaders refuse to donate provisions to Gideon's hungry men (Judg 8:5–7) and a second village, Penuel, where the same scenario is replayed (Judg 8:8–9). The third and final stage of the journey brings Gideon and his three hundred to Karkor where Zebah and Zalmunna are captured (Judg 8:10–12). Leaving Transjordan, Gideon settles all three scores in turn, in ways that echo details from Gideon and the Winepress. Gideon, who had once "threshed," $\sqrt{hbt}$, wheat (Judg 6:11), now "threshes," $\sqrt{dwš}$, the leaders of Succoth, dragging them across an array of thorns and briers (Judg 8:7, 16).[59] Gideon, who had once "torn down" ($\sqrt{nts}$) the shrine of Baal at Ophrah (Judg 6:25), now "tears down" ($\sqrt{nts}$ again) the fortification tower of Penuel (Judg 8:17). The lone remaining account in the ledger, the blood feud, is settled with the ceremonial execution of Zebah and Zalmunna (Judg 8:18–21).[60]

This violent little story about the satisfaction of slights offers readers the narrative satisfaction of a tripartite structure: three villages, three feuds, three shaming rituals of torture, arson, and manslaughter. This story has not satisfied interpreters troubled by clannish vendettas and bent on exposing the sins of Gideon.[61] But no narratological aside—whether from author or redactor—interrupts the matter-of-fact description of Gideon's fierce defense of personal, family, and militia honor.

There is, however, explicit and emphatic condemnation of Gideon's cultic activities. According to Judges 8:27,

> Gideon made an ephod . . . and put it in his town, in Ophrah; and all Israel prostituted themselves to it there, and it became a snare to Gideon and his family.

In terms of the final form of the story in Judges 6–9, which details the fall of Gideon's family in the Abimelech story, this editorializing condemnation of Gideon's shrine makes perfect sense. It was the *ephod*. That was where Gideon went wrong and look what happened to his family. In terms of the final form of the book of Judges, which casts the entire frontier era as socially chaotic and cultically corrupt, the condemnation of Gideon's shrine is pivotal. That was where Israel went wrong. The axis of the cycle of apostasy, humbling oppression, prayer for relief, and recovery through a divinely appointed rescuer that characterizes the formulas in the accounts about Othniel, Ehud, Deborah, Barak, and Gideon begins to spiral downward after this note. We never hear again in Judges that the land had rest after Judges 8:28, which closes the story of Gideon, and the protagonists of the rest of the book, Abimelech, Jephthah, and Samson are fratricidal, filiocidal, and feral misfits, respectively.

But surely this condemnation of Gideon's *ephod* and his Samarian highland village shrine in the half verse of Judges 8:27b reflects the religious sensibilities of a later era, and the historiography of priestly historians offended by the religious practices—under sacred trees, around monoliths, at shrines in rural villages—that violated the standards held among exiled Judahite priests in Babylon in the sixth century B.C.E., when these materials were brought into something approximating their present form. Aside from this single sentence ("and all Israel prostituted themselves to [the ephod] there"), there is nothing in Judges 6–8 to suggest that Gideon's construction of an *ephod* was anything more than a fitting conclusion to the story of an Abiezer martial and cultic hero. Though we can never be sure about earlier versions of the story, the conclusion of the story of Gideon could be read, apart from the intrusive remark in Judges 8:27b, as its own kind of happy ending. The warrior who founded a shrine at Ophrah now furnishes it. The warrior with "an exceptional penchant for oracle seeking and divinatory inquiry"[62]— whether via a theophany under a terebinth, sacrificial rites at an altar, ritual tests with fleece on a threshing floor, martial ordeals at a spring, or an interpreted dream—now provides his community with a mediating object for divination.

ABIMELECH AND THE STONES

THE STAKES

The final section of Judges 6–9 is the account of Abimelech, Gideon's putative son, of his murderous quest for warlordship in the Shechem region, and of his divinely appointed demise. The filial connection between Gideon and Abimelech is most likely a literary fiction designed to bridge two originally unrelated traditions in order to create a multigenerational family saga. Whether Abimelech was the son of Jerubbaal, a.k.a. Gideon, as the extant text insists, or the son of a different personage, Jerubbaal, a legendary warlord of the era (1 Sam 12:11), is an academic question whose adjudication does not affect our appreciation of the literary symmetry in the story.

Abimelech, introduced as the son of a secondary wife, *pilegeš*, of Jerubbaal, "namely, Gideon" (Judg 8:35), conspires with the men of Shechem, home of his mother, to murder his seventy brothers in Ophrah, home of his father, so that he alone might inherit his father's estate and status. The warlord Gideon/Jerubbaal had presumably earned the loyalty of Shechem and the other villages in the vicinity by driving the Midianite raiders from the region (Judg 9:16–17). We can speculate that "the house of Gideon"—his family, his clan militia, his "organization"—could thus expect economic tribute and social gestures of fealty from local villages in return for this great benefit.

These are the stakes: the economic and political benefits accruing to the heir(s) of the House of Gideon/Jerubbaal; the honor, the "respect," due to a godfather-like patron in this eastern Mediterranean culture.[63] Ancient Mediterranean societies, as analyzed in the recent study of J. David Schloen, can be viewed as a network of households, and social order was imagined as maintained by a network of father figures: in the house, the patriarch; in the clan, the chief; in the larger group, a warlord or ruler or king; ultimately, in the cosmos, a patriarchal deity.[64] Father/son, patron/client, master/servant, ruler/subject, deity/worshiper: all these relationships, according to Schloen, were governed by a common ideology of reciprocity.[65] The superior party in the relationship provided care, or patronage, in exchange for obedience and tribute from the inferior party in the relationship. One dimension of such a system, often overlooked by analysts of modern bureaucratic states but easily recognized by any participant in the actual commerce of "big-city" or "small-town" politics, is the personal nature of these relationships. By way of example, Niels Peter Lemche discusses the patronage society of ancient Israel and cites, in a different context, the functional analogy of the prologue to Hammurapi's Code, where the great king appeals to readers of his stela, his subjects, as their friend, i.e., their father figure, the promoter of their welfare, the defender of their rights, accessible to rich and, especially, poor, through the terms inscribed on the stela.[66]

As Schloen observes, this "patrimonial household model," conceived of as a vertical arrangement of nested patron-client relationships—where the household member honors the patriarch who honors a regional patron who honors a ruler who honors, ulti-

mately, a deity—fails when "the system breaks down into its component parts," every household, every village, every regional network,
every ruling family for itself.[67] In this light, the final refrain in the
book of Judges (Judg 17:6; 21:25) might mean that, in those days,
when there was no king, it was every "patriarch," every "warlord,"
every "patron"—perhaps those ideas are implicit in the word,
"man," *'îš*—who did what was right in his own eyes, without the
moderating influence of larger, or higher, networks of relationship.

THE STORY

"The lords of Shechem" provide Abimelech with seventy pieces of
silver from what amounts to the local bank, the treasury of the city's
temple, with which he hires "empty men" to murder his Ophrah-
based rivals (Judg 9:1–6). The members of Gideon's gang get their
silver and, presumably, the lords of Shechem get a regional warlord
of "their bone and flesh" (Judg 9:2). For three years, Abimelech's
position is unchallenged (Judg 9:22).

But the lords of Shechem, bought with these expectations, do
not stay bought. As the narrator puts it, "Elohim sent an ill wind
(*rûaḥ rāʿâ*) between Abimelech and the lords of Shechem" (Judg
9:23). The latter shift to side with a different warlord, named Gaal, a
more promising patron from their perspective, and with his kinship-
based gang, in opposition to Abimelech (Judg 9:26–31). Gang warfare ensues. At one point in the narrative, the men of Shechem
siding with Gaal set an ambush for Abimelech (Judg 9:25); at
another, Abimelech sets an ambush for the men of Shechem (Judg
9:34). Abimelech survives long enough to defeat Gaal (Judg
9:39–41). In retaliation for the disloyalty of the lords of Shechem,
Abimelech destroys the perimeter fortifications around their town
and massacres its commoners (Judg 9:45). When the lords and
ladies of Shechem retreat to the citadel of the town's tower, Abim-

elech torches it, killing them and avenging their treachery (Judg 9:46–49).[68] In the final scene, at a neutral village, an outsider with no stake in any of the preceding conspiracies, ambuscades, and murders, serves as the agent of divine retribution (Judg 9:50–57). A woman in Thebez drops a millstone from the city tower and this stone, among the sea of besiegers, providentially finds the head of Abimelech.

LOYALTY

Abimelech and the Stones is a morality tale about one, perhaps the central, moral quality or virtue of ancient Israelite society: fidelity to covenant. The emphasis in biblical scholarship on formal political covenants and the way such contracts were used to formulate theological worldviews tends to obscure the significance of covenant in everyday life.[69] In societies without strong central political, legal, and religious institutions, the guards against chaos were faiths made good, loyalties repaid, and promises kept.[70] Social and economic life were governed by expectations of mutuality, whether they were formulated in explicit contracts deposited in shrines or embedded through custom in family and clan culture. Whether or not there were social or political institutions strong enough to enforce fidelity and punish the faithless, it was thought that the deity witnessed every covenant, championing the cause of those without social standing—the widow, the orphan, the stranger—and prosecuting, in time, those who did not meet obligations. The book of Judges in its final form is a cautionary tale about the consequences of forsaking covenants made with God, as formulated by priestly historians. This story in the center of the book of Judges concerns the consequences of forsaking social covenants.

Abimelech and the Stones introduces the theme before the action even begins.

The Israelites did not remember Yhwh their God, who had snatched them from the hand of all their enemies on every side. And they did not perform loyalty (*ḥesed*) with the house of Jerubbaal/Gideon [in recognition] for all the benefits he had performed for Israel. (Judg 8:34–35)

The theme is reinforced in the middle of the story when Jotham, the lone survivor of the initial fratricide that inspires this chain reaction of treachery, delivers a jeremiad about the consequences of faithlessness to the assembled motley crew of murderous conspirators, hired killers, ambitious warlords, and opportunistic town fathers (Judg 9:7–21). Jotham says, "If you have acted truthfully (*be'emet*) and with integrity (*bĕtāmîm*)"—terms synonymous with loyalty, ḥesed—then, in effect, blessings to you all (Judg 9:19)." "But if not," Jotham continues, a pox on all your houses.

> "May a fire come out from Abimelech and devour the lords of Shechem . . . and may a fire come out from the lords of Shechem and devour Abimelech." (Judg 9:20)

Events play out as Jotham predicts. The faithless, ruthless, and reckless take turns double-crossing, ambushing, and incinerating each other. The social order cannot be maintained in the face of such murderous opportunists so all the principals must die. After defeating his rival, Gaal, and repaying the lords of Shechem for their treachery, Abimelech is the last man standing. Since none of the other principals survives to serve as Abimelech's nemesis, an unnamed woman from a village, Thebez, which had no role in the preceding story, functions as the agent of divine retribution. In a case of *deus ex machina*, or *femina ex turrī*, a character from outside the story, an innocent bystander at a neutral site, is imported to serve as the agent through whom "Elohim repa[ys] Abimelech for his evil" (Judg 9:56).

THE STONES

Robert O'Connell observes the idea of *lex talionis*, the law of punishment in kind, at work throughout Judges 8:29–9:57.[72] The story works out this principle, Barry Webb writes, "with almost mathematical precision."[73] The key example of *lex talionis* is the way the story focuses on two stones, located at the beginning and end of the story, to mark Abimelech's rise and fall.[74] Abimelech gains power by murdering all but one of his seventy brothers "on a certain stone," *'al-'eben 'eḥāt* (Judg 9:5, 18). Abimelech is mortally wounded in the final scene by "a millstone," *pelaḥ*, thrown by "a certain woman," *'iššă 'eḥat* (Judg 9:53). The "certain stone" on which Abimelech kills his rivals (by beheading them?)[75] was probably a stone butchering table where blood and other fluids could be drained from carcasses.[76] Presumably, Abimelech does not want the blood of his brothers to fall to the ground, where it would "cry out," arousing a response from the divine *go'ēl* (Gen 4:10). Working in this realm of taboo and custom, Abimelech captures and disposes of the blood, as if it were possible to avoid the consequences of his crime through ritual.[77]

But "God is not mocked" (Gal 6:7) and the one who gains power through murder at the site of a "certain stone" dies by the stone dropped by the "certain woman" in Thebez. She serves as yet another female nemesis in Judges, alongside Jael who killed the Canaanite general Sisera (Judg 4:17–21; 5:24–27).[78] The detail of the stones serves as yet another physical object utilized as the key motif of a Judges narrative, alongside the monoliths, *pěsîlîm*, in the story of Ehud (Judg 3:19, 26) and the troughs of the winepress, *gat* and *yeqeb*, in the story of Gideon (Judg 6:11; 7:25). A single detail cast by the storyteller boomerangs through the story. The repetition of the motif near the end of each story brings stylistic closure and adds narrative depth. In the story of Ehud, the monoliths provide a short adventure tale with an epic, even mythic, background, comparable in popular American cinema to the filming of relatively simple stories about nineteenth-century blood feuds, tribal wars, and larcenies grand and petty against the primeval landscapes of the Southwest.[79] In the stories of Gideon and Abimelech, the terminal repetition of winepress and stone, respectively, impart a sense of poetic justice.

*   *   *

HEROIC MOTIFS

Heroic Culture and Conventions in the Story of Gideon

The narrative of Gideon preserves the most complete series of martial rituals, a full catalogue of Holy War, of any single biblical narrative. The sequence is initiated by the appearance of an intermediary, described here as a "herald of YHWH" who "sits under the Terebinth at Ophrah." The language here is very similar to that which begins the account of the Israelite battle against the Canaanites in Judges 4 where the female prophet Deborah, "sitting under" a different sacred tree, "the Oak of Deborah," issues the summons to war (Judg 4:5).[80] Like Ehud's monoliths, sacred trees (or groves) were thought of as gates between cosmic realms.[81] Through such a gate, the divine messenger enters our story.

The message delivered to Gideon contains sentences of encouragement drawn from the idiom of war oracles, "YHWH is with you," "Do not be afraid."[82] Divinatory rites are performed to confirm the authenticity of the call to war; cereal and animal sacrifices are offered. The description of warfare is delayed by an episode in which Gideon removes the elements of rival deities—Baal's stone table, Asherah's wooden totem—from the very same shrine where the intermediary emerged (Judg 6:25–32). Below the surface description, we see here the deep structures of Israelite religious syntax: a "passionate" deity (Ex 20:5) demands fidelity before committing divine companionship to any enterprise.

Gideon is described as a *gibbôr ḥayil*, a warrior of means, a clan warlord, and can count on the resources of a family with status sufficient to sponsor a shrine (Judg 6:11, 25).[83] Gideon can count on a clan militia to respond when he pulls sound from the *shofar* (Judg 6:34). When he enters a battle, Gideon has his own squire (Judg 7:10), and after another battle (in the story of Gideon's blood feud), he offers ceremonial honors, the ritualistic killing of captive enemy leaders, to one of his sons (Judg 8:20).

The breath of YHWH inspires Gideon as the prelude to battle (Judg 6:34).[84] He blows the ram's horn to summon the militia (Judg 6:34) and initiate a charge (Judg 7:18).[85] The battle itself is described as the unlikely triumph of a war party of outnumbered men, using stealth and surprise, and is reminiscent of the account in Joshua of the battle at Jericho, where underdog Israelites blew rams' horns and toppled a city wall (Josh 6:1–21). Though our standards of historiographic realism may be beside the point, it is worth mentioning that the use of horns against a fortified camp in the Gideon narrative is not identical to that in the attack on Jericho. Here, the noise does not supernaturally liquefy mortar and collapse stones; rather, the sudden disruption of nocturnal silence liquefies the hearts of stout warriors and collapses morale, leading to panic, retreat, and rout.[86] The actual killing though, just like at Jericho, is wholly of the natural variety (Josh 6:21).

So YHWH has breathed battle fury into the Israelites and has thrown panic into the Midianites.[87] All that remains is the collection of trophies. Special attention is given to the pursuit and capture of enemy leaders, Raven and Wolf in one version (Judg 7:25), Zebah ("Sacrifice") and Zalmunna ("Shelter-Withheld") in a second (Judg 8:4–21). Indirectly and directly, there are references to the retrieval of booty (Judg 8:1–3, 21).[88] The story begins with a ritual of cereal and animal sacrifice (Judg 6:19–24) and it ends with the ceremonial slaughter of the enemy elite (Judg 8:21), a form of human sacrifice.[89] The importance of the supreme martial virtue, bravery, though a secondary motif here, is given thorough treatment (Judg 6:23, 27; 7:3, 10; 8:20).[90]

Abimelech's Empty Men

Before leaving Abimelech, we must note the appearance, for the first time in Judges, of the phrase, 'ănāšîm rēqîm, "empty men."[91] Abimelech hires a group of empty men in order to kill his cohort of kinship peers and gain the holdings of his bêt 'āb (Judg 9:4–5). Jephthah (Judg 11:3) and David (1 Sam 22:2) also attract empty men. Eighth sons (David), concubine's sons (Abimelech and Jephthah), mercenaries, misfits, the penniless and landless: empty men fell between the cracks of kinship structures and operated beyond the bonds of filial honor codes.

The full phrase in Judges 9:4 is "'ănāšîm rēqîm ûpōḥăzîm," "empty (Moore: 'portionless') and reckless men."[92] That Abimelech pays these desperadoes from the border town of Shechem with silver drawn from the treasury of a temple known as "Baal-berith" (Judg 9:4) or "El-berith" (Judg 9:46) is another irony in the story. Both names probably refer to the same shrine, the house of "El, lord [i.e., ba'al] of [the] Covenant," a site where pacts were ritually solemnized before a divine witness.[93] These men without a stake in the traditional land system are strangers to every covenant except the contracted killing for which Abimelech hires them. Their ḥesed, covenant loyalty, is worth the seventy silvers used to hire them. The ḥesed of the lords of Shechem is not worth even that much. Like the flower of the field, the ḥesed of these men from Shechem fades (Isa 40:7) once an (evil) spirit from Elohim blows over the landscape (Judg 9:23), and they repay Abimelech's treachery with their own. When Abimelech kills his brothers, this prince makes himself an empty man.

POETIC JUSTICE

To summarize: the longest narrative of the three contained in Judges 6–9, Gideon and the Winepress, has a certain structural coherence, best seen in the use of the winepress as a rhetorical bracket. Gideon and the Winepress (Judg 6:1–8:3) is thematically coherent as well, in its emphasis on the triumph of an outnumbered group, Gideon and his band, over a multitude. This episode, as well as Gideon and the Three Villages and that of Abimelech and the Stones, is dense with motifs from Israelite heroic culture and storytelling. With all three episodes in view, representing many layers of literary development, let us take one more look at the characterization of Gideon.

In the final version of the story, Gideon is a fearful hero (Judg 6:23, 27; 7:10) who habitually requires oracular reassurance (Judg 6:17, 36, 39; 7:10–11). The ritual in which a divine messenger stokes a sacrificial fire with a staff, creates a conflagration, and disappears in the smoke, is the sign that authenticates the divine source of Gideon's call to arms (Judg 6:17–24). The two rituals with the fleece represent divinatory experiments (Judg 6:36–40). Only after the deity produces supernatural results in the controlled and safe ritual laboratory of the threshing floor does Gideon venture out into the killing fields confident that God will rescue Israel "by [his] hand" (Judg 6:36). The ordeals at the "Spring of Trembling" certify the divine election of the three hundred men who accompany Gideon into battle (Judg 7:2–8). The dream and its interpretation overheard in the vicinity of the "Hill of [Oracular] Seeing" confirm that Gideon and his men will triumph (Judg 7:9–14). In the end, the insecure warrior with the penchant for oracles constructs his own *ephod* (Judg 8:27) so that he never lacks the comfort of divinatory tokens that offer a transcendent "yes" or "no" to any question.

Taken as a whole, the narrative symmetries in the three major episodes of Judges 6–9 remind us of another horizon of divination, the plumbing of human experience and fortunes for their revealed lessons. In Gideon and the Three Villages (Judg 8:4–28), form and content combine to remind readers that bad hombrés like Gideon do not leave accounts unsettled. In Gideon and the Winepress (Judg 6:1–8:3), the winepress serves both as the starting and finishing line in a desperate, deadly competition for food between Iron Age ethnic groups. In Abimelech and the Stones (Judg 8:29–9:57), the final, fitting stroke of Providence that guides a falling stone represents the most heavy-handed example of this kind of symmetry.

Variations on the theme of retribution in due kind occur in enough places in the Bible to suggest that it was a component of the Israelite world view. Consider first these sentences from a grisly little anecdote about just deserts in Judges 1:4–7.

> Adoni-bezek fled; and [the Judahites] pursued him, and caught him, and cut off his thumbs and his big toes. (Judg 1:6)

Why this particular torture? Its victim, Adoni-bezek, himself explains, and offers the moral to the story.

> Adoni-bezek said, "Seventy kings, their thumbs and big toes cut off, gathered food under my table. Just as I have done, so Elohim has repaid (*pi'el* of √*šlm*) me." (Judg 1:7)

The words attributed to the warlord of Bezek do not mention the men of Judah who mutilated him. The larger truth, explicitly formulated, is that it is the deity who has restored the cosmic balance, the *šālōm*. This larger truth was probably an article of popular wisdom; namely, that such a punishment, the amputation of a sadist's digits, so expertly tailored to fit the crime, must be the product of divine handiwork.

Another example, in legal literature, is the teaching in Exodus 22:21–23 (22:22–24 ET) about just treatment of widows and orphans.

> You shall not abuse any widow or orphan. If you do . . . , then as surely as they cry out to me, just as surely will I hear their cry. My anger will be aroused and I will kill you. . . . Then your wives will become widows and your children orphans.

The connection between a fit punishment and divine judgment is even more explicitly formulated in Psalm 9:16–17 (9:15–16 ET).

> The nations have sunk into the pit they made.
> In the very net they hid, their feet are caught.
> Yнwн is [thus] revealed; [Yнwн] has made justice
>   (*mišpāṭ*):
> the wicked is ensnared by the work of his hands.

This view, that punishments aptly fit crimes, that "whatsoever a man soweth, that [precisely] shall he also reap" (Gal 6:7 KJV) is reflected in many sapiential observations (Job 4:8; Pss 7:16 [7:15 ET]; 57:7 [57:6 ET]; Prov 1:11–19; 1:31; 5:22; 22:8; Hos 10:13; Matthew 26:52). In some cases, this type of proverb is translated into a imprecatory prayer, such as in Psalm 35:8, "Let the net that they hid ensnare them; let them fall into it—to their ruin" (cf. Pss 10:2; 141:10), to arouse God to restore *šālōm* and render *mišpāṭ* in the uniquely fitting way that evidences divine management of human affairs.

This idea is present in the observations of wisdom literature, the didactic formulations of legal literature, and in the maledictions of liturgical literature. It is also revealed in the formulation of narratives that emphasize the symmetry of crime and punishment. One pharaoh initiates a murderous pogrom to kill Hebrew boys (Ex 1:22), prompting the cries ($\sqrt{z^c q}$) of the Israelites (Ex 2:23); his successor loses his firstborn son (Ex 12:29), prompting a great cry, $\text{s\'e}^c \bar{a}q\hat{a}$ $g\check{e}d\bar{o}l\hat{a}$, from the Egyptians (Ex 12:30). Haman is executed on the gallows he had prepared for Mordecai (Esth 7:10).[94] Abimelech, who killed on a stone, is killed by a stone. The trophy site of the campaign against an oppressor is marked by a winepress that, earlier, had symbolized the marginal state of the oppressed group.[95] These stories do not bother to add the moralism so deeply inscribed that it could go without saying: God is the author of poetic justice.

Occasionally, uncanny symmetries between what a man, woman, or group sowed and what he, she, or they reaped presented themselves with the force of revelation. More often, I suspect, the symmetry had to be detected by interpreters as expert in their divinatory crafts as the priests who read omens and the prophets who translated visions. Storytellers extracted divine communications from the chaotic flow of raw, mute experience, drew inferences from them, and translated them into the patterns of narrative. The primary object of human divination is not some esoteric realm of sheep entrails and skins, but common reality. The primary oracular mediators are neither priests nor prophets but those who sift through the residue of experience, seek to divine its larger meanings, and then translate these into ordered, meaningful, and memorable patterns: storytellers.

NOTES

1. See Isa 11:12; Ezek 7:2; Rev 7:1.

2. If one prefers word counts to verse counts as a measure of comparing the lengths of the Gideon and Ehud narratives, then there are 2,645 words in Judges 6–9 (the Gideon-Abimelech narrative) as opposed to 312 words in the Ehud narrative of Judg 3:12–30. The ratio (in verses, 157 to 19; in words, 2,645 to 312) is roughly the same: the Gideon narrative is more than eight

times as long as the Ehud narrative (as suggested to me by David Noel Freedman, private conversation).

3. As detailed below, the account of the raid on the Midianite camp, with the attackers holding torches and jars in one hand, and *shofars* in the other, is conflated. The story also contains two rival expressions for the theme of the triumph of a small band of warriors, through the motifs of Gideon and the Abiezer militia, on one hand, and of Gideon and the three hundred warriors from Manasseh, on the other hand. My basis for linking the motif of the three hundred with the tactic of the *shofars* is twofold, the reference to the "three hundred trumpets" in Judg 7:22, and the relative proximity of the terms, "three hundred" and "trumpets," in Judg 7:16, 20. That leaves the tactic of jars containing torches to the Abiezer motif.

4. See the discussion of the culture of raiding on p. 67.

5. For "Slasher," see R. Boling, "Gideon," 1013.

6. R. Boling, *Judges*, 132. Gideon's call narrative has many parallels to the call of Moses in Ex 3:1–4:17, including the phrase "I will be with you," *'ehyeh 'immāk* (Judg 6:16; Ex 3:12), the protest of inadequacy (Judg 6:15; Ex 3:11; 4:1, 10), and the request for a sign (Judg 6:17; Ex 3:11–12; 4:1–9).

7. For the Ephraimite/Deuteronomistic prophetic tradition, with its veneration of Moses, associations with the ancient shrine of Shiloh where Samuel received his call, and relationship to Hosea, see R. Wilson, *Prophecy and Society in Ancient Israel*, 135–252.

8. D. Gunn, "Joshua and Judges," 114.

9. In Ex 28:6–30, the *ephod* is a priestly garment with an attached breastplate containing the sacred dice, the Urim and Thummim (see also Lev 8:7–8; 1 Sam 2:18; 22:18). In this story, as in Judg 17:5; 18:14, 17, 20; 1 Sam 2:28; 14:3; 23:6, it is an undefined ritual object. P. King and L. Stager conjecture that the latter object was a box containing the Urim and Thummim

(*Life in Biblical Israel*, 10, 325). C. Van Dam also considers the *ephod* in Judg 8:24–27 to be a priestly garment containing the oracular equipment of the Urim and Thummin (*The Urim and Thummim*, 148). For a different position, that the *ephod* in Judg 8:24–27 refers not to a garment but to a type of ritual box or "ark" (that could also serve a divinatory function), see K. van der Toorn and C. Houtman, "David and the Ark."

10. See 1 Sam 2:18, 28; 14:3; 22:18; 23:6.

11. Cf. Judg 8:27b, "all Israel prostituted themselves (√*znh*) to it there, and it became a snare [*môqēš*] to Gideon and his family," with Dt 7:16, Josh 23:13, and Judg 2:3.

12. Cf. the seventy-sevenfold measure of revenge the legendary Lamech takes in response to an injury (Gen 4:24) with the number of men, also seventy-seven, that Gideon tortures in the village of Succoth in retaliation for their lack of hospitality (Judg 8:14).

13. A. Auld, "Gideon," 257.

14. The comments of C. Burney (*The Book of Judges and Notes on the Hebrew Text of the Book of Kings*, 176): "The narrative of . . . Gideon is highly composite throughout" and J. Soggin (*Judges*, 103): "The complex character of the Gideon tradition is immediately evident" are representative. See also G. Moore, *A Critical and Exegetical Commentary on Judges*, 175–77.

15. G. Moore, *Judges*, 207.

16. Traces of a blended narrative in Judg 6–8 are unmistakable and are best demonstrated by the fact that two parallel outlines of events can be isolated (see table on p. 161). But beyond these lines of evidence, it is impossible to separate two self-standing sources. Both build from the common foundation laid in Judg 6:1–6, 11–18 of the description of the Israelites' plight and of the call of the hero Gideon.

17. The name "Jerubbaal," understood as "May the Lord (or 'Master') contend on [my] behalf," a meaning contrary to that given in Judg 6:32 but his-

The Abiezer Design	Motif	The 300 Manassite Design
YHWH manipulates fire (by igniting a drenched sacrificial assemblage) (Judg 6:17–23)	**Gideon receives supernatural confirmation of divine support**	
in response to a fiery theophany (Judg 6:24)	**Gideon founds a shrine at Ophrah**	by divine command; after demolition of Baal shrine (Judg 6:25–32)
the Abiezer militia (Judg 6:34)	**Gideon musters a select force**	(a) the troops of Manasseh (Judg 6:35a)
	Gideon receives supernatural confirmation of divine support	Elohim manipulates moisture (the test with fleece) (Judg 6:36–40)
	Gideon musters a select force	(b) the troops of Manasseh are reduced by ordeal to 300 (Judg 7:1–7)
with torches/jars (e.g., Judg 7:19b)	**Gideon and company attack the Midianite camp at night**	with *shofars* (e.g., Judg 7:19a)
Oreb and Zeeb (Judg 7:24–8:3)	**Gideon and company execute a pair of Midianite leaders**	Zebah and Zalmunna (Judg 8:4–21)

torically more likely, could have been borne by an Israelite worshiper of
YHWH. The word *ba'al*, an epithet meaning "lord," "master," or "patron,"
was applicable to YHWH, as evidenced by the biblical name "Bealiah" (i.e.,
"Yah[weh] is my lord [*ba'al*]") in 1 Chr 12:6 (12:5 ET). A text originating in
the eighth century B.C.E., Hos 2:18–19 (2:16–17 ET), explicitly states that
the title "Baal" was used by Israelites for YHWH even as it admonishes its
audience to abandon this usage. For a discussion of biblical names that in-
corporate the divine element *b'l*, see J. Fowler, *Theophoric Personal Names
in Ancient Hebrew*, 54–63.

18. An analogous case is the figure of Isaac in Genesis. As a character,
Isaac is largely a cipher: the passive son in stories about Abraham and
Sarah (Gen 17; 21–22; 24–25), the duped father and husband in stories
about Jacob and Rebekah (Gen 27–28). For a single chapter, Gen 26, Isaac

takes the patriarchal stage alone for a set of stories that transparently parallel earlier tales about Abraham (cf. Gen 26:1 with 12:10, 20:1; Gen 26:6–11
with Gen 12:10–20, 20:1–18; Gen 26:12–33 with Gen 21:22–34). But the
character Isaac is necessary to combine genealogically two rich bodies of
tradition about legendary ancestors, Abraham and Jacob, into a single
multigenerational family saga.

19. J. Barrera, "4QJudg[a]," 162; "Textual Variants in *4QJudg[a]* and the Textual and Editorial History of the Book of Judges."

20. A. Auld, "Gideon," 263; J. Wellhausen, *Prolegomena to the History of
Ancient Israel*, 234.

21. A. Auld, "Gideon," 263; J. Barrera, "Textual Variants in 4QJudg[a]," 236,
245. R. O'Connell has a different opinion, namely that it is more likely that
4QJudg[a] has omitted Judg 6:7–10 than that the MT has added it (*The
Rhetoric of the Book of Judges*, 147, n. 178).

22. Cf. Judg 6:8–10 with Ex 20:2; Dt 5:6; Josh 24:17–24; Judg 2:1–2; 1 Sam
10:18.

23. The manuscripts from Qumran Cave 4 have been dated to a period
between the mid-second and mid-first centuries B.C.E. (F. M. Cross and
E. Ulrich, *Qumran Cave 4*, 2).

24. As R. O'Connell argues (*Rhetoric of the Book of Judges*, 147, n. 178).

25. As in the Ehud narrative (Judg 3:12–30) where a note in the introductory section lists the Israelites' oppressors as Moab, Ammon, and Amalek
(Judg 3:13) even though only Moab is mentioned subsequently.

26. For an outline of possible constitutive traditions, see p. 161, n. 16.

27. E.g., G. Moore, *Judges*, 175–77; Burney, *Judges*, 176–84.

28. *Aristotle's Poetics* (trans. S. H. Butcher), 65.

29. G. Moore, *Judges*, 215; Auld, "Gideon," 266.

30. R. O'Connell, *Rhetoric of the Book of Judges*, 140.

31. The mention of "Amalek" and "the sons of the East" is probably a secondary expansion of the story. Neither group has an active role in the story itself, although both are mentioned again in Judg 6:33. Biblical references to these traditions outside Judges (Isa 9:3 [9:4 ET]; 10:26; Ps 83:10 [83:9 ET]) mention only Midian as the enemy of Israel. This expansion of the enemy forces from single groups to larger coalitions (seen also in Judg 3:13) parallels the editorial expansion of Israelite forces from single tribes to larger coalitions in the narratives of Judges; see p. 108, n. 43.

32. H.-J. Fabry, "דל *dal*," 217–18.

33. Just as in Judg 4:5, a religious intermediary, the prophet Deborah, is described "sitting under" a sacred tree.

34. J. Gray, *Joshua, Judges, Ruth* (NCB), 292.

35. See p. 49.

36. P. King and L. Stager, *Life in Biblical Israel*, 100–101.

37. P. King and L. Stager, *Life in Biblical Israel*, 100–101.

38. In addition to Isa 10:26, the Israelite victory over Midian is also alluded to in Isa 9:23 (9:4 ET) and Ps 83:10–13 (83:9–12 ET). We do not know whether Isaiah knew of literary or oral traditions about it. His allusion to "the day of Midian" and to "the rock of Oreb" confirm that by the late eighth century B.C.E., he could assume that traditions about the defeat of Midian in the era of Judges were known by his audience. Ps 83 is probably postexilic (M. Tate, *Psalms 51–100*, 345). It refers to the killing of both pairs of Midianite leaders. If we assume that this doublet arises from the mixing and narrative harmonization of two independent accounts, in which each

pair of names occurred separately, then Ps 83:10–13 (83:9–12 ET) is probably drawing on some form of the written source of the Judges scroll.

39. G. Moore, *Judges*, 174.

40. See p. 35.

41. G. Mendenhall ("The Census Lists of Numbers 1 and 26") formulated
the idea, in a 1958 article, that *'elep* sometimes means, not a "thousand,"
but a "militia-unit." He was trying to rationalize the suspiciously high
counts of Israelite warriors in the lists of Numbers 1 and 26. For instance,
in Num 1:35, the tribe of Manasseh is credited with "32 *'ălāpîm* [i.e., thou-
sand] and 200," i.e., 32,200 men. Mendenhall's innovation was to reinter-
pret *'ălāpîm*, "thousand," as "militia unit," and, in effect, to add a comma
to the clause, reading the formula as "32 militia-units, 200 men," or "32
militia-units *totaling* 200 men."

According to Mendenhall, the term *'elep*, when used in military contexts, meant simply "militia unit" in the premonarchical period, but came
to mean "a thousand" in the monarchical period because the standard size
of an army unit came to be a thousand men (p. 57). Mendenhall's argument, based on the kind of low dating typical of the Biblical Archaeology
movement in its heyday (1958), is dated by his assumptions that the list
from Numbers stems from the second millennium.

In Proto-Semitic, the form **'alpu* was used both for "ox" and "a thousand" (S. Moscati et al., *An Introduction to the Comparative Grammar of
the Semitic Languages*, 118). If biblical Hebrew *'elep* sometimes means
"militia unit," it is more likely that this meaning stems from the meaning
"herd [or group] of cattle" (B. Levine, *Numbers 1–20*, 138–39). When *'elep*
means "a thousand," whether in reference to fighting men or any counta-
ble noun, it is unlikely that the usage stems from the size of a monarchical
army "unit whose normal strength was a thousand men" (Mendenhall,
p. 57). According to Levine, the word *'elep* in Numbers, since it stands in
sequences next to *mē'â*, "hundred," and other words for numerals, must
mean "thousand" in the census lists (pp. 139–40).

The LXX version of Num 1:35 gives the number of men as three hundred, rather than two hundred. Mendenhall (prompted by a suggestion of

D. Freedman, journal editor of Mendenhall's 1958 article) noted the striking correspondence between these numbers for Manasseh in this census list and the numbers of Manassite warriors in this episode of the Gideon narrative in Judg 7:2–8: thirty-two *'ălāpîm* and three (again, reading Num 1:35 in the LXX) hundred (pp. 63–64, n. 53). The correspondence of these amounts is striking but the process that yields their equivalence, with textual emendations, questionable literary stratifications, and debatable philology, is convoluted.

Let us leave Numbers aside and concentrate on the figures given in Judg 7–8. According to Judg 7:3, Gideon led thirty-two *'ălāpîm* to the Spring of Trembling for the ordeal. This process eventually yielded three hundred men (Judg 7:7). If *'elep* in Judg 7:3 means "militia unit," and we assume that such units averaged around ten men, then thirty-two *'ălāpîm*, the number who began the ordeal, and three hundred, the number that passed it, are roughly equivalent. To confuse matters even more, if the ten *'ălāpîm* who passed the first stage of the ordeal (Judg 7:3b) represents ten militia units (say, eighty to a hundred men), then the second part of the ordeal (Judg 7:4–6) somehow *increased* Gideon's ranks rather than reducing them.

This hardly leaves us any conclusion save that *'ălāpîm* in Judg 7:3 must mean "thousands," not militia units. Gideon's troops are reduced from the (grossly exaggerated) number of 32,000 to three hundred. When these three hundred engage the Midianites in Judg 7:19–22 (whose ranks are numbered in a later verse, Judg 8:10, at 135 *'ălāpîm*), the ratio of Israelite to Midianite is 300 to 135,000. It is inconceivable that any ancient state, and early Iron Age Midian was hardly that, could put 100,000 men in the field. According to the Mesha Stela, the king of Moab led a force of two hundred men against Israel in the ninth century B.C.E. It is tempting, then, to read *'ălāpîm* in Judg 8:10, when it refers to the number of the Midianites, as militia-units rather than thousand. The underdog motif is preserved if Gideon and a band of three hundred men triumph over a Midianite camp of about a thousand men. To picture the Midianite force as numbering a thousand men, in light of the Mesha Stela, is exaggeration enough.

In the end, the effort to rationalize the astronomical numbers of troops in this story may be doomed to failure. Still, it is entirely possible that *'elep*, from **'alp*, "(herd of) oxen" could sometimes mean "group of men." Since I am at a loss, I will defer to Professor Freedman, who wrote the following to me.

> The writer is playing games with the word *'elep*, but the original story simply specified that Manasseh and its allies put together their muster of 32 units of about 9 men each, totaling 300 men. They fought against a group about [three or] four times larger, which is brave enough, but they had to win by a ruse because man-to-man they would not have succeeded. (David N. Freedman, personal communication)

42. For "fear," see Judg 6:23, 27; 7:1–3, 10; 8:20; for divination, 6:17–23, 36–40; 7:4–8, 9–15; 8:27.

43. Another piece of evidence for the composite texture of Judg 6–8 is the contrast between sections that betray no anxiety about attributing the victory to Gideon and "his hand" (Judg 7:9, 15, 18b, 20b) and the note in Judg 7:2 that considers such an assertion as boastful.

44. The phrase in brackets is from the LXX.

45. Josephus, *Jewish Antiquities* 5:215–217; *Josephus* (trans. H. Thackeray and R. Marcus), 5:98–99).

46. Josephus, *Jewish Antiquities* 5:216.

47. See n. 42, p. 166.

48. J. Soggin, *Judges*, 137.

49. T. Gaster, *Myth, Legend, and Custom in the Old Testament*, 420. R. Boling (*Judges*, 145–46) apparently misunderstood Gaster, assuming that the latter meant that the kneeling men, the eliminated group, were more alert.

50. G. Moore, *Judges*, 202; J. Gray (*Joshua, Judges, Ruth*, 291) also imagines that the "lappers" were prostrate.

51. T. Gaster, *Myth, Legend, and Custom in the Old Testament*, 420–22.

52. J. W. Johnson and J. R. Johnson, *The Book of American Negro Spirituals*, 156–57.

53. J. Lovell, *Black Song*, 259.

54. See p. 63.

55. R. Boling, *Judges*, 152.

56. C. Burney, *Judges*, 228–29.

57. See p. 103, n. 7.

58. F. M. Cross, *From Epic to Canon*, 3.

59. G. Moore (*Judges*, 225) and J. Slotki ("Judges," 227) refer to a similar torture of scoring and scratching in Plato's *Republic* (X:616), visited upon the tyrant Ardiaeus in the afterlife. "They dragged [him] along the wayside, carding [him] like wool on thorns" (*The Republic of Plato*, trans. A. Bloom, 299).

60. See p. 49.

61. The behavior of this Iron Age warlord in a blood feud is analyzed anachronistically in psychological language in three recent literary studies. For R. O'Connell, Gideon's behavior in the blood feud betrays an obsession, fueled by his attempt to (over-) "compensat[e] for his own lack of significance (cf. Judg 6:15) by a personal triumph" (*Rhetoric of the Book of Judges*, 156). B. Webb talks about Gideon's "frenzied determination" (*The Book of the Judges*, 151); L. Klein of Gideon as a "Jekyll-and-Hyde" character (*The Triumph of Irony in the Book of Judges*, 63).

62. R. Boling, "Gideon," 1013.

63. N. Lemche ("Kings and Clients") uses the figure of the Mafia god-father as an analogue for the patrons of ancient Mediterranean societies.

64. J. Schloen (*The House of the Father as Fact and Symbol*, 51) writes:

> In a patrimonial regime, the entire social order is viewed as an extension of the ruler's household—and ultimately of the god's household. The social order consists of a hierarchy of subhouseholds linked by personal ties at each level between individual "masters" and "slaves" or "fathers" and "sons."

65. J. Schloen, *House of the Father*, 77.

66. N. Lemche, "Kings and Clients."

67. J. Schloen, *House of the Father*, 58.

68. Regarding the tower at Shechem, see L. Stager, "The Shechem Temple."

69. N. Lemche, "Kings and Clients," 126–27.

70. As N. Lemche puts it, "Loyalty is a governing concept [of the patronage system], and without it the organization will have no chance to survive" ("Kings and Clients," 122).

71. N. Lemche discusses the significance of *hesed* and *'emet* as key virtues in patronage systems ("Kings and Clients," 126).

72. R. O'Connell, *Rhetoric of the Book of Judges*, 168.

73. B. Webb, *Judges*, 154.

74. L. Ginzberg, *The Legends of the Jews*, 4:41; T. Boogaart, "Stone for Stone"; J. Janzen, "A Certain Woman in the Rhetoric of Judges 9"; S. Ackerman, *Warrior, Dancer, Seductress, Queen*, 48.

75. S. Ackerman suggests that Abimelech beheads his brothers (*Warrior, Dancer, Seductress, Queen,* 48). In 2 Kgs 10:1–11, the seventy sons of Ahab are killed in this fashion.

76. In accordance with Israelite purity codes, blood had to be drained from slaughtered animals (Lev 19:26; 1 Sam 14:31–35).

77. G. Moore writes that Abimelech's "motive was to dispose of the blood, in which was the life of his victims, in such a way that they should give him no further trouble" (*Judges,* 243).

78. R. O'Connell, *Rhetoric of the Book of Judges,* 169, n. 219; S. Ackerman, *Warrior, Dancer, Seductress, Queen,* 48.

79. Best seen in the Western films of John Ford, such as "The Searchers" (1956), set in Monument Valley, along the Arizona-Utah border.

80. G. Moore, *Judges,* 184.

81. See pp. 95–99.

82. For war oracles, see pp. 64–67.

83. The shrine at Ophrah belonged to his father (Judg 6:11, 25). For another family-held shrine in the book of Judges, see Judg 17:1–13.

84. The idiom here ("the breath of YHWH clothed [itself with] him") is phrased in a way more reminiscent of the diction of Chronicles than Judges and Samuel (cf. 1 Chr 12:19 [12:18 ET]) (J. Soggin, *Judges,* 129; A. Auld, "Gideon," 265) and, accordingly, may represent a secondary reformulation.

85. For the *shofar,* see J. Braun, *Music in Ancient Israel/Palestine,* 26–29.

86. For the idiom of hearts "melting" in descriptions of panic, see p. 63.

87. See p. 61.

88. See pp. 49–50.

89. See pp. 25–27, 49–50.

90. See pp. 64–67.

91. For more on "empty men," see pp. 36–38.

92. G. Moore, *Judges*, 244.

93. For the Temple of El/Baal-Berit, see T. Lewis, "The Identity and Function of El/Baal Berith."

94. This observation addresses the absence of any explicit mention of God in the Hebrew version of Esther. To ancient audiences, it went without saying that God, "behind the scenes . . . carefully arrang[ed] events so that a justice based on the principle of 'measure for measure' . . . triumph[s]" (J. Levenson, *Esther*, 21).

95. For "trophy," see pp. 63–64.

6

SAMSON AND THE

THREE WOMEN

SAMSON'S DREADLOCKS

The Bible says nothing about Samson's size, nothing about his physical appearance with the sole exception of a singular detail: Samson wore his hair, uncut since birth, in seven braids (Judg 16:13, 14, 19).[1] Bible readers are accustomed to minimal description.[2] A single detail—Jacob's limp, Moses's "thick tongue" (Ex 4:10), Ehud's left handedness, Saul's height, David's ruddy complexion—is often the most we can expect and more than we can say for Noah or Abraham or Sarah or Joshua. Characterization in the Bible is revealed most often through speech and deed, not physical description, and, like all revelation, is open to interpretation.

Given Samson's expansive speech and outlandish deeds, it is hardly surprising that interpreters have imagined him as larger-than-life, as gigantic. How else, as reflected in the Talmudic tradition that Samson was a giant, could he have, walking, shouldered the city gate of Gaza (Judg 16:3) or, standing, spanned the space between the two supporting pillars of the temple of Gaza (Judg 16:29)?[3] Still, nowhere in Judges 13–16, the four chapters that comprise the saga, is there any description of Samson as gigantic. We have only our imaginative projections based on these hints from Judges 16.

Prior to Judges 16, Samson is portrayed not so much as gigantic but as feral. By tearing apart a lion in his inaugural feat (Judg 14:5–6), the lion a popular symbol of royalty throughout the biblical world, Samson shows himself to be king of the beasts.[4] The narrator compares the ease with which Samson handles his rival with that of a lion itself tearing apart a goat (Judg 14:6), as if this deed established a new pecking order in the wilds of the Judean Shephelah.[5]

By catching and enlisting three hundred jackals, šûʿālîm, to race ablaze through the Philistine fields (Judg 15:4–5), Samson shows himself to be master of the beasts.[6] In the Bible, jackals are associated with images of agricultural and architectural ruin and it is natural to assume that Samson would encounter a pack of these stray predators on the outskirts of the Philistine town of Timnah.[7] Samson's choice of comrades, though born of necessity, is nonetheless fitting for a hero who himself wreaks much agricultural and architectural devastation, raiding Philistine towns (earning from them the epithet, "The Ravager of Our Land," maḥărîb ʾarṣēnû; Judg 16:24) and retreating in feral isolation to rocky haunts (Judg 15:8, 11). Fierce as a lion, as socially marginal as a jackal, this animalistic portrait of Samson in Judges 14–15 is capped off when he happens upon and wields the most improbable of weapons, the jawbone of an ass (Judg 15:15–17).

This introduction of Samson, emphasizing his superhuman strength and subhuman ferocity, hardly does justice, however, to the legend of Samson, which surely began before the Bible and which has continued to generate new tellings and import new details long after the Bible was formed.[8] Here I refer not only to the biblical narrative in Judges 13–16 but to the myriad presentations in art, music, literature, storytelling, and common speech of Samson, and of Samson and Delilah.[9] In a manner rivaled only by his Greek counterpart Hercules, the character Samson has become a platform for heroic projections in many cultures and eras, through many media.[10] The character Samson has become an emblem of brute strength, physical desire, and foolish love. And the biblical story has provided Samson, in his own way a caricature of hypermasculinity, with a suitable partner. The character Delilah, despite the lack of detail about her in Judges 16, has also become a platform for heroic and narrative projections. From an androcentric perspective, Delilah has become a caricature of, in traditional terms, a certain brand of seductive hyperfemininity.

I will not attempt to chart Samson, or Samson and Delilah, through the ages. Still, any analysis of Samson must acknowledge that this larger-than-life character is in many ways larger than the Bible. Popular interpretations of Samson ignore many of the details of Judges 13–16, and this study will concern itself with the careful analysis of these very details in the biblical account and with the way they exemplify aspects of a larger Israelite heroic tradition. Still, the power of popular interpretations of Samson is a force to be reckoned with, and is neither a debasement nor a trivialization of the biblical character. In all likelihood, the biblical version is itself not the beginning of the Samson tradition but represents one (and may contain fragments of another; see "Samson and the Three Vows" below) telling of a story about a folktale character about whom many stories may have circulated in ancient Israel. The character of Delilah may also be built from traditional materials about Ishtar-like figures or *femme fatales* in ancient Levantine myths and legends. Just as in Greek tradition, the figure of Hercules became a magnet attracting all manner of heroic motifs, secondarily organized in one tradition under the rubric of twelve labors,[11] the Samson story incorporates nearly every motif from the Israelite heroic tradition and, many assert, freely imports motifs from outside Israelite culture.[12] In the end, the enduring popularity of the Samson tradition—that despite the breadth of its treatments it contains space for more—is based on the fact that this biblical story is a pool fed by and connected to many other stories.

Before we can view Samson against this broader array of stories, however, we must begin with his biblical portrait, and with the sole physical glimpse it offers, of his seven "braids," *maḥlĕpôt* (Judg 16:13, 14, 19). Mesopotamian art contains dozens of examples of a similar motif: of male figures, often in contests with animals, sporting, most often, six braids.[13] These dreadlocks apparently represent a "heroic hairstyle." Samson's seven, as opposed to six, braids, are best understood as an Israelite variation on this Mesopotamian theme.[14] Samson, like the braided characters on Mesopotamian seals, has his contests: near the beginning of the story, with the lion; near its end, in gladiatorial "play," √*śḥq* (Judg 16:25).

In the next section, we will consider the structure and themes of the biblical story contained in Judges 13–16. In the final section, we will compare Samson with mythic figures and legendary characters. Samson's strength, and implied mass, opens him to comparison with titanic deities, demons, and supermen. Samson's ferality opens him to comparisons with a menagerie of hairy men, natural men, wild men, and theriomorphic hybrids. But though his dreadlocks, as discussed below ("Samson as Chaos Monster"), are reminiscent of an artistic image and mythological character in Mesopotamian art and literature, these mythic and legendary categories must not obscure the image of an all too human hero. Certainly the strongest; to be sure, the rawest: Samson, as depicted in the Bible, is most of all a warrior, and he has the dreadlocks to prove it. In Milton's terms, Samson is *agonistes*, "combatant, wrestler"; in biblical terms, a *gibbôr*.

SAMSON AND THE THREE VOWS

Below I will devote considerable attention to the way that certain details in Judges 13, the story of Samson's birth, relate uneasily to details in Judges 14–16, his adult adventures. In some scholarly circles, where the goal is to uncover the earliest literary stratum of a biblical narrative, or to reconstruct some primal historical moment which gave birth to a tradition, an analysis such as I offer below is unnecessary. After all, birth stories, in terms of the sequence by which heroic biographical materials develop, are almost always secondary constructions. Heroes acquire their reputations before they acquire the accounts of how they were abandoned in the wilds and nursed by beasts, or announced by angels and born to the infertile. Birth episodes and adventure episodes, though eventually combined, draw on conventions distinct to each respective genre and chronologically emerge in reverse sequence from their narrative arrangement. If my goal were to reveal the first Samson, the *real* Samson, it would be unnecessary to belabor the handful of discrepancies I note between the birth account and the adventures.

But my goal is not to recover the first Samson, though my approach is not ahistorical. My goal is to recover the first Samsons. That is, in my view Samson is a character about whom many stories were told. Did he exist? I cannot know though my childhood religious training and adult immersion in his story have brought him to life in my imagination. There, I imagine that the uncommon feats of an extraordinary—and criminally dangerous—misfit have been inflated to near-mythic proportions by the workings of popular storytelling over generations.

My analysis will concentrate on one of these Samsons, a version of the story which assumed the literary form extant, primarily, in Judges 14–16, the adventure cycle. This Samson narrative portrays the drama of a one-man army against Philistia, and is divided

into three acts, each revolving around Samson's amorous relationship with a woman. There are, however, traces of other versions, of
other Samsons, within Judges 13–16, as I suggest below. I do not
claim that the Samson of "Samson and the Three Women" is any
more or less authentic, or more or less deserving of scholarly analysis or imaginative sympathy, than any of the other Samsons. I contend, merely, that the Samson who goes searching for love across a
border, leaving a path of destruction in his wake, is the version most
fully presented in Judges 13–16.

Judges 13 contains the story we will call "Samson's Birth." The
story begins on familiar terrain for biblical birth stories: a divine
messenger visits a barren woman and announces that she has
conceived (Judg 13:2–3).[15] Later, she gives birth and names her son
šimšôn, a diminutive of šemeš, "sun." Samson's name means
"Sunny." The birth story continues on a bright note with Judges
13:24, "The child grew up and YHWH blessed him." The final sentence of the birth account, however, begins to map a different narrative territory. About the same place in the story that, for instance,
the Samuel story proudly observes a boy "ever growing, in as good
[stead] with YHWH as with people" (1 Sam 2:26), the narrator of the
Samson story seems to register the onset of some disturbance, "The
breath of YHWH began to trouble him among the camps of Dan, between Zorah and Eshtaol" (Judg 13:25).

There is not space here to analyze Judges 13 systematically;[16] I
will allude to it as needed in my analysis of the adventure stories in
Judges 14–16. But one issue in the birth story must be addressed.
One of the major motifs of Judges 13, the nāzîr conditions imposed
on mother and child, is never fully realized in Judges 14–16, notwith-
standing the energetic attempts of many interpreters to discover
them. The Nazirite motif is emphasized in the birth story by its
threefold repetition (Judg 13:4–5, 7, and 14). At the same time, however, the emphatic effect of this repetition loses much of its force

because the conditions of the *nāzîr* state are formulated differently in each instance. We must look at these verses in some detail.

The first version of the Nazirite motif appears in Judges 13:4, where a divine messenger appears to a barren woman, announces that she has conceived, and issues her these instructions: (1) she is to avoid drinking *yayin*, grape wine, or *šēkār*, beer or date wine; (2) she is to avoid eating *ṭāmē'*, ritually unclean food; and (3) her child's hair is not to be cut. Her child, the messenger explains, is to be *nāzîr*, consecrated, separated, set apart from birth (Judg 13:5).

The second version appears in Judges 13:7. The woman reports the above encounter to her husband and reprises the messenger's instructions. She repeats, almost verbatim, the parallelistic formulation of the first two elements of this consecration ("Do not *drink* X/do not *eat* Y") but she omits the third entirely, saying nothing about the child's hair.[17]

The third version of the Nazirite motif appears in Judges 13:14, in an extended scene (Judg 13:8–23) which comically contrasts the knowing ease of Samson's mother in this most delicate of social situations—an encounter with an angel—with the ineffectual bustle and bluster of Manoah, Samson's father.[18] Though Manoah prays for a second visit of the messenger, so that *they* might know what *they* are to do (Judg 13:8), the messenger returns to visit the woman alone. After she summons her husband, and Manoah directly asks for instructions, the messenger refers only to Samson's mother, "Let the woman carefully perform the things I said to her" (Judg 13:13). In this formulation, it is unclear whether there are two stipulations of consecration or three. According to the messenger's words in Judg 13:14, the woman is prohibited from eating anything that comes from the grape vine; from drinking *yayin* or *šēkār*; and from eating that which is unclean.

Here, again, there is no mention of Samson's hair. If we retreat even a single step from the details of these three formulations and look at the entire Samson story, we can see that, of the three *nāzîr* stipulations mentioned in Judges 13:4, which contains the fullest expression of the formula, the issue of the child's hair is the most significant. Surely Samson's hair—braided, shorn, full again—is too important a motif in the story to be omitted or under emphasized in this prefatory section. Yet it is, not only in Judges 13:7 but in Judges 13:14.

Stipulations for the Nazirite condition are given in the priestly legislation of Numbers 6:1–21. In Numbers 6, this consecrated state is a form of religious devotion, analogous to fasting, where, for a given period, men and women adopt three special strictures: abstaining from alcoholic beverages or any product of viticulture, avoiding contact with human corpses, and keeping their hair unshorn. At the end of the cycle, the worshiper shaves his (or her) head as part of the ritual for rejoining normal life. Note that the consecrated conditions mentioned in Judges 13, which vary in and of themselves, are not wholly identical to these; neither is their context. In Numbers 6, the Nazirite state is a temporary withdrawal from everyday life; in Judges 13, it is, for the woman, a prenatal regimen; for her child, a lifelong condition. These two descriptions of ritual behavior described by the same Hebrew word, *nāzîr*, "separated [from normal practice or custom]," differ enough to suggest either that they represent different understandings of the Nazirite vow and, assuming that Nazirite practice evolved over time, stem from different eras; or that, simply, the regulations in Numbers 6 merely reflect a single, but not the sole, denomination of a host of loosely or closely related devotional practices grouped under the name *nāzîr*.

Robert Boling, protesting too much, offers three explanations for the omission of any reference to the child's hair in 13:7 and 13:14.[19] I cannot explain the variations among the three descriptions of the Nazirite condition in Judges 13. The deeper issue is this: the account of Samson's birth introduces the Nazirite motif, underscores it through repetition, and, yet, curiously, underplays the very aspect of Naziritism, the uncut hair, that turns out to be its most crucial component in the adventure cycle. Before attempting to explain this anomaly, we must look at how the Nazirite motif is dealt with in the adventures of Samson.

Based on the threefold stipulation of the Nazirite condition in Judges 13:4, the messenger's initial instructions to the woman, one might expect that the narrator is preparing us for a certain story. Let us call it "Samson and the Three Vows."[20] We might anticipate episodes in which the hero is tempted to drink wine, then eat unclean food, and, climactically, following the order of their formulation in the birth story, cut his hair. Note that this assumes that the injunctions placed upon Samson's mother, the first two of the above, can be transferred to her child. This also assumes that, despite the variant forms in Judges 13:7 and 14, we can base our analysis on the fullest expression of the formula in Judges 13:4. In fact, guided by these assumptions, many interpreters have discovered such a story, Samson and the Three Vows, in Judges 14–16.

Joseph Blenkinsopp's argument is representative.[21] I will begin with the third vow, since there can be no dispute about its presence in the adventure cycle. The third vow, concerning the cutting of hair, is explicitly broken in the Delilah episode (Judg 16:15–19). Judges 16:17 drops a footnote to the birth story ("A razor has never come upon my head; for I have been a Nazirite to God from my mother's womb"), leaving no doubt that a sacred vow has been violated.

According to Blenkinsopp, Samson first violates a vow, the second in the series, when, in Judges 14:9, he scrapes honey from a lion-carcass, a violation of the prohibition against eating impure food (food in contact with dead matter was ritually contaminated; cf. Lev 11:27, Num 9:10).[22] Unlike in Judges 16:17, however, there is no note here from the narrator or aside from a character to underscore the significance of this violation. Other interpreters find Samson in violation of this injunction when he touches the donkey jaw-bone in Judges 15:15.[23]

What of the first vow, to abstain from alcoholic beverages? On the surface, there is no mention anywhere in the story, no direct evidence, of Samson drinking *yayin* or *šēkār*. Blenkinsopp uses circumstantial evidence to accuse Samson of violating Prohibition, citing Judges 14:10–18 where Samson participates in a Philistine wedding "banquet," *mišteh*. As Blenkinsopp notes, "*Mišteh* [from √*šth*, "to drink"] speaks for itself."[24] But does it? Lillian Klein contends that this violation, that Samson had fallen off the wagon of temperance, is underscored when, the text reports, he descends into the Sorek ("Choice Vine") Valley (Judg 16:4), the site of his encounter with Delilah.[25]

Provisionally, let us allow Blenkinsopp's interpretation and say that we have here the story of Samson and the Three Vows. If so, the adventure cycle has a curious shape. Within the first nine verses of the adventure cycle (which comprises a full three chapters, 71 verses), Samson violates the vow against eating unclean food (Judg 14:9) (again, a vow which was not imposed upon him, but upon his mother). Then, in the very next verse, 14:10, Samson begins his, in Boling's words, "drinking bout."[26] If this is the case, then the plot of three vows bears no relation to the arrangement and structure of the episodes. A full chapter, Judges 15, in which a brawl initiated at the wedding escalates into a regional conflagration, and a brief but self-contained episode, the story of Samson's visit to the prostitute in Gaza in Judges 16:1–3 (perhaps some suspect he drank or ate something unclean there?) become superfluous, as we wait for the third trial.[27]

There is a kind of midrashic impulse at work in these scholarly discoveries inspired by clues in the birth story. But, in fact, the Nazirite motif has an ambiguous presentation in the birth account—it is repeated, but the effect of the emphasis is weakened by the variations in its formulation—and is only partially realized in the adventure stories. The only unambiguous realization of a broken vow occurs in Judges 16:19, when Samson's hair is shaved.

Samson can be accused of eating unclean food, the honey from the lion, but the story does not pause there, either in structure or diction, to underscore the violation. What, then, is the function of this odd episode about bees hiving in a lion carcass—which seems so artificial—if it does not represent a violation of one of Samson's vows? I prefer Michael Patrick O'Connor's explanation.[28] He calls it "a shaggy dog story," that is, a secondary episode constructed to provide a narrative platform for a popular riddle that had become associated with the Samson tradition. Though improbable and illogical on its own, the account of bees nesting in the lion carcass (Judg 14:8) does create a narrative background for the riddle in Judg 14:14:

> Out of the eater came something to eat.
> Out of the strong came something sweet.

The text never reports that Samson drank *yayin* or *šēkār,* or, for that matter, ate a raisin.[29] If Judges 13–16 were the story of Samson and the Three Vows, surely it would not leave us with such ambiguous preparation, amorphous episodic arrangement, unfulfilled expectations, and unrealized motifs.

Below I will champion a different view, held by many, about the structure and plot of the Samson narrative. Still, the polemical tone of my rhetoric and my support for a rival theory cannot fully erase the traces of the three vows from the story. You can draw a direct line from the initial formulation of the vow against Samson cutting his hair (Judg 13:4) to its violation (Judg 16:17). There are some gaps and ambiguities in the presentation and fulfillment of the other two vows but, as clearly evidenced in the scholarship noted above, they invite perceptive readers to fill the gaps and clarify the ambiguities.

What should we make of this? Blenkinsopp and others have accurately observed the residue of another Samson story. Such a story was, in the end, left unfinished in the book of Judges but circulated in Israelite oral tradition and is preserved in fragmentary literary form here.[30] The Bible preserves only a sample of the literary output of ancient Israel, to say nothing of the thousand-and-one tales never composed in writing. These traces of another Samson story, fascinating in themselves, indirectly, stand in for an entire lost narrative world, a full and varied, living tradition of Samson legends mainly lost; though postbiblical Samson legends may preserve, here and there, bits and pieces of oral traditions as old or older than the Bible.[31] The adventure cycle in Judges 14–16 contains fragments of Samson and the Three Vows, a story for which the birth account in Judges 13 partially prepares us. In the end, however, Judges 14–16, the adventures of Samson, are organized around a different tripartite scheme.

SAMSON AND THE THREE WOMEN: STRUCTURE

The structure which holds together Judges 14–16 is a simple, traditional tripartite structure: Samson's adventures are organized around his relationships with three women.[32] In Judges 14:1 Samson sees a woman from Timnah; in Judges 16:1 Samson sees a woman from Gaza; in Judges 16:4 Samson *loves* a woman from the Sorek Valley. Not all of the material in the narrative is directly concerned with this dance card, Samson's romantic itinerary. Nevertheless, though the story does not concern in every instance Samson's relationships with women, the device of the three women provides the structure for this version of the Samson legend.[33] This organizational scheme provides more than structure, as I will detail below. But before looking at each of the episodes (14:1–15:20; 16:1–3; 16:4–31) in more detail, we must note other structural elements in Judges 14–16.

Double-Judgeship Notices

At two places in the narrative, near its middle and at its very end, there are formulaic editorial notices of the sort found elsewhere in material about the Minor Judges, a group of ancient potentates for whom Judges includes brief, highly conventionalized anecdotes.[34]

> He judged Israel in the days of the Philistines
> 20 years. (15:20)

> He, he had judged Israel 20 years. (16:31)

There are differences between these variants of the formula used to close the notices of the Minor Judges: the second is shorter, omitting the "in the days of the Philistines," and, more important, the second has inverted word order (indicated above by the repetition of "he" in the second example), a personal pronoun followed by a suffix conjugation verb as opposed to the earlier prefix conjugation verb prefixed with a *wāw*-relative.[35] This inversion is disjunctive and helps mark the end of the entire Samson cycle.

The fact that there are two notices is puzzling. To be more precise, it is the earlier notice, in Judg 15:20 that is the puzzle. What is a concluding formula doing in the middle of the story? Is this a source-critical or tradition-critical seam? Have two independent Samson blocks of tradition, each with its own concluding formula, been joined?[36]

However one accounts for the origins of a terminal formula in the medial position (Judg 15:20), it is useful to ask whether this has interpretative value. Boling, for instance, takes the medial formula as a structural marker, dividing the narrative into two parts, a hero's rise and fall.[37] Certainly the imposition of a piece of editorial structure into the middle of the story, even if it was the type of formula we would expect only at the end of a story, frames the story in a certain way. Perhaps, reading with the biblical editor who inserted this formula, we see yet another version of the Samson story, "Samson's Rise and Fall." A moralistic reading of the story could follow this arc. During his innocent ascent, Samson has the opportunity to make his mistakes and learn from them; his descent occurs because he fails to heed the lessons of experience.

I resist the idea, however, that Samson rises or falls; he is the same on both sides of this juncture. He follows his impulses (14:1; 16:1); reveals secrets to women who betray him (14:17; 16:17); and, when in a tight spot, prays (15:18; 16:28). J. Cheryl Exum has noted the above parallels, and more, between the episodes, demonstrating that the entire Samson narrative coheres, that the beginning and the end of the story are thematically related.[38] In short, however one accounts for the presence of the judgeship notice in Judges 15:20, the internal dynamics of plot and character development do not hesitate at this boundary. Such a narrative line, of rise and fall, if it is present, is much fainter than the more deeply inscribed tripartite pattern noted below. The two judgeship notices are further evidence of the complicated compositional history of this text. In the end, I invoke the term of Edward Greenstein, who talked about textual "noise," features of a text which "cannot be incorporated into any interpretive pattern."[39] To my ears, the first judgeship notice (Judg 15:20), evidence of the friction between strata in a text which was touched and retouched by many hands, is this kind of noise.

Ups and Downs

Another structural feature of the story is the repetition of verbs of ascent, √ʿlh, and descent, √yrd. Sixteen times, a character is described as going up or going down, or bringing (i.e., carrying or accompanying) another character up or down (using the hipʿil forms of the same verbs). Consider this table (reading left to right; "S" stands for "Samson").

14:1 S descends ↓   14:2 S ascends ↑   14:5 S descends ↓

14:7 S descends ↓   14:10 Parents descend ↓   14:19 S descends ↓

14:19 S ascends ↑   15:6 Philistines ascend ↑   15:8 S descends ↓

15:9 Philistines ascend ↑   15:11 Judahites descend ↓

15:13 Judahites bring S up ↑   16:5 Philistines ascend ↑

16:21 Philistines bring S down ↓   16:31 S's brothers descend ↓

16:31 S's brothers bring S up ↑

In every case, the verb is a form of either ʿālâ or yārad. These ups and downs conform to the topography of the story as Danites—Samson and his family members—descend from the Shephelah to Philistia on the coastal plain and ascend when returning home. The Philistines ascend when moving inland and descend when moving toward the Sea.

This feature is not noise: the repetition of ascent and descent is part of the score. Every time a character goes up or goes down, important boundaries are crossed: the boundaries between Dan and Philistia; between "cut," mûl, and "foreskinned," ʿārēl; between highlanders and lowlanders; between a decentralized kinship society with its tribal leaders, šōpĕṭîm, and a centralized society with its city leaders, sĕrānîm; between the "campsites," maḥănîm, of Dan (Judg 13:25) and the cities, ʿārîm, of the Philistine Pentapolis; between rural economy and urban economy; between, as Hermann Gunkel put it, nature and culture.[40]

This repetition of ascent and descent does not match the plot as it unfolds. To use Levi-Strauss's analogy of myth to music, this repetition is not the melody of the piece but, rather, its rhythm.[41] Up/down, up/down, up/down, the story beats, and each move evokes a bundle of contrasts.

The Three Women

What, then, is the melody of the Samson saga? The Samson narrative has a traditional structure. It is a kind of outlaw ballad with three stanzas (of unequal length), each beginning with a form (with degrees of variation) of the same line.

> Samson descended to Timnah and he saw a woman (Judg 14:1)

> Samson went to Gaza and he saw there a woman (Judg 16:1)

> After all these events, Samson loved a woman in the Sorek Valley: her name was Delilah. (Judg 16:4)

I use the term, outlaw ballad, with the folk music of the British Isles, its borderers and highwaymen, and of the American West and Deep South, its outlaws and rounders, in mind. Consider, for instance, how in Anglo-American folk music, an Ozarks bank robber, Jesse James, is transformed into a populist Robin Hood who "stole from the rich and gave to the poor."[42] In African-American folk music, "Stag" Lee Shelton, a St. Louis pimp who murdered a man on Christmas Day, 1895, is transformed into "Stagolee," the archetypal "Bad Nigger," who proudly defies the authority, first, in terms that reach back to English balladry, of "the High Sheriff" ("I don't run, white folks,/When I got my forty-one"); and, then, even of the very Principalities and Powers.[43]

> Stagolee, he told the Devil,
> Says, "Come on and have some fun—
> you stick me with your pitchfork,
> I'll shoot you with my forty-one."

In both cases, those of Jesse James and Stagolee, unsavory characters, socially marginal, murderously dangerous, become emblems of resistance to unjust power structures in the popular imagination of folks in the Dust Bowls and Deltas. I cannot know this, but I imagine Samson as a rough and rowdy character of the Danite-Philistine frontier, whose exploits and misadventures were transformed into near-mythic proportions in oral tradition.[44] His self-serving violence directed against Philistine urban culture was idealized by Iron Age folks in the camps of Dan and Israelite villages of the Shephelah as resistance to oppression. The outlaw, in tradition, became a *šōpēṭ*, a "judge." The Samson narrative is not a song, and the analogy with outlaw ballads only suggestive, suggestive of the stanza-like prose organization of the story, with its episodes framed by Samson's visits to three women, and suggestive of the way that stories about morally ambiguous antiheroes might have found their way into Holy Writ.

STORY

The Woman from Timnah

The adventure stories begin in Judges 14, set in motion by Samson's encounter with the first of three women. There is more to the adventure cycle than Samson's search for female companionship in a foreign land. In fact, a basic function of Samson's search for a wife in Philistia, like Saul's errand to find his father's lost livestock (1 Sam 9:3ff), is that it serves as a means for getting our hero off the farm and into town, so that the adventures may begin.

Samson goes down, √*yrd*, from Dan to the Philistine village of Timnah (Judg 14:1)[45] and in Timnah Samson sees, √*r'h*, a Philistine woman. Later, to his parents, Samson explains that the Timnite woman is "right in [his] eyes" (Judg 14:3; note the echo here of the editorial formula used in Judg 17–21).[46] This simple act, arising from the amorous wanderlust of our hero, sets in motion a violent chain reaction of reprisal and counter-reprisal that leaves in its wake thirty stripped corpses outside Ashkelon, scorched grain fields and orchards outside Timnah, a thousand dead Philistines at Lehi, three hundred charred foxes, and one very dead lion.

This dizzying sequence is set in motion by Samson's simple desire to marry the woman from Timnah.[47] But YHWH's desire is mixed up in this too. The narrator reminds us in Judges 14:4 that Samson's romantic interest, and, we can assume, the ensuing carnage as well, is all according to divine plan.

> His father and mother did not know that it (i.e., Samson's extramural romance) was from YHWH, because he was seeking an opportunity (*tōʾānâ*) against the Philistines.[48]

Who is the subject of the verb "he was seeking" in the second clause, a participial construction of the independent masculine singular pronoun *hûʾ* and a masculine singular participle *měbaqqēš*? It must be YHWH, the previous noun.[49] The other possibility is that Samson is the antecedent, that Samson had an ulterior motive for the marriage, to gain entrance into Philistia under false pretenses and there, then, begin to destroy things.[50] The latter interpretation is more theologically palatable, as Judah Slotki explains: "Modern commentators define *he* as God; but it is contrary to Hebraic thought that God required an *occasion* in the circumstances here described."[51] Perhaps it is my modern perversity that finds this apologetic interpretation less satisfying than its alternative, which suggests that it is the deity here who is scheming.

And what of the woman at the center of all this? She has an instrumental role: YHWH uses her to lure Samson into Timnah; the Philistines use her to discover Samson's secret. When they are unable to solve the riddle posed by Samson at the wedding feast,[52] they threaten her and her family if she does not discover and disclose the answer to them. For the most part she is passive and mute while Samson and his Philistine counterparts engage in their violent play of chicanery, arson, and murder all around her.

She is not mute, however, when she persuades Samson to reveal the answer to his riddle. She accuses him of not loving her, "You only have hate for me and you do not love [√'*hb*] me" (Judg 14:16). After seven days of weeping, she succeeds in wearing Samson down. Even here, the Timnite woman has an instrumental role, foreshadowing the Delilah episode in which another woman extracts a secret from Samson.[53] It is also interesting to note the word used to describe her effect upon Samson. Judges 14:17 says that she "pressured" or "squeezed him" (*hĕṣîqatĕhû*); the verbal element a causative form of √*ṣwq*, "to be narrow." The same verb is used in Judges 16:16 to describe Delilah's effect upon Samson. Judging from all his comings and goings, it is safe to say that Samson's essential nature is to roam and he cannot stand to be constricted. When bound, √'*sr*, by ropes of men, as happens several times (Judg 15:13; 16:8, 12), or squeezed, the *hip'il* of √*ṣwq*, by women's words (Judg 14:17; 16:16), Samson explodes: he bursts bonds; he blurts secrets.

There is one more detail in the Timnite episode that is crucial to the plot of Samson and the Three Women, namely, the Philistine formulation of their answer to Samson's riddle. Samson's riddle is, "Out of the eater came something to eat; / Out of the strong came something sweet" (Judg 14:14), and it is not solvable through any amount of cleverness. The answer has to do with the extraordinary accident of the bees hiving in the lion carcass, and only an eyewitness could know it.[54] The Philistines solve the riddle by deceit, not by mental agility.[55]

Their cleverness, however, is on display when they give their answer to Samson in the form of their own riddle.

What is sweeter than honey?
What is stronger than a lion? (Judg 14:18)

The answer to Samson's riddle lies on the surface of their answer—the honey and the lion—but this second riddle has its own depths. By formulating their answer in terms of a riddle of their own, Samson's Philistine competitors up the ante considerably.

Their riddle goes unanswered in the Bible. This may be the most extraordinary feature of this extraordinary narrative: this second riddle, posed as much to the audience as to Samson. Even though the narrative does not supply the answer, the solution of the riddle is crucial to understanding the Samson narrative. What is stronger than a lion? What is sweeter than honey? Put another way: what proves stronger than the lion slayer Samson? What proves more irresistible to Samson than his wild honey, his natural foods regimen, out in Nature? The answer to all these questions, as Gunkel and many others have noted, is "love."[56] We will have more to say about love and of its effect on Samson.

The Woman from Gaza

Samson's second adventure, the briefest, is contained in the first three verses of Judges 16. Samson this time goes to Gaza and, again, he "sees," √*r'h,* a woman, a prostitute (Judg 16:1). He "enters her," as the text puts it, but while he is at her place, the Philistines learn of his presence and set up an ambush. At midnight, Samson sneaks by them and, on his way out of town, uproots the city gate, hoists it onto his shoulders, and carries it away to Hebron, a distance of twenty miles.

Though this brief adventure can be read didactically,[57] its tone betrays nothing about the dangers of visiting prostitutes. Rather, this episode is an entertaining (and, mercifully, bloodless) adventure inserted between two longer, more violent ones, a broadly comic interlude which emphasizes Samson's larger-than-life strength and potency.[58] In its effect, Samson's feat is roughly similar to Ehud's: both enter an enemy city, wreak havoc, and manage to escape unharmed. But the differences are telling: Ehud's heroics are the result of design; Samson's, the accidental by-product of impulse. Still, this brief episode, about the length of one of the *gibbôrîm* traditions in 2 Samuel 23, has a function beyond comic relief. It serves as a dress rehearsal for the conclusion of the entire saga: here, in Gaza, Samson topples a structure, the city gate. He will do so again (Judg 16:30).

Delilah

As in most verbal constructions with three parts—whether stories, jokes, or arguments—the first two elements set up the third. Our text signals this in many ways. Samson "sees" the woman from Timnah; Samson "sees" the woman from Gaza; but Samson "loves," √'*hb*, a woman from the Sorek Valley (Judg 16:4). While the other two women were unnamed, we are told the name of the third woman. She is *dĕlîlâ*, "Delilah."

It would seem then that the fact that her name is given is important, one more signal that we have reached the final and most important woman in the story.[59] But we cannot be sure what "Delilah" means; not because the name, though rare,[60] or its root is so obscure, but because the story offers no etymological aside or pun to help us choose among the most likely candidates. The root √*dll* can mean, in Hebrew, "to hang down, to dangle";[61] in Akkadian, "to praise";[62] and in Arabic, "to flirt."[63] "Delilah," a feminine adjective (e.g., **qaṭīlâ*) in form, could thus mean "Dangling [Hair]" or "Devotee [of, e.g., Ishtar]" or "Flirtatious," respectively.[64] Another popular interpretation, though it is linguistically the most unlikely, has been to relate the name *dĕlîlâ* to the Hebrew word for "night," *layĕlâ* (cf. the famous female lover of Arabic/Persian poetry, "Layla"), as in "[The-]One-of-the-Night."[65] Juxtaposed, the above names together read like a list of burlesque show performers: "Dangling Hair," "The Devotee," "Flirtatious," "The One of the Night." But even if we are not sure what her name means, the fact that this third woman bears a name, in contrast to the first two women in the adventure cycle, marks her as significant.

We have already noted how certain elements in the previous adventures, and even the birth story, anticipate the Delilah episode: Samson here will once again be bound by ropes, and squeezed by words.[66] This episode begins somewhere in the Sorek Valley—the first episode took place in Timnah, a town in the Sorek Valley—before it moves to Gaza, the venue of the second adventure, and ends where everything began, as Samson is buried in the family tomb in Dan (cf. Judg 13:2, 25; 16:31). In the Delilah story, Samson's susceptibility to the love of a woman, already implicit through deed and riddle, becomes explicit as the verb √'*hb* is introduced in the opening sentence.

Briefly, let me outline the episode. Samson falls in love with Delilah. The Philistines offer her eleven hundred silver pieces to discover the secret of Samson's strength, so recently displayed at Gaza. Samson and Delilah play four rounds of a game in which she asks about the source of his strength, and three times, he gives her a false answer. In the fourth round, he tells her the truth. The language of these exchanges is repetitive. Delilah asks Samson about his strength and how he might be bound. Samson always answers, "If you do X to me, then I will become weak," followed by in Hebrew, *wĕhāyîtî kĕ'aḥad hā'ādām*, "and I will become like one of the humans"—the word *'ādām*, "Adam," here used in its broadest sense. In the fourth and final exchange, Samson's words are slightly different, another sign that we have reached the end of a series, "I will become like *all* humans." Delilah's words to Samson the fourth time are also more emphatic; like the Timnite woman, she accuses Samson of not loving her, "How can you say, 'I love you' . . ." (Judg 16:15).

After Samson reveals the truth about how his strength is related to his unshorn hair, the Philistines seize him, blind him, and take their captive to Gaza, the site of his latest crime against society. There he is made to grind at the prison mill. Parenthetically, we are told that his hair begins to grow back (Judg 16:22). The Philistines then display Samson at the temple of Dagon, their god, in Gaza, and force him to "make sport" or "compete" (√*ṣḥq*), like a gladiator.

Samson prays that YHWH would strengthen him once more. His strength returns, he topples the temple, killing himself and the three thousand assembled Philistine men and women.

How should we understand Samson's encounter with Delilah? I would like to frame this encounter in the terms of a well-known theme: the humanization, or domestication, of a wild man by a woman. When Samson meets Delilah, he has preternatural strength and unshorn hair. When he leaves her, he has shorn hair and reduced strength. Delilah transforms Samson, albeit briefly, from wild man to human.

I have not yet discussed whether Samson is a wild man, or hairy man, a hybrid creature of folklore, but these issues emerge even from a surface reading of the text and I have alluded to many of them.[67] His mastery over the beasts is reminiscent of the wild man: he kills a lion and controls jackals. So is the way he performs his feats without tools: he kills the lion bare handed, he uproots the city gate and topples the temple without a lever. When he does use a weapon, it is drawn directly from the animal world, the jawbone of an ass. All of these are suggestive of the folklore wild man, a topic to which we will return in the final section of this chapter, "Measuring Samson."

Here we must momentarily leave the Bible and note the similarities between this story and the account of the humanization of Enkidu in the Akkadian Gilgamesh Epic.[68] In brief, Enkidu is the quintessential wild man. He lives as an animal on the steppe.[69] He comes to the attention of urban society because a hunter spies him and realizes that he is the one who has been spoiling the hunter's traps. The king of the city of Uruk, Gilgamesh, sends a prostitute to the watering hole, the place where hunters and animals meet in the wilderness. Enkidu and the prostitute named Shamhat make love for seven days. Afterwards, Enkidu tries to gallop away with the animals, as he used to, but finds that his knees are paralyzed. The animals now run away from him, signaling his alienation from them and his changed status. It is not just coitus that changes Enkidu, for he is still rough around the edges. As Shamhat leads him back to the city, she provides a tutorial on urban life along the way. Like a mother, she teaches him the basics that every child must learn: eating, drinking, dressing himself.[70] The end result of this love and maternal instruction is that Enkidu, in the words of one version of the Epic, "became a human," *awēliš īwe*.[71]

The theme of the humanization of the wild man by a woman is also present in the story of Samson and Delilah. Delilah is Samson's guide through a similar rite. Though there is no mention of lovemaking in the biblical Samson-Delilah story, there is of love. After Samson's surrender to Delilah, he too becomes like one of the humans. Through the cutting of his hair, which symbolizes Samson's feral strength, Delilah transforms Samson from wild man, hairy man, to *'ādām*.

In the final exchange with Delilah, Samson mentions his mother, "A razor has never touched my head for I have been consecrated [*nāzîr*] from my mother's womb" (Judg 16:17). After hearing his secret, Delilah puts Samson to sleep on her lap, literally "on her knees," before cutting his hair (Judg 16:19).[72] This may be a significant detail too for the phrase "on the knees" and the term "knees" have associations with childbirth and adoption rituals in the Hebrew Bible.[73] There is then a maternal aspect to Delilah in this scene, as there was with Shamhat in the Enkidu story. As Mieke Bal says, it is as if Samson is reborn in this scene: he awakens on Delilah's lap bald and helpless.[74] When Delilah assumes this maternal posture and shears Samson, she severs the vow that had tied the Nazir to his biological mother and Samson, through the agency of this second mother, becomes something he had never been before, an ordinary man. Delilah then delivers the former man of nature over to the urban men, the Philistines.

Love Story

What, then, is the story, Samson and the Three Women about? It is about love. The theme of love—typically the humanization of a wild man through the love of a woman—is implicit in narratives about wild men. Furthermore, this theme is made explicit in Judges 14–16 in four ways. (1) The plot revolves around the hero's search for female companionship. (2) The second riddle—which we have to judge as the winning entry in the contest—has for its solution "love." (3) In both cases in which Samson capitulates and reveals a secret to a woman, to the Timnite in Judges 14:15–17 and to Delilah in 16:15–17, the ultimate weapon in their verbal assault against Samson is to accuse him of not loving them.[75] (4) Finally, in retrospect, the notice in Judges 16:4 that Samson "loved" Delilah—in Hebrew the first word of the episode after an introductory adverbial clause—gives the whole thing away.[76] Once Samson falls in love, he is doomed. Marvin Pope's translation of Song of Solomon 8:6 is apt: "For love (*'ahăbâ*) is strong as Death, Passion fierce as Hell."[77] Like Luther's Prince of Darkness, Samson, a giant in haggadic legend, is felled by one little word: *'ahăbâ*, love.[78]

Didactic Story

Judges 14–16, however, is more than a love story; it is also a didactic story with lessons about many topics. As Yair Zakovitch has noted, the story cautions against hubris: twice Samson, the strong man, is reduced to weakness after a triumph—the first time by thirst (Judg 15:18); the second time by the shearing of his hair and torture—and forced to acknowledge his dependence on God through prayer (Judg 15:18; 16:28).[79] J. Cheryl Exum notes something similar, that the story teaches that God answers prayer.[80] James Crenshaw has drawn attention to the theme of marrying within one's ethnic group, a message that gets inscribed in many folk narratives: If only Samson had listened to his parents (Judg 14:3) and settled down with a nice Danite girl, he would not have met his ruin.[81] There are also lessons here about the consequences of breaking vows and the dangers of foreign women.

Political Story

In terms of the wild man tradition, Samson's capitulation to Delilah is a variation on an ancient and persistent theme: the transformation of the animalistic male into civilized man through the love of a woman, as mentioned above. However, our love story, with its conventional hero and traditional form and motifs, does not run true to form and diverts sharply from the pattern at this point. For in the Samson story, unlike in a fairy tale such as "Beauty and the Beast," the movement from nature to culture is viewed as a lapse, as something negative and Samson, with YHWH's help (Judg 16:28) reverts to wildness. YHWH apparently wants Samson in the raw. Why? Part of the answer to why Samson reverts to wildness is related to the wild man type, because wild men often have an instrumental function in stories. They solve problems for society—winning battles and slaying monsters—but, often, find no place in that society for themselves.

The narrative provides another answer: Samson's mission is to kill as many of the enemy as he can. This is made explicit in the birth story where the divine messenger tells Samson's mother that her son "will begin to deliver Israel from the Philistines" (Judg 13:5). In Judges 14:4 we are reminded of this destiny when the narrator informs us that Samson's interest in the Timnite is all according to the plan of YHWH, who wanted to pick a fight with the Philistines. In Judges 16:30, after all the sex and all the violence is over, we are told that Samson had killed more Philistines in his death than in his life; in other words, mission accomplished.

Love story and didactic story, the Samson narrative is also, then, a political story concerning the Israelite-Philistine conflict. In this light, the feat when Samson carries the gates of Gaza to Hebron has political significance, linking Samson with another Israelite hero of the Philistine Wars. The next time Hebron appears in the Bible, it will be David's provisional capital (2 Sam 2:1–4). In this light, the feat when Samson topples the temple in Gaza is an ideological statement. YHWH's servant bests the servants of Dagon, just as in the Ark narrative (1 Sam 4–7), the Israelite icon bests the icon of Dagon.[82]

In its present location, the Samson narrative stands near the end of the book of Judges, which reinforces the didactic aspects of the story: Samson is the last of the šōpĕṭîm and, in many eyes, the worst, representative of Israel's decline into ethical, religious, and societal chaos.[83] What if we look forward instead of backward? It may be said that Samson begins the era of the resistance against the Philistines. His assaults, to be followed by those of Samuel, Saul, Jonathan, David, and Joab (and, in 1 Sam 4–7, of the inanimate Ark of the Covenant), represent the first skirmish of the Philistine Wars: "He will begin to deliver Israel from the hand of the Philistines" (Judg 13:5). Samson draws first blood. This is the political reading of the Samson narrative.

The African-American spiritual, "Samson and Delilah," perhaps because the social location of its performers and audience was roughly analogous to early Israel, provides a remarkably accurate historical exegesis.[84] The spiritual describes "a nachul man . . . [who] t[ore] that building down." In the song, Samson is a liberationist hero invoked to tear down the oppressive structures of, first, King Cotton, and then, Mister Jim Crow. For early Israel, Samson was a liberationist hero who tore down the temple of a social rival, whom they perceived, rightly or not, as oppressing them.

MEASURING SAMSON

Samson is so many things: the biblical judge; the giant of Jewish folklore; the Semitic Hercules for patristic apologists eager to translate the biblical tradition into classical categories; the blind artistic hero of Milton; the tree-uprooter of medieval Central Europe; the liberationist folk hero of the African-American spiritual; even the doomed *Noir*-ish hero played by Victor Mature in Cecil B. DeMille's movie "Samson and Delilah." Based on my reading of Judges 13–16, there were at least two literary versions of the Samson legend in ancient Israel, to say nothing of the possibility of multiple oral traditions (surely, for instance, there were ancient versions that included details of love-making between Samson and Delilah).[85] On what heroic scale can we measure such a larger-than-life character?

Roughly a hundred years ago, George Foot Moore and Hermann Gunkel rescued Samson from the genre of mythology. At that time Samson was being exhibited in the display cases of Victorian solar mythologists who uncovered allusions to astral activity throughout Judges 13–16: Samson's hair, the rays of the sun; the donkey jawbone, lightning; Delilah, goddess of the moon.[86] The other prevalent, and more persistent, mythological interpretation of Samson was to compare Samson with Hercules, an analogy as old as Eusebius in the early fourth century C.E. and that reached its limit with the discovery of Samson's *twelve labors* by enterprising Victorian scholars.[87] How did Moore and Gunkel redirect the discussion? Moore argued that the Samson narrative be considered primarily as a folk-story rather than a myth, that it is best interpreted in comparison and through analogies with heroic legends, not stories about the gods. "The [Samson] legend," Moore wrote in 1895, ". . . has its roots in the earth, not in the sky."[88] Gunkel also looked in the earth for Samson and found him there: running through forests, wrestling wild animals, eschewing tools and barbers; the ancient Semitic ancestor of a character in European folklore: *ein Naturmensch,* a Natural Man.[89]

Perhaps, it is time to remythologize Samson; that is, to compare Samson to a figure who appears in a myth. The myth is the Babylonian Enuma Elish. The figure is *lahmu,* one of the helpers of the Babylonian goddess, Tiamat, herself a symbol of saltwater, chaotic yet essential for life.

SAMSON AS WILD MAN

This approach to Samson leads directly from Moore and Gunkel, especially the latter's characterization of Samson as a wild man. The case for Samson as an Israelite variant of this traditional character has been updated by David Bynum, Susan Niditch, and Mobley.[90] Wild men are often hairy, eschew human tools and weapons, have an affinity for animals and natural habitats, and are prone to domestication by women. Samson conforms in certain respects to this folklore character.

There are many similarities between the biblical Samson and the literary character and artistic image of the wild man, best known from medieval sources.[91] Though the Bible does not say a word about body hair, Samson's hair, uncut since birth, is his signal trait. Samson establishes his credentials as master of beasts in his inaugural feat of wrestling a lion (Judg 14:5–6) and, later, by capturing and controlling the jackals (Judg 15:4–5): Samson leads an army of jackals, rather than men, against the Philistines.[92] Samson sleeps in a rock crevice (Judg 15:8), and, in terms of diet, he eats wild honey (Judg 14:9), and drinks neither wine nor beer (Judg 13:4, 7, 14); i.e., he eschews city food. Samson usually works without tools—he tears the lion apart and uproots the city gate of Gaza bare handed (Judg 14:6; 16:3)—and when he does require a tool, it is drawn directly from the animal world, the jawbone of an ass (Judg 15:15).[93] Samson displays the perpetual aggressiveness of the wild man in his episodes of frenzied violence (Judg 14:6, 19; 15:14–15). His relationships with culture are of the wild man type: he is irresistibly drawn to culture by women and, once in culture, he is pressured to divulge secrets (Judg 14:15–17; 16:5–17). Like so many wild men of myth and fairy tale, a woman, Delilah, can be said to have humanized the

Danite beast since the text repeatedly notes that after his hair is cut, Samson will "become like one of the human beings."[94] As it turns out, however, Samson's humanization or, if you prefer, domestication, does not take, and, in the end, he reverts to wildness.

SAMSON AS CHAOS MONSTER

A more interesting and less discussed issue is that Samson shares some traits in common, not with this ideal type from a catalogue of international folklore, but with a specific figure in Mesopotamian art and literature, the *laḥmu*. The term *laḥmu*, "the hairy one," appears in ritual and mythological texts and F. A. M. Wiggermann has identified the *laḥmu* with a character in Mesopotamian art: a naked, bearded human figure whose distinguishing feature is long hair, parted down the middle, usually worn in six braids, three on each side.[95] This figure, once known as "the naked hero" or "the six-locked hero," is sometimes depicted in combat scenes with animals; occasionally unarmed but often holding a staff or spade. In literature, the *laḥmu*, though not formally a hybrid, is yet another specimen in the Mesopotamian menagerie of *Mischwesen*, alongside, for instance *kusarikku*, the bull-man, and *girtablullu*, the scorpion-man.[96] The *laḥmu* is one of "the Eleven," a team of chaos monsters created by Tiamat and led in battle by Qingu in the Babylonian creation epic, *Enuma Elish*.[97]

What is the fate of the Eleven in the *Enuma Elish*? Tiamat and Qingu are defeated by Marduk and recycled, their carcasses and body parts integrated into the physical structures of the orderly world brought into existence after the primordial cosmic conflict.[98] "The Malificent Eleven" are also defeated but they are not obliterated. Instead the language used is that of control. In his translation, Benjamin Foster describes the Eleven as "held," "drawn in," "cast in a net," "to prison confined," and "put on lead ropes."[99] If we artifi-

cially constructed a Babylonian meta-narrative of the chaos monsters around the time of the end of the second millennium (as Wiggermann does in scholarship, and as the *Enuma Elish* does in
literature), it would go something like this: in the Olden Days, the
patron deity of Babylon, Marduk, representing hopes for cosmic
order, defeated these chaos monsters. Now they are his servants.
Accordingly, they appear on portals and walls and the sides of char-
iots, fierce trophies that give evidence of the power of their master,
but also acting as watchdogs, warding off other evil powers.[100] Foster
calls them "beneficent monsters."[101]

The chaos monster that figures most prominently in the Bible
is "Leviathan," *liwyātān*.[102] Leviathan is the Hebrew name for the
primordial sea serpent found in many mythologies, such as the
seven-headed Hydra of Greco-Roman lore. The standard creation
narratives in the Bible found in Genesis 1–3 reject any hint of a primordial combat between God and chaos personified in a form such
as Leviathan.[103] But many biblical poetic texts allude to Leviathan
and to a primeval or eschatological battle in which God defeats a
dragon or sea monster.

Psalm 74 sketches God's creation of the world, "You established light and the sun, you set in place all the boundaries of the
earth, you fashioned summer and winter" (Ps 74:16–17). The pre-
requisite to the creation of this orderly world of fixed boundaries
and predictable seasons, however, was the defeat of chaos, mentioned in an earlier line of the poem, "You crushed the heads of
Leviathan" (Ps 74:14). Isaiah 27:1 invokes the theme of the combat
between God and Leviathan to describe the day of Kingdom Come:
"On that day, YHWH will punish, with his inflexible, great, and strong
sword, Leviathan the fleeing serpent, Leviathan the twisting serpent." These poetic allusions suggest that the myth of combat between God and Leviathan was a component of Israelite lore.

One text about Leviathan, Job 3:8, indirectly alludes to the relationship in ancient thinking between the chaos monsters and destruction. Job refers to Leviathan in his initial speech, following the prose narrative (Job 1–2) that introduces the story of "the greatest of all the peoples of the east" (Job 1:3) and his "very great trouble" (Job 2:13). "After this Job opened his mouth and cursed the day of his birth" (Job 3:1). In terms that inversely echo the creation account in Genesis 1, Job asks for the rewinding of the tape of history, first back to the day he was born, then further back to the night he was conceived, so that they might be removed from the calendar. If living means burying his ten children and seeing his skin dissolve, Job wishes never to have been born.

> Perish the Day on which I was born,
> the Night that said, "A male is conceived." (Job 3:3)

In Genesis 1, creation begins with the divine command, "Let there be light," *yĕhî 'ôr* (Gen 1:3a). Job asks for the reverse, "Let there be darkness," *yĕhî ḥōšek* (Job 3:4). To accomplish this negation, Job calls for specialists, "those who are adept at awakening Leviathan" (Job 3:8), flautists capable of charming the primordial snake from its basket. The implication is that awakening the sleeping or inactive monster would unleash chaos and undo creation all the way back to the primeval darkness of the abyss (Gen 1:2). The logic of awakening the monster and unleashing chaos, whether through esoteric "black magic" or ethical trespass, is the foundation of many narratives and is as ancient as Pandora's Box and as contemporary as horror stories and films in which the moral lapse of some unsuspecting sinner provides the occasion for the emergence of some monster or serial killer.[104] The chaos monsters, whether Leviathan of Israelite lore or the Eleven in Mesopotamian, are agents of destructive energy. In some instances, the chaos monsters, such as Leviathan in Psalm 74:14 and Isaiah 27:1, are the opponents of divine order; in others, the monsters are under the control of beneficent powers, such as in Psalm 104:26 and Job 40:25–29 (41:1–5 ET), where Leviathan is pictured as YHWH's domestic pet.

At least a handful of scholars has noted two parallels between the Samson of Judges 14–16 and the *laḫmu* of Babylonian seals: both wear their hair in braids; both are described or pictured in combat with beasts.[105] Could Samson, whose biblical characterization has superficial similarities to the Babylonian *laḫmu,* have a similar function to this Babylonian chaos monster? Is there a way in which Samson functions as a chaos monster or plague or personified divine weapon unleashed on Philistia in order to combat this nation? Samson is controlled; Samson is as deadly as a plague. From a Philistine perspective, Samson is merely one of the many names—plague, blight, drought, an invading army—for chaos.[106]

This is Samson as a bundle of chaotic destruction, wielded, handled by a corner man, used, as Judges 14:4 admits, as a "pretext," an occasion, for YHWH against the Philistines. This is Samson as the most personified of a roster of harmful divine agents, *malā'kîm,* in YHWH's entourage (Ps 78:49), alongside *Mašḫît* ("the Destroyer"),[107] *Qeṣep* ("Anger"),[108] *Deber* ("Plague"),[109] and *Ṣir'â* ("the Hornet"? "Terror"?),[110] the last a demonic intermediary sent against the nations in the wars of conquest. This is Samson—who in Gaza uproots the structures of the city wall, topples the temple, and buries thousands alive; who in Timnah, sets orchards and fields ablaze; who in Ashkelon, kills and plunders thirty men—as the living embodiment of the terms of a prophetic oracle against Philistia, such as that issued in Zephaniah 2:4: "Gaza shall become a ghost town, / and Ashkelon an ash heap."[111]

So much depends on how we understand the little riddle of the meaning of Judges 14:4 and the big riddle of human freedom and divine sovereignty. If Samson had a choice, if *he* was seeking an occasion against the Philistines, then this is the story of a man who is little lower than the angels, a man who laid down his life for God and country. If we take Judges 14:4 as referring to a divine pretext, as

I think we must, then this is the story of a character who is a kind of Israelite *laḥmu*, little higher than Leviathan, Yʜᴡʜ's chaos monster sent to destroy Philistia.[112]

SAMSON AS A *GIBBÔR*

There is a grave danger in this mythological comparison if it obscures the humanity of our folk hero. I would not and could not flatten Samson into a type, or depersonalize him. The enduring power of the story is based in the tension between the sex and the violence, between Samson's hearty, larger-than-life adventures in search of love, and his grim mission. Samson in Judges 13–16 is a character human enough to invite our identification with his desire and our sympathy for his frustration. Despite the gargantuan elements of his characterization, the story in the end invites readers to identify more with Samson's weakness than his strength. On a human scale, against the backdrop of Iron Age heroic tradition, how, then, does Samson appear? Samson is the complete package, the ultimate *gibbôr*, according to the categories discussed in chapter 3.

Samson crows about his "great victory," his *tĕšûʿâ gĕdōlâ*, when, after three militia units of Judah had surrendered him to a Philistine raiding party, he slays the "foreskinneds" by himself (Judg 15:9–18).[113] Samson has impressive numbers: his thirty at Ashkelon; his "thousand" at Lehi, his three "thousand" at Dagon's temple in Gaza (Judg 14:19; 15:15; 16:27, 30).[114] Samson certainly uses inferior technology, killing a lion with his bare hands, slaying Philistines with the jawbone of an ass, uprooting a city gate and toppling a temple without a lever.[115] Samson receives a dose of "the breath of Yʜᴡʜ" as a prelude to several of his feats.[116] Samson is the raider who sabotages fields and orchards around Timnah.[117]

Above all else, Samson is the supreme solo combatant.[118] Samson inhabits the arena, the fields and wilderness outside villages and towns, that other *gibbôrîm* entered only on the occasions of rit-

ual ordeals and desperate circumstances.[119] He seems constitutionally incapable of acting in the context of a group. On one occasion
he does enter the very arena of gladiatorial combat, in Dagon's Temple in Gaza, when the Philistines, their hearts merry, bring him out
of his cell to "play," √śḥq, before them.[120] On the single occasion
that he requires companions, he enlists jackals (Judg 15:4–5).

All this is to say that the primary image of Samson, under however many overlays, is that of an Israelite warrior, many of his feats
akin to those of other *gibbôrîm* in Judges and Samuel. Samson slays
a lion (Judg 14:5–6) but so do Benaiah (2 Sam 23:20) and David
(1 Sam 17:34–37). Samson, handed over to the Philistines by Judahites, defeats a thousand men in single combat (Judg 15:9–13). Two of
the *gibbôrîm*, Eleazar and Shammah, are abandoned by comrades
and then defeat Philistines in solo combat (2 Sam 23:9, 11). Samson
fights Philistines at Lehi (Judg 15:9–17); so does Shammah (2 Sam
23:11). Motifs can be combined in similar sequences. In both Judges
15 and 2 Samuel 23, a story about the thirst of a hero follows directly
a Lehi tradition (Judg 15:18; 2 Sam 23:11–17).

If we expanded this comparison to other heroic materials in
Judges and Samuel, we would find that the Samson story draws on
various elements of an Israelite heroic repertoire, and shares certain features in common with stories about Shamgar, Gideon, Jephthah, Saul, Jonathan, and David.[121] Samson displays virtually every
possible motif of the Israelite heroic tradition with a few telling exceptions. Samson does not slay an elite rival: he is that for the
Philistines.[122] Samson does, in fact, take trophies, garments stripped
from corpses outside Ashkelon, the city gate of Gaza which he carries to Hebron, but, more than that, Samson is the sacred trophy,
captured by the Philistines and deposited in their temple, the
House of Dagon.[123] However, like another Israelite sacred object
taken as a Philistine trophy, the Ark, his capture functions, in this
respect at least, like the Trojan Horse, and ultimately proves to be
an agent of destruction, one planted in the very center of the Philis-

tine town; an agent—if I can invoke again the Babylonian hairy man, the *laḥmu*—of chaos.

COMEDY, TRAGEDY

There is something comic about Samson: he is the bull in a china shop; the rube, the hillbilly, who topples all the carefully arranged structures of Philistine urban society.[124] But there is also something tragic about Samson. The tragedy is that Samson never had a chance.

Judges 14:4 ("[YHWH] was seeking an occasion against the Philistines") suggests that Samson is an instrument. Looking for love, giving as good as he gets, Samson violently careens through Philistia, burning things, killing people, and tearing buildings down. He is the embodiment of chaos and, from a Philistine perspective, he raises Hell. All the while he is simply, unintentionally, practicing his divinely ordained vocation: mayhem. Samson's mission was to begin to deliver the Israelites from the Philistines (13:5). This Terminator does that and more. And so the story does not end with Samson's marriage or with the news that he headed back into the hills, gathering a group of empty men around him to raid before either passing into legend or, like David, going legitimate and competing for political power. No, the story ends with a body count: "So [the number of] those he killed as he died were more than [the number of] those he killed while he was alive" (Judg 16:30).

In order to equip Samson for his job, YHWH set him apart from birth (Judg 16:17), sent the divine breath to disturb and rush over him, and gave him feral power. Susan Ackerman has parsed the deep grammar of biblical narratives about special births and has articulated "the Israelite understanding that a child given to a barren woman is a gift of Y[HWH]" and that "the God who fills a woman's womb has the right to demand, in some fashion, the life that comes forth from it."[125] She notes, for instance, how Isaac (Gen 16–17; 21:1–7) is demanded as a sacrifice (Gen 22:1–14), and how Samson and Samuel are dedicated to God as Nazirites (1 Sam 1:11). I would take her analysis one step further. Through a series of editorial reflections (Judg 13:5; 14:4; 16:30b), the Samson narrative frames its hero's life and death in terms of a grim, divinely ordained mission. Here, then, the LORD, within "his" rights, giveth and the LORD taketh away, in order to liberate, from the perspective of the book of Judges, Israel from Philistine oppression.

At times it seems as if Samson is a mule, powerful but producing no offspring, used to clear the field of Philistines so that a new people can be planted in their stead. But the more dominant image is thoroughly human, of a young man searching for love across a border. For all his ups and downs, and criss-crossings of topographic and cultural borders, he remains betwixt and between. Samson is human enough to be aware of love, but he is too wild ever to experience it. In the end, then, in the Temple of Dagon, Samson pulls down the columns, kills the Philistines, and completes his destructive mission. In the same action, he buries himself, erasing himself from the surface of the earth. There was nowhere else for Samson to go. He is the ultimate empty man.

NOTES

1. The Hebrew word is *maḥlĕpôt* (Judg 16:13, 19), from √ḥlp, "to change"; here, perhaps in the sense of hair which has been styled, i.e., "changed," in a certain way for ritual purposes (S. Tengström and H.-J. Fabry, "חלף *chālaph*," 434).

2. As illustrated by E. Auerbach's comments about the character Isaac in Gen 22: "[H]e may be handsome or ugly, intelligent or stupid, tall or short, pleasant or unpleasant—we are not told. Only what we need to know about him as a personage in action, here and now, is illuminated. . . . [T]he narrative . . . is 'fraught with background' " (*Mimesis*, 10–12).

3. *b. Soṭah* 10a.

4. D. Fowler, "Lion."

5. The syntax of Judg 14:6 ("[Samson] tore apart the lion [as easily] as the rending of the kid"), with a verbal noun (i.e., "as the rending," *kĕšassaʿ*) rather than a simple noun, makes the subject of the second clause grammatically ambiguous. Its plain sense is captured by J. Milton's gloss, "[Samson] tore the Lion, as *the Lion* tears the Kid" (emphasis mine) ("Samson Agonistes," line 128; *John Milton* [ed. M. Hughes], 554).

"Shephelah," though it means "lowlands," refers to the low hills adjacent to the southern coastal plain. This ridge is "low" only in relation to the central mountains of Judah (Y. Aharoni, *The Land of the Bible*, 25).

6. The word *šûʿāl*, though often translated as "fox" (i.e., "the little foxes" of Song 2:15), probably refers to the jackal, *canis aureus* (HALOT 4:1445; O. Margalith, "Samson's Foxes," 225).

7. See Ezek 13:4; Song 2:15; Lam 5:18; Neh 3:35 (4:3 ET).

8. For instance, A. Scheiber has found artistic images from medieval central Europe of Samson uprooting trees, a motif found nowhere in the Bible or premedieval sources ("Samson Uprooting a Tree"; "Further Parallels to the Figure of Samson the Tree-Uprooter"). This motif may have been borrowed from medieval legends about wild men who wielded tree trunks and saplings as weapons (G. Mobley, "The Wild Man in the Bible and the Ancient Near East," 230).

9. For a partial list, see J. Crenshaw, *Samson*, 154, n. 20.

10. Regarding Hercules, "the greatest of Greek heroes," note the comment of A. Schachter, "Legends arose early of his epic feats, and they were added to constantly throughout antiquity" ("Heracles," 684). For general treatments, see W. Burkert, *Greek Religion*, 208–11; G. Kirk, *The Nature of Greek Myths*, 176–212.

11. B. Lincoln, *Priests, Warriors, and Cattle*, 112.

12. In a series of articles, O. Margalith argues for Greek influence on the Samson narrative: "Samson's Foxes"; "Samson's Riddle and Samson's Magic Locks"; "More Samson Legends"; "The Legends of Samson/ Heracles." Though I view the Samson legend as primarily emerging out of Israelite and Near Eastern heroic traditions, the latter often itself cited as a matrix of Greek heroic traditions (e.g., the Oriental motifs in legends about Hercules noted by W. Burkert [*Greek Religion*, 209]), it is entirely possible that motifs from East and West attached themselves to the Samson material.

For a survey of the array of Israelite heroic conventions present in the Samson narrative, see pp. 204–6. For a literary analysis of the way in which the Samson story, the last in the series of heroes profiled in Judges, echoes themes and motifs from the previous chapters of Judges, see E. Greenstein, "The Riddle of Samson."

13. For examples, see D. Collon, *First Impressions*, 33 (#'s 95, 99, 101); 46 (#'s 158, 159, 161, 165); 64 (# 275); 98 (# 445); 124 (# 522, 529); 133 (# 566); 156 (# 706); 164 (# 760); 188 (#'s 903, 904); 195 (#'s 953, 954); 196 (# 964).

14. For more discussion, see pp. 200–204.

15. For charts that sketch the profile of biblical birth stories, see R. Brown, *The Birth of the Messiah*, 156; and Y. Zakovitch, חיי שמשון (*The Life of Samson*), 84. For analysis of this type of story, "the birth of the hero to his barren mother," see R. Alter, *The Art of Biblical Narrative*, 51; cf. "How Convention Helps Us Read." For an analysis of Samson's birth story, see S. Ackerman, *Warrior, Dancer, Seductress, Queen*, 181–215.

16. See J. Exum, "Promise and Fulfillment: Narrative Art in Judges 13."

17. In her report of the encounter to her husband, the woman omits any mention of the third Nazirite stipulation, that the child's hair remain uncut, but adds something else. As J. Exum observes, the woman omi-

nously previews the child's destiny: "the boy shall be *nāzîr* to God from birth *to the day of his death*" (the addition in italics) ("Promise and Fulfillment," 49).

18. J. Exum's analysis details the contrast between "extremely positive portrayal" of the woman (p. 48) and the marginal role Manoah has in the proceedings ("Promise and Fulfillment," 51–59). Indeed, the birth story has two major scenes (Judg 13:2–7; 13:8–23), depicting two appearances of the divine messenger. The first scene provides all the information necessary for reading the adventure stories of Samson in Judg 14–16. The second scene functions mainly to develop the contrast between these two minor characters, the discerning, knowing woman and her clueless husband; as S. Ackerman puts it, the pious woman and her "bumbling" husband (*Warrior, Dancer, Seductress, Queen*, 112).

19. R. Boling, *Judges*, 221. Boling contends, first, that uncut hair was so central to the Nazirite status that it needed not be mentioned. Second, Boling reminds us that it is the woman who is talking in Judg 13:7, reporting the angel's instructions to her husband; and that since the cutting of the hair did not apply to her, she did not need to report it in her speech. This does not account for the omission of any reference to hair in 13:14, in which the messenger again gives instructions to the parents. For Boling's third explanation, see p. 221 of his commentary on Judges. There, he braids together strands from the Nazirite rules of Num 6 and from the story of Judg 13 concerning hair into a knot of innertextual assumptions that I cannot untangle.

20. Many such stories exist; in fact, G. Dumézil (*The Destiny of the Warrior*) has observed that a common pattern in Indo-European heroic tradition is that of "the three sins of the hero." I am not suggesting that the Samson saga, in this respect, has borrowed or is influenced by the Indo-European pattern; merely that this body of comparative data demonstrates that such a story, about a hero's three trials, or three temptations, could have existed.

21. J. Blenkinsopp, "Structure and Style in Judges 13–16."

22. J. Blenkinsopp, "Structure and Style," 66.

23. For instance, D. Olson, "The Book of Judges," 853.

24. J. Blenkinsopp, "Structure and Style," 66. Again, Blenkinsopp insists that the transparent etymology of *mišteh* "speaks for itself"; for E. Greenstein such an assumption "must be supposed" ("Riddle of Samson," 251).

25. L. Klein, *The Triumph of Irony in the Book of Judges*, 119.

26. R. Boling, *Judges*, 231.

27. As J. Exum notes, "A major objection to Blenkinsopp's thesis that the plot of Judg xiii–xvi centers on the broken Nazirite vow is its failure to account for major portions of the saga" ("The Theological Dimension of the Samson Saga," 32).

28. M. O'Connor, "Judges," 142.

29. Nazirite regulations emphasize that the prohibition extends beyond drinking intoxicants; "they shall not . . . eat grapes, fresh or dried" (Num 6:3; cf. Judg 13:14).

30. J. Exum also argues that a Samson narrative which gave more prominence to the Nazirite vow existed. In her view, it was "part of the tradition which the narrator of our present story received . . . but, at the same time, moved beyond to make another theological point;" namely, that God answers prayer ("Theological Dimension," 33). In a more recent article, Exum describes the conundrum that the ambiguous presentation of the Nazirite motif presents to interpreters, "Though I am not entirely persuaded that the narrator presents Samson as breaking the Nazirite regulations against contact with what is unclean or drinking wine or strong drink . . . , I acknowledge the potential for such a reading" (*Fragmented Women*, 75–76, n. 32).

31. Among the more colorful Jewish legends are that Samson was a giant (*b. Soṭah* 10a) and that the Philistines put him out to stud (i.e., his "grind-

ing" [Judg 16:21], a euphemism for sexual intercourse in Job 31:10), hoping he would sire gigantic offspring (*b. Soṭah* 9b–10a), a labor that, according to one version, sired Goliath! (L. Ginzberg, *The Legends of the Jews*, 6:250).

Y. Zakovitch uses postbiblical Jewish tradition, prudently, to uncover traces of older Samson legends. He suggests that the biblical version of the tale has suppressed certain mythological and erotic details of ancient popular tradition, namely that Samson was gigantic, that he had a divine paternity (according to Judg 13:6, 9, 10, the angel "came to," *bô' 'el-*, the woman; this phrase is often used to describe sexual intercourse in the Bible; including later in the Samson narrative, i.e., Judg 15:1; 16:1), and that he had sexual intercourse with Delilah (*Life of Samson*, 236–39).

32. G. Moore, *A Critical and Exegetical Commentary on Judges*, 312–13; J. Crenshaw, *Samson*, 98.

33. Furthermore, as J. Crenshaw observes, Samson's mother is the leading character in Judg 13; thus, women are central throughout the narrative (*Samson*, 98). Taking the birth story into account, we have the story of "Samson and the Four Women."

34. E.g., Judg 10:2, 3; 12:7, 9b, 11.

35. The grammatical nomenclature (i.e., "prefix conjugation," *waw-relative*,") are the terms used by B. Waltke and M. O'Connor (*An Introduction to Biblical Hebrew Syntax*, 543. The traditional term for the phenomenon is "Imperfect with Wåw Consecutive" (E. Kautzsch and A. Cowley, *Gesenius' Hebrew Grammar*, 326).

36. One explanation is "the subtraction-addition theory," according to which, the Samson narrative originally included some version of what we now know as Judg 14–16, but a later editor (the Deuteronomist?) subtracted the Delilah episode, and inserted the closing formula of Judg 15:20, thus concluding the story on a heroic rather than tragic note. A later editor then added it back, along with the final closing formula of Judg 16:31. For discussion and rejection of this theory, see J. Exum, "Literary Patterns in

the Samson Saga," 36. Without an ancient scroll of Judges which preserves a variant, such a thesis remains unverifiable.

37. R. Boling, "Judges, Book of," *ABD* 3:1112.

38. J. Exum ("Aspects of Symmetry and Balance in the Samson Saga," 4) demonstrates "that Judg 14–15 and Judg 16 are constructed as thematic parallels: what happens in the first cycle (chs. 14–15) is repeated in the second (ch. 16)."

39. E. Greenstein, "Riddle of Samson," 238.

40. H. Gunkel, "Simson," 40.

41. C. Lévi-Strauss, *The Raw and the Cooked,* 15–32.

42. The nineteenth century American folksong, "Jesse James," has as many variants as it has performers. For the version that includes the line, "He stole from the rich and he gave to the poor," see M. Boni, *The Fireside Book of Favorite American Songs,* 224–26. In another version, collected by J. and A. Lomax, the same theme—the outlaw Man-of-Sorrows—appears in different form:

> "Jesse was a man, a friend to the poor, / He never would see a man suffer pain" (J. Lomax and A. Lomax, *American Ballads and Folk Songs,* 128–31).

43. For the song, "Stagolee," see A. Lomax, *Folk Songs of North America,* 571–72; for commentary, see G. Marcus, *Mystery Train,* 65–68; *Invisible Republic,* 78–79; and the definitive recent study of C. Brown, *Stagolee Shot Billy.* Marcus's description of the Stagolee of the song is memorable: "dispatching his enemies, humiliating white sheriffs, . . . dethroning the devil" (*Invisible Republic,* 79). For Stagolee as "the Bad [or 'baaad'] Nigger," see Brown, *Stagolee Shot Billy,* 14–15.

44. There does seem to be a functional parallel between the characters of Samson in Israelite folk tradition and the Stagolee figure in African-

American culture. Compare, for instance, the following birth account of Willie Dixon's "Hoochie Coochie Man" with the story in Judg 13 about how Samson's birth and mission were announced to his mother by an angel (the reference to Dixon as found in B. Filene, *Romancing the Folk,* 101):

> The gypsy woman told my mother
> Before I was born
> You got a boy child comin'
> He's gonna be a son of a gun.

45. The last time that the Danites had been mentioned in the book of Judges prior to the Samson story was in Judg 1:34, where it says that "the Amorites had pushed them toward the hill country." Judg 14:1 ("Samson descended . . .") serves notice: the Danites are coming back down from the hills, with a vengeance.

46. E. Greenstein notes that the phrase "right in his eyes" indicates more than mere physical attraction, an idea expressed through other idioms in biblical Hebrew ("Riddle of Samson," 249–50). The phrase anticipates the editorial refrain in Judg 17:6 and 21:25, and marks, from the standpoint of the editorial arrangement of the book of Judges as a whole, the progressive deterioration of this society without a king.

47. The episode of Samson and the woman from Timnah, from a certain analytic distance, has a plot roughly parallel to Gen 34. In both cases, members of a woman's host culture scheme to thwart the marriage and kill a suitor from a foreign group. One might expect a culture to preserve stories about the defense of its womenfolk from outsiders. The Samson story reverses this pattern and adopts the point-of-view of the outsider. For more on the unusual point-of-view of the story, see G. Mobley, "The Wild Man in the Bible and the Ancient Near East."

48. 2 Kgs 5:7 uses a different form of the same verbal root (*'nh*) in a similar way, "[The king of Aram] is picking a quarrel with me." For the construction, "It was from Yhwh," compare Josh 11:20. There, an editor explains, the refusal of various Canaanite peoples to make peace with the Israelites

was "from Yʜᴡʜ," i.e., divinely destined, because it allowed Joshua and the Israelite tribes the opportunity to face and exterminate their rivals in battle. Cf. also 1 Sam 2:25.

49. G. Moore, *Judges*, 328; J. Soggin, *Judges*, 239.

50. The 1917 JPS version of the Bible, for instance, explicitly makes Samson the initiator of the plot by using lowercase for the masculine pronoun in its translation of Judg 14:4: *"he* [not *He;* italics mine] sought an occasion against the Philistines." Pronouns whose antecedents are names for the deity are always rendered with uppercase in this translation (*The Holy Scriptures* [ed. M. Margolis]).

51. J. Slotki, "Judges," 269.

52. "Out of the eater came something to eat; out of the strong came something sweet" (Judg 14:14).

53. J. Exum, "Literary Patterns," 46–55; "Aspects of Symmetry and Balance," 3–5.

54. As noted above, M. O'Connor ("Judges," 142) contends that the entire episode about the lion and the bees (Judg 13:5–9) is a narrative contrivance growing out of the terms of this riddle.

55. D. Bynum, "Samson as a Biblical φὴρ ὀρεσκῷος," 62–63.

56. H. Gunkel, "Simson," 54; O. Eissfeldt, *The Old Testament*, 85; P. Nel, "The Riddle of Samson"; J. Crenshaw, *Samson*, 117–18; J. Exum, *Fragmented Women*, 77–78; M. O'Connor, "Judges," 142; C. Camp and C. Fontaine, "The Words of the Wise and their Riddles," 140–42.

Admittedly, the term, "love," can be banal; I use it only because forms of the Hebrew word, "love" (√'hb) occur elsewhere in the narrative (Judg 14:16; 16:4, 15), but the answer to the riddle can be formulated in more explicitly erotic terms, e.g., O. Eissfeldt, "semen" ("Die Rätsel in Jdc 14," 134);

J. Crenshaw, "copulation" ("The Samson Saga," 490); C. Camp and C. Fontaine, "cunnilingus" ("Words of the Wise," 141).

57. J. Crenshaw, for instance, in a study of the Samson story from the perspective of the Hebrew wisdom tradition, draws this lesson: "supplanting a normal marriage relationship is fraught with danger" ("Samson Saga," 472).

58. H. Gunkel cannot resist commenting on the humor of the episode—that after a night of lovemaking, Samson was still capable of hoisting the city gates on his shoulders—but he shifts to Latin to avoid offending his gentle readers, noting that Samson's feat is all the more remarkable since *"omne animal post coitam triste"* ("every living creature is spent after intercourse") ("Simson," 44).

59. See A. Reinhartz (*"Why Ask My Name?"*) for an analysis of anonymous *vis-à-vis* named characters in the Hebrew Bible.

60. In Ugaritic, the name *Dalil[u]* appears as a masculine name. Its feminine form would be **dalilat,* though we do not know the quality of its vowels (either *dālilu/at,* an active participle, or *dalīlu/at,* a passive participle). The latter would be cognate to the Hebrew *dĕlîlâ* (F. Gröndahl, *Die Personennamen der Texte aus Ugarit,* 124; J. Huehnergard, *Ugaritic Vocabulary in Syllabic Transcription,* 212).

61. See under √*dll* II in *HALOT* 1:223.

62. *CAD* 3:46–47, 50–51.

63. H. Wehr, *Arabic-English Dictonary,* 289.

64. Consider: M. Noth, "falling curls" (*Die israelitischen Personennamen im Rahmen der gemeinsemitischen Namengebung,* 227); J. Exum, "loose hair" ("Delilah," 133) and also, from √*dll* I, "small, slight" (*HALOT* 1:223); C. Burney, "worshipper [of Ishtar]" (*The Book of Judges and Notes on the Hebrew Text of the Book of Kings,* 407); R. Boling, "flirtatious," (*Judges,* 248) and J. Crenshaw, "affectionate" (*Samson,* 18).

65. As in A. Palmer, *The Samson Saga and its Place in Comparative Religion,* 129–31. Linguistically, there are two problems with this interpretation. First, the Aramaic relative particle *dĕ-* is not attested in Hebrew. Second, the *yod* in Hebrew *layĕlâ* is consonantal but the *hireq yod* in *dĕlîlâ* does not reflect an original *yod* but rather, a lengthened i-class vowel. It must be said, however, that such philological considerations are irrelevant to those who coin and trade in punning folk etymologies.

66. J. Exum, "Aspects of Symmetry and Balance," 4.

67. See also, "Samson as Wild Man," pp. 199–200.

68. For English translations of the Gilgamesh Epic, see A. George, *The Epic of Gilgamesh;* S. Dalley, *Myths from Mesopotamia,* 39–153.

For comparisons between Enkidu and Samson, see C. Burney, *Book of Judges,* 407; J. Gray, *Joshua, Judges, Ruth* (NCB), 221; J. Crenshaw, *Samson,* 17–18; D. Bynum, "Samson as a Biblical φὴρ ὀρεσκῷος," 63; S. Niditch, "Samson as Culture Hero, Trickster, and Bandit," 613; G. Mobley, "Wild Man," 220–23.

69. These events are described in Tablets I–II of the Standard Babylonian Version (A. George, *Epic of Gilgamesh,* 1–14; S. Dalley, *Myths from Mesopotamia,* 50–60) and in the Old Babylonian Pennsylvania Tablet (A. George, *Epic of Gilgamesh,* 101–05; S. Dalley, *Myths from Mesopotamia,* 136–39).

70. E. Reiner sees two stages in Enkidu's development: humanization through intercourse with the human woman, then, urbanization under her tutelage along the journey to the city ("City Bread and Bread Baked in Ashes," 118). Regarding the humanization of Enkidu, see also W. Moran, "Ovid's *Blanda Voluptas* and the Humanization of Enkidu."

71. M. Jastrow and A. Clay, *An Old Babylonian Version of the Gilgamesh Epic,* 65 (i.e., *Gilgamesh Pennsylvania* III:105); cf. A. George, *Epic of Gilgamesh,* 105; S. Dalley, *Myths from Mesopotamia,* 138.

72. I follow J. Sasson's interpretation that Delilah shaved Samson's head ("Who Cut Samson's Hair?").

73. See Gen 30:3; 2 Kgs 4:20; Isa 66:12; Job 3:12.

74. M. Bal, *Lethal Love,* 59.

75. J. Exum, "Wife of Samson."

76. J. Crenshaw puts the answer to the Philistine's riddle and the note that Samson loved Delilah together this way: " 'After this he *loved* a woman.' At last Samson has fallen prey to a power sweeter than honey and crueler than a lion" ("Samson Saga," 502).

77. M. Pope, *Song of Songs,* 653.

78. In Frederick Hedge's translation of Martin Luther's *"Ein' Feste Burg* (A Mighty Fortress)," stanza 3: "The Prince of Darkness grim / We tremble not for him; / His rage we can endure, / For, lo, his doom is sure, / One little word shall fell him."

79. Judg 15:18; 16:19ff; Y. Zakovitch, *Life of Samson,* 236–39.

80. J. Exum, "Theological Dimension," esp. 33, 39–43.

81. J. Crenshaw ("Samson Saga," 503): "One could even say, therefore, that the Samson saga develops in highly dramatic fashion one facet of the thought of Gen 2:24 ('Therefore a man leaves his father and his mother and cleaves to his wife, and they become one flesh')."

82. Although the significance of the connection varies, others have also juxtaposed the Samson narrative and the Ark narrative; cf. M. O'Connor, "Judges," 141; J. Crenshaw, "Samson Saga," 502.

83. Consider, for instance, the remarks of D. Olson ("Judges," 841): "The last rogue judge, Samson, is the reverse image of the first model judge, Othniel."

84. Seen in A. Lomax, *Folk Songs of North America*, 478–79. On a rhetorical level, the term "nachul man" in the song, found elsewhere in African-American folk songs, makes for an appealing parallel to the folklore term, "Natural Man" (another term for "Wild Man") often invoked in this chapter. But within their respective linguistic systems, the African-American "natural man" (or "woman") and the German *Naturmensch* or English "Natural Man" are not equivalent expressions. The latter implies a sub-human, animalistic quality; the former, an assertion of authentic, fully realized, "normal" personhood over against a demeaning cultural environment.

85. Y. Zakovitch, *Life of Samson*, 234.

86. For these and others, see H. Steinthal, "The Legend of Samson."

87. See G. Moore's review of mythological interpretations of Samson (*Judges*, 364–65).

88. G. Moore, *Judges*, 365.

89. H. Gunkel, "Simson," 38–64.

90. For more recent treatments of Samson as a wild man, see D. Bynum, "Samson as a Biblical φὴρ ὀρεσκῷος"; S. Niditch, "Samson as Culture Hero"; G. Mobley, "Wild Man"; "Samson, the Liminal Hero."

91. The best general study of the wild man remains R. Bernheimer, *Wild Men in the Middle Ages*. See also R. Bartra, *Wild Men in the Looking Glass*.

92. For examples of ancient Near Eastern iconographic depictions of the master of the beasts motif, see O. Keel, *Jahwes Entgegnung an Ijob*, 88–124.

93. As S. Niditch writes, Samson fights "not with a culture-intensive, humanly designed weapon, but with a found or gathered tool worthy of a cave-man" ("Samson as Culture Hero," 614).

94. Judg 16:7, 11, and, with a slight variation, v. 17 in the MT; see also v. 13 in the LXX, which has fallen out of the MT due to a haplography (G. Moore, *Judges*, 354–55).

95. F. Wiggermann, "Exit *TALIM!*"; *Babylonian Prophylactic Figures*, esp. 286–89.

96. For the *Mischwesen*, see illustrations in J. Black and A. Green, *Gods, Demons and Symbols of Ancient Mesopotamia*, 64–65; and discussion in the articles by F. Wiggermann ("Mischwesen A") and A. Green ("Mischwesen B").

97. For English translations of *Enuma Elish*, see B. Foster, *Before the Muses*, 1:351–402; and S. Dalley, *Myths from Mesopotamia*, 228–77.

This ancient version of "Ocean's Eleven" is introduced in Tablet I of *Enuma Elish* [hereafter *EE*]: "[Tiamat] . . . gave birth to monster snakes, . . . fierce dragons, . . . serpents, dragons, and hairy hero-men [i.e., *laḫmū*], [l]ion monsters, lion men, scorpion men, [m]ighty demons, fish men, bull men. . . . Eleven indeed on this wise she crea[ted]" (*EE* I:132–47; translation by B. Foster [*Muses* 1:358–59]). This block of text is repeated in *EE* II:18–34; III:15–38, and III:72–97.

Lawrence Wills once wondered aloud to me if the odd number of Tiamat's corps, eleven as opposed to the numerologically charmed ten or twelve, was itself a marker of their chaotic nature.

98. *EE* IV:93–104, 119–20; 128; V:65; VI:25–33. Implicit in this Babylonian myth of creation, in which the structures of cosmic order are built from the raw material of Tiamat and Qingu, i.e., mythic personifications of chaos, is the idea that chaos, though threatening, is essential for creativity.

99. *EE* IV:110–12, 114, 117; B. Foster, *Before the Muses*, 1:376.

100. Just as scorpion-men, *girtablullū*, guard a threshold in sacred space— Shamash's domain at Mt. Mashu—in the Gilgamesh Epic (Tablet IX; A. George, *Epic of Gilgamesh*, 71), hybrid creatures, the cherubim, are posted at liminal posts in the Bible (Gen 3:24; 1 Sam 4:4, 2 Sam 6:2; Ezek 1:5–14).

101. B. Foster, *Before the Muses*, 2:534.

102. For Leviathan in the Bible, see C. Uehlinger, "Leviathan."

103. For a discussion of the way that the Hebrew Bible both draws on and, at times, eschews, the creation combat myth, see J. Levenson, *Creation and the Persistence of Evil*.

104. "Psycho," the well-known 1960 film of Alfred Hitchcock, illustrates the pattern: When the character Janet Leigh embezzles money from her employer in the opening scene, the deep logic of the film is that, unwittingly, at a great distance, she has awakened and made herself vulnerable to the chaos monster, Norman Bates, played by Anthony Perkins. More obvious is the treatment of the theme in T. Geisel's (Dr. Seuss) *The Cat in the Hat:* When the mother goes out shopping, she leaves her two children alone with explicit instructions that they not open the door to anyone. Violation of this commandment, allowing the Cat in the Hat to enter, leads to the emergence of the chaos monsters, in this case, Thing 1 and Thing 2. The rest of the story is devoted to getting the chaos monsters back into their suitcase.

105. C. Burney, *Book of Judges*, 379; A. van Daalen, *Simson*, 116–17; R. Wenning and E. Zenger, "Der siebenlockige Held Simson: Literarische und ikonographische Beobachtungen zu Ri 13–16"; R. Mayer-Opificius, "Simson, der sechslockige Held?"; G. Mobley, "Wild Man," 230–31.

106. For the phrase, "the many names of chaos," I am indebted to Davis McCombs' poem, "Farming" (*Ultima Thule*, 45):

> My father stands in the barn's wide upper doors,
> flicks a cigarette into the twilight and scans
> the fields for what we both know lies in wait:
> chaos with its many names—frost or drought
> or thistles or the herd that breaks the fence.

107. Ex 12:23; 2 Sam 24:16 ‖ 1 Chr 21:15; S. Meier, "Destroyer."

108. Num 17:11 (16:46 ET); J. Milgrom, *Numbers*, 142. See also the Deuteronomistic formula in Dt 29:27 (29:28 ET); Jer 21:5, 32:37.

109. Hab 3:5; Ps 91:3, 6; G. del Olmo Lete, "Deber."

110. Ex 23:28; Dt 7:20; Josh 24:12.

111. I have attempted to capture the word-play of the Hebrew of Zeph 2:4:

kî ʿazzâ ʿăzûbâ tihyeh
wĕʾašqĕlôn lišmāmâ.

112. Leviathan is described as controlled by YHWH, "on a leash," in Job 40:29 (41:5 ET).

113. For this motif, see p. 52.

114. See pp. 49–50. The word for "thousand," *ʾelep*, could mean "military unit" in Judg 15:15, but "thousand" must be intended in the description of the crowd at Gaza that included men and women in Judg 16:27.

115. See pp. 56–59.

116. See pp. 59–61.

117. See p. 67.

118. See pp. 51–55.

119. Cf. J. Pedersen remarks about Samson's lifelong Nazirite status: "He was to be constantly in a similar state to that in which warriors found themselves while under the law of war" (*Israel*, 36).

120. See p. 54.

121. Shamgar (an ox goad) and Samson (the jawbone of an ass) both use primitive weapons against Philistines (Judg 3:31; 15:15). Along with Gideon,

Jephthah, and Saul, Samson is inspired to heroic performance by "Yhwh's breath" (Judg 6:34, 11:29; 1 Sam 11:6 for the former three heroes; Judg 14:6, 19; 15:14 for Samson). Jonathan and Samson unexpectedly find honey in the wilds (1 Sam 14:27; Judg 14:8–9). Both Samson and David see their intended given to another, and are offered her younger sister in return (Judg 14:20–15:2; 1 Sam 18:19–27). Both Samson and David kill wild animals with their bare hands (Judg 14:6; Sam 17:34–35).

122. See pp. 50–52.

123. See p. 50.

124. For comic and tragic elements of the story, see J. Exum and J. Whedbee, "Isaac, Samson, and Saul" and the response of Y. Zakovitch, "∪ and ∩ in the Bible"; J. Exum, *Tragedy and Biblical Narrative*, 121–48.

125. S. Ackerman, *Warrior, Dancer, Seductress, Queen*, 192–93.

7

THE HEROIC AGE

AFTER SAMSON

Samson is not the last biblical warrior though this one-man army separated *(nāzîr)* from peers at birth by a divine messenger (Judg 13:5a), agitated *(*nip'ām)* during his youth by an otherworldly spirit (Judg 13:25), and irresistibly drawn in adulthood toward *amour fou* by divine purpose (Judg 14:4), is at once the ultimate *gibbôr* and the most empty of men. The proving grounds for the Iron Age Israelite warrior were arenas of solo combat, whether the physical space arranged by martial convention for dueling, the serrated edge of opposing lines where men closed, or the narrative space arranged by literary *mise-en-scène* for combat between a single hero and a beast, a foe, or a host of foes. Samson, constitutionally incapable of teamwork, knows no other way to function. He is a caricature of the solo combatant.

But once Samson draws first blood in the long conflict between the sons of Israel and the Philistines (Judg 13:5b), and after he completes his killing spree through the villages of the coastal plain, he himself has no place left to stand. Like the wild man from Northern European folklore, *Rumpelstilzchen,* who once his alchemical usefulness to society is exhausted buries himself with a titanic earth-shaking stomp, Samson pulls himself into the chthonic vacuum of Dagon's ruined temple once his deadly mission is fulfilled. Announced by YHWH's messenger, agitated and inspired by YHWH's breath, seduced by YHWH's grim design to seek but never find love across the border, no rescuer comes to deliver Samson from the Philistines who gouge out his eyes, harness him to a mill wheel, and, finally, exhibit him at their Circus Maximus in Gaza (Judg 16:21–25). He does receive one small kindness. His family members retrieve his body so that Samson can sleep with his Danite ancestors (Judg 16:31).

The book of Judges continues after the conclusion of the Samson narrative in Judges 16 with a collection of unhappy stories, each closed by a sad refrain. The short version of the refrain is, "There was no king in those days"; the longer version adds another sentence, "Every man (every warlord? every *pater familias?*) did what was right in his eyes" (Judg 17:6; 18:1; 19:1; 21:25). Judges 17–18, the first of two narratives in this final section of the book, reveals the *shocking truth* about the tribe of Dan and their perverted forms of worship, a story that held more attraction for ancient Judahites than it does for moderns. Judges 19–21, the final section of the book, contains a dirty little epic that includes gang rape, ritual dismemberment, internecine warfare, and bride capture. Though the locale of Judges 19–21 is a mere twenty or so kilometers from Jericho, the site of Ehud's heroics, the distance from that heroic narrative near the beginning of Judges to this destination is immense, between the latter story's buoyant reversals and the former's widening gyre of societal self-destruction, between one Benjaminite warrior and a Benjaminite mob, between the portals of the sacred monoliths from which Ehud emerges after assassinating an oppressive warlord and the threshold of a house in Gibeah where rapists abandon the body of a spent woman.

How did we end up here? The *Retterbuch,* the old Ephraimite core of what became the book of Judges (i.e., Judges 3–9, according to Richter), contained a cyclical view of history.[1] The relationship it sketches between the Israelites and Yнwн was that of a troubled marriage: a good week at work followed by a weekend bender followed by reconciliation. A consistent rhetorical formula—cultic impurity and intermarriage with foreigners leads to dissolution, followed by pleas to Yнwн, followed by the emergence of a divinely appointed rescuer—was woven into the narratives of Ehud, Deborah, and Gideon. A subsequent editor, probably Deuteronomistic, appended the stories—Abimelech and Jephthah, each with their empty men, and Samson—with baroque elaborations of or passing, patently secondary insertions of elements from the above formula (Judg 10:6–16; 13:1).[2] This changed the direction of the history. The Israelites were no longer going in circles, they were losing ground. The addition of the final section of Judges, the graphic and chaotic events recounted in Judges 17–21, accelerates the slope of the decline.

This kind of historical patterning is artificial. Every era has its catalogue of atrocities. Biblical interpreters who take this characterization of the frontier era at face value, bemoaning the chaotic days of the Judges, obviously never read their local newspapers. Exilic historians with a stake in the dynastic and religious culture of Judah, and with its imagined renaissance following the Exile, have selectively remembered the worst stories about the era in order to rhetorically prepare the way for, first, the emergence of monarchy and, second, the cultural hegemony of Judahite religious and social culture.[3] Note that the arch villains of Judges 19–21 are the Benjaminites, the tribe of Saul and the ethnicon for the non-Judahite element in postexilic Southern society.[4] Furthermore, the final two sections of Judges, chapters 17–18 and 19–21, respectively, bundle narrative denunciations of the shrines of Dan and Gilgal, the Northern alternatives to Jerusalem's Mount Zion, in a single appendix. The horrific final chapters of the Deuteronomistic account of the premonarchical era, with their spiraling eddies of self-destruction, have pulled all the protagonists of Judges into their vortex.

The scroll, now books, of Samuel, recounts how this decline was arrested through the introduction of kingship, specifically the kingship of the Davidic dynasty and the religious culture fostered by its priests around Solomon's Temple in Jerusalem. In Samuel, the same martial culture and heroic conventions that we saw in the narratives of Judges appear. Warriors will count their kills (1 Sam 14:14; 2 Sam 23:8, 18). YHWH will inspire Israelite and Judahite *gibbôrîm* (1 Sam 10:10; 11:6) and throw panic into their opponents (1 Sam 7:10; 14:15). Outmanned and ill-equipped underdogs will overcome the enemy through cunning and divine favor (1 Sam 17; 2 Sam 23:9–10).[5] The resolute will be sifted from the fearful on the threshing floor of battle by the winds of warfare (1 Sam 28:5). But the texture of the storytelling changes once we cross the threshold from Judges to Samuel.

Whereas the heroes of Judges—Ehud; Deborah, Barak, and Jael; Gideon; Jephthah; Samson—took the stage one at a time, the heroes in the scroll of Samuel—Samuel, Saul, Jonathan, David, Abner, Joab—occupy the same stage. Not only did the prose narratives of Judges concentrate on a single hero (except for Judg 4–5, with its three: the religious intermediary, Deborah; the false male hero, Baraq; and the unlikely female hero, Jael) but the plot of each had simple constructions. Each story was built square, by the arrangement of a few, sturdy, interlocking motifs. The titles we have given to these stories, Ehud and the Monoliths, Gideon and the Winepress, Gideon and the Three Villages, Abimelech and the Stones, and Samson and the Three Women, are at once descriptive titles of and blueprints for each story. The design of these stories betrays their origins in oral narrative; the mnemonic devices that aided transmission—the bracketing style of the Ehud narrative, the three stanzas of the outlaw ballad of Samson—remain close to the surface. The structures undergirding the stories in Judges 6–9, about Gideon and Abimelech, are more complicated but even there remnants of the bracketing style, the motifs of the winepress and the stones, respectively, bear the imprint of the oral style. The high degree of patterning in these stories encoded the mnemonic genes necessary for self-replication through generations of storytelling while allowing for the admixture of new traits from each new transmitter. The density of the patterning also reinforced a consistent solid-state worldview, a certain moral cause-and-effect whose gravity was eased by entertaining, impish reversals.

The architectonic simplicity of the narratives in Judges, like the four-room house style of Iron Age village life, yields to an extended, busy, stratified palatial narrative in Samuel. Though it is possible, here and there, to detect boundaries around narrative units such as the Ark Narrative in 1 Samuel 4–7, the scope of the contents is broad and the narrative progress practically unbroken from the birth of Samuel, the religious intermediary who will legitimate the monarchy, to the royal competition between Saul and David, first, and among David's heirs, second, until the tribes and the narrative are united under a single Davidide, Solomon, at the beginning of 1 Kings.

From a literary standpoint, the books of Samuel advance the Israelite heroic tradition from the episodic to the epic. The material is more complicated: its narratives more intricately braided, its character portrayals more richly ambiguous. The same repertoire of heroic motifs evident in the narratives of Judges is being drawn upon in the stories about Saul and David but the medium has changed, and the terrain has shifted from the oral to the literary. Military lists, royal annals, and court sponsored histories designed to legitimate the rule of its patrons—conscious literary constructions all—are the building blocks of Samuel.

PERIODIZATION

The period represented in the biblical account by Judges and Samuel was Israel's heroic age. For rhetorical purposes, we might say that it begins in the early chapters of Judges, in a Deuteronomistic preface to the *Retterbuch*:

> These are the nations that YHWH allowed to remain in order to test Israel; that is, all those who had not known ($\sqrt{yd^c}$) any wars in Canaan. It was only to teach warfare to the generations of the sons of Israel who had not known ($\sqrt{yd^c}$) them earlier (Judg 3:1–2).[6]

According to this explanation, subsequent Israelite generations would not be able to luxuriate down by the riverside of the Jordan. Instead, they would need to beat plowpoints into spears, take up their swords and shields, and study war under the guidance of their tutor, YHWH. The heroic age ends with the ascension of Solomon. The words of a prayer attributed to King Solomon in 1 Kings 3 rhetorically marks the end of this era with its speaker's remarkable confession that he did not know ($\sqrt{yd^c}$ again) even the first thing about warfare.

> "And now, O YHWH my God, you have made your servant king in place of David my father even though I am a small lad (*na'ar qāṭōn*). I do not know ($\sqrt{yd^c}$) going out or returning." (1 Kgs 3:7)

The latter phrase, "going out and returning," is an idiom for battle. Solomon makes no claim to be a *gibbôr*; he admits to being its opposite, a *na'ar*. Solomon's basis for leadership is not valor tested in battle but wisdom, "a heart attentive to judging people and to discriminating between good and evil" (1 Kgs 3:9).

The advent of Solomon, the advent of a leader without the

knowledge (√*yd'*) necessary for survival in the era of the Judges, seals the end of the Israelite heroic age. In the first place, because it explicitly replaces the former platform of martial heroism for leadership with a new platform of wisdom (1 Kgs 2:6, 9; 3:3–15, 16–28; 5:9–14 [4:29–34 ET]; 10:1–10, 23–25). In the prayer above, Solomon, though by now a married man in story time (1 Kgs 3:1) and hardly an innocent (see his treatment of Adonijah in 1 Kgs 1:49–53; 2:13–25), compares himself to a boy too young to have tasted battle. In any age, this is a great disadvantage for a political leader, to have no record of military service and to lack the symbolic aura of physical vitality and superiority. To compensate for this deficit, Solomon's court apologists portray their patron as a paragon of wisdom. Anecdotes about Solomon's legendary cultured worldliness and sagacity (e.g., 1 Kgs 3:16–28; 5:9–14 [4:29–34 ET]; 10:1–10) serve as his credentials rather than accounts of derring-do. Solomon does not wrestle beasts, like David did (1 Sam 17:34–37); Solomon catalogues them (1 Kgs 5:13 [4:33 ET]). Solomon's great duel, his solo combat, is not a fight to the death against a Philistine pituitary giant but a contest of wits against the Queen of Sheba (1 Kgs 10:1–10).

In the second place, following Solomon's ascension, there are hardly any accounts of martial heroism throughout the remainder of the Deuteronomistic History, that is, in the books of 1 and 2 Kings. The scroll of Kings does contain formulaic asides, drawn from sources in royal annals, about the military accomplishments of many kings of Israel and Judah, e.g.:

And the rest of the deeds of Asa, and all his heroism (*gĕbûrātô*; a cognate of *gibbôr*), and all he made, and the cities that he built: are they not written on the scroll of the Annals of the Kings of Israel? (1 Kgs 15:23)

And the rest of deeds of Joash, and all that he made, and his heroism (*gĕbûrātô*), how he fought (*nilḥam*; √*lḥm*)

with Amaziah, king of Judah: are they not written on the
scroll of the Annals of the Kings of Israel? (2 Kgs 13:12)

And the rest of the deeds of Hezekiah, and all of his heroism (*gĕbûrātô*), and how he made the pool and the conduit
and brought water into the city: are they not written on
the scroll of the Annals of the Kings of Judah? (2 Kgs
20:20)

Similar formulas, all with *gĕbûrātô* or *nilḥam,* are found in 1 Kings
14:19; 16:5; 16:27; 22:46 (22:45 ET); 2 Kgs 10:34; 14:15; 14:28. Incidentally, a comparison of the above formulas with its cognate in the account of Solomon's reign reinforces our first point, that Solomon's
wisdom compensates for his lack of martial experience. For the corresponding concluding formula about Solomon's reign does not
mention any heroism, any *gĕbûrâ,* but instead, chronicles his wisdom, his *ḥokmâ.*

And the rest of the deeds of Solomon, and all that he
made, and his wisdom (*ḥokmātô*): are they not written on
the scroll of the Annals of Solomon? (1 Kgs 11:41)

Kings rather than warriors—*mĕlākîm* rather than *gibbôrîm*—
exhibit martial prowess in 1 and 2 Kings but this is marked only
through routine citations from annals, not the crafting or retelling
of heroic narratives. There are plenty of battles in the era of Kings
but the combatants, as in 1 Kings 20, are anonymous soldiers in
standing armies, usually under the remote guidance of monarchs.
No *gibbôr* wins a name. Military victories are recorded only in royal
ledgers. In the books of Kings, which chronicle over three centuries
of history, there are only three occasions when kings are credited
with specific feats, with something more than the above routine references to heroics in annals. The coup leader Jehu kills his rival,

King Joram of Israel, with a bowshot (2 Kgs 9:24). Amaziah of Judah kills (that is, leads a force that kills) ten thousand Edomites (2 Kgs 14:7). Regarding Hezekiah, one of only two Judahite kings (along with Josiah) to approach the standard of David, we get this Davidic refrain, "YHWH was with him: every time he went out [to battle], he succeeded" (2 Kgs 18:7; cf. 1 Sam 18:13–14).

Second Kings 13:3–5 is one place in Kings, however, where the rhetoric of the Judges formula reappears, and where a narrative about individual martial heroism lies in wait.

> The anger of YHWH burned against Israel, and [YHWH] gave them into the hand of Hazael, king of Aram, and into the hand of Ben-hadad, son of Hazael, for many days. (v. 3)

In Judges, this is the moment when the people cried out to YHWH for rescue. Here, Jehoahaz, king of Israel, voices their entreaty:

> Then Jehoahaz sought the face of YHWH. YHWH heard him, for [YHWH] saw the oppression of Israel, how the king of Aram oppressed them. (v. 4)

The widespread use of this formula earlier in the Deuteronomistic History, in Judges, has conditioned readers ancient and modern for the next development, the emergence of the hero who will deliver them. We are not disappointed, yet.

> So YHWH gave to Israel a rescuer (*môšîaʿ*) and they got out from under the hand of Aram. (v. 5a)

But that is as far as the formula goes. The identity of this *môšîa* is not given, and while commentators engage the fair question of whether the rescuer was king Jehoahaz or the prophet Elisha or someone else, what is most striking is the lack of commitment to the pattern. Just as the sons of Israel cried out for deliverance in the days of Judges, these verses in 2 Kings 13 call for the narrative response of a heroic anecdote. But the same historians, whether we imagine them as editors or authors, who gave us the tales from Judges and Samuel about warriors, here let the pattern fall, abandoning the narrative arc at its apogee.

The form of heroic narratives about warriors is replaced, in the books of Kings, by the same kind of narratives, only now they involve prophets rather than *gibbôrîm*. This is the third way in which the Deuteronomistic History betrays its sense of periodization. The repertoire of motifs and style of storytelling characteristic of the material in Judges and Samuel is now utilized in legends about prophets. The prophet Elijah triumphs in solo contests against legions, the four hundred priests of Baal on Mount Carmel (1 Kgs 18:20–40), and two units of fifty men along with their respective officers somewhere outside Samaria (2 Kgs 1:9–16). An anonymous "man of God" faces off against King Jeroboam I in the royal sanctuary of Bethel and wards off the king's attempt to capture him through priestcraft (as Jeroboam extends his arm to strike or seize the prophet, the king's arm withers) (1 Kgs 13:4). Back in Judges, Samson controlled foxes (Judg 15:4–5); in Kings, it is prophets who control wild animals, lions (1 Kgs 20:36; cf. 13:20–24) and bears (2 Kgs 2:23–24). Though these prophets do not lead men in battle, they do act in league with bands of angels, the chariot corps of YHWH *Ṣĕbā'ôt*, commander of the heavenly armies (2 Kgs 2:9–12; 6:15–19; cf. 7:6). In Kings, it is prophets, not warriors, who intervene to bring victory over foreign opponents (e.g., Elisha in 2 Kings 3 and Isaiah in 2 Kings 19).

Since the historians who produced the scrolls of Judges and Samuel also produced the scroll of Kings, this shift from tales of *gibbôrîm* to those of *nĕbî'îm*, and the routinized, colorless references to the martial accomplishments of kings, clearly demarcate epochs. The turning point is the ascension of Solomon, which marks the ideal template of Judahite culture, the unification of the twelve tribes under a single Davidic monarch ruling in Jerusalem, a dynasty whose patron deity YHWH receives pilgrims and accepts tribute in Solomon's Temple on Mount Zion. As the frontier era closes, as David trades roaming the Shephelah and Judean wilderness with his *gibbôrîm* for sitting in his palace and dispatching troops (e.g., 2 Sam 11:1), there is also a cosmic relocation. The deity who once moved around in a tent, inspiring warriors, is given his own house. As the age of warriors closes, even Israel's divine warrior is domesticated.

THE LAST WARRIOR

The first warrior to appear in the Deuteronomistic History is Joshua. But for all the battles he fights and rituals he leads, Joshua remains colorless, "a kind of carbon copy of Moses," Michael Coogan writes.[7] Joshua is a type of Moses, an idealized figure, the runner who receives the baton from Moses and leads Israel through its final lap, across the finish line of the Jordan River. But there is little drama or tension in the contest; the outcome of the race had already been fixed by divine promise and Joshua, as a character, rarely, if ever, descends from his Mosaic pedestal.[8] As Coogan puts it, "the most that can be said is that Joshua was . . . perhaps a local hero who became the focus for the idealized reconstruction of early Israel."[9] In contrast, the final warrior left standing in the Israelite heroic age as sketched in the Deuteronomistic History is the most fully realized secondary character in the Hebrew Bible.

Joab is best known as the first commander of David's nascent army, as the son of Jesse makes the transition from guerrilla warlord and rebel during Saul's reign to territorial ruler.[10] Introduced without fanfare as a background character in one of David's adventures in 1 Samuel (1 Sam 26:6), Joab comes to center stage after Saul's death, in 2 Samuel, leading David's men to victories over the rival ethnic militias loyal to the House of Saul under the command of Abner (2 Sam 2–3) and then the Ammonites, the conflict that dominates the action in 2 Samuel 10–12. Once David's supremacy against internal and external rivals is initially secured, Joab becomes David's fixer, plugging all the leaks that threaten to erode the foundation of the newly built royal house.

Joab is portrayed as a convincing tangle of contradictions. David says of him and of his brother Abishai, "the sons of Zeruiah [David's sister according to 1 Chr 2:16] are too hard (*qāšâ*) for me,"[11] too violent, too clannish, too fierce; too old country, we might say. The remark functions to distance David from the blood-feuding ways of Joab, who never let *Realpolitik* stand in the way of a vendetta.

But for the most part, Joab's loyalty to David is portrayed as unsurpassed, especially in the Ammonite campaigns where, no questions asked, he exposes a valiant warrior, the cuckold Uriah the Hittite, to certain death in the front line of the battle with the Ammonites in order to clean up David's messy affair with Bathsheba (2 Sam 11:14–25), or, in the same campaign, when Joab prolongs a siege merely to allow David the triumphal entry into Rabbah (2 Sam 12:26–31). Indeed, Joab's defense of David was rock solid, so long as deference did not violate the two fundamental principles at the core of Joab's code: (1) always protect your position in the chain-of-command, and (2) never leave a score unsettled. Happily, these two principles occasionally overlapped. Joab murders the two rival commanders, Abner and Amasa, whom David, his eyes ever on a kingdom and always eager to extend an olive branch, had drawn into his service (2 Sam 3:26–30; 19:14 [19:13 ET]). Joab's assassination of Abner satisfies a blood feud, for Abner had earlier—reluctantly according to the text—slain Joab's brother Asahel (2 Sam 2:18–23). Joab's killing of Absalom, David's son, quells a revolt but also balances an outstanding account; earlier in the story, Absalom had set Joab's barley field on fire (2 Sam 14:28–33). Though David protested that Joab was too hard, David benefited politically from all of Joab's murders.

Joab was not only a hard man, he was also a capable man. Joab managed David's team of twelve in a duel between special forces, arranged complicated field maneuvers involving three units, raided, apprehended, besieged, killed external enemies, assassinated internal rivals, took David himself to task (2 Sam 19:6–9 [19:5–8 ET]), and, in perhaps his greatest and (I want to believe) most distasteful work of martial artistry, succeeded in realizing the unevenly shaped design demanded by his patron, David, in the Ammonite campaign: gain the city of Rabbah but lose one specific *gibbôr*, Uriah. According to the account in 1 Chronicles 11:6, it is Joab who began the assault on Jerusalem, staking David's claim to the city he would make his capital. Maybe Joab was too hard, too violent, for David, but his mastery of any situation was the cornerstone of David's house.

But Joab was not always hard, and this apparent truth both complicates and humanizes our apprehension of him as a character. He initially acts as a mediator in the oedipal drama between David and Absalom (2 Sam 14:1–24). On a mission to execute a fugitive, Joab acquiesces to the intervention of a wise woman from the village of Abel of Beth-maacah, agreeing to withdraw from her village, and from unnecessary carnage, as long as the townspeople hand over the rebellious Sheba, who had fled there for refuge (2 Sam 20:14–22). This portrait of a man equally adept at force and finesse, at faithful service and decisive initiative, at gripping and relaxing, at going out and coming in, makes Joab among the most vividly drawn characters in Scripture.

In the story of the court masquerade Joab produces in 2 Samuel 14 in order to reconcile Absalom with his father, after David is moved by the brilliant performance—deferential and pointed, obsequious and manipulative—of the wise woman from Tekoa, it finally dawns on the king that he is witnessing a play scripted by a master whose signature he recognizes. David asks, "Is the hand of Joab in this?" (2 Sam 14:19). Indeed, the hand of Joab is prominent in most of the events in 2 Samuel. Modern scholars, conditioned to reject biblical hagiography and official versions of events, have now asked whether Joab's hand, specifically his fingerprints, are not too prominent, conveniently prominent, perhaps even planted, around too many crime scenes in 2 Samuel.

Kyle McCarter was the first to delineate, beneath the text of Samuel, a thematic subtext of carefully drafted responses to charges that threatened to undermine David's legitimacy.[12] For example, the first charge, according to McCarter, was that "David sought to advance himself at Saul's expense." The narrator counters this charge by showing "that David came to court at Saul's behest (1 Sam 16:19–22) and that as long as he was there he was completely loyal and indeed did much to help Saul's own cause (cf. 1 Sam 19:4–5)."[13] One by one, the charges are countered. David was not a deserter from Saul's court; he was driven away (charge #2). David was not an outlaw; he was a fugitive from Saul (#3). David was not a Philistine mercenary (#4). David had no hand in Saul's death (#5), etc.[14]

Joab figures in this subtext of what McCarter has entitled the "Apology of David." Did David have a hand in the death of Abner, Saul's commander and the most powerful warlord among the Northern tribes following Saul's death? Absolutely not, according to 2 Samuel 3. Abner had abandoned the cause of Saul's heir Ishbaal and had made peace with David at Hebron, pledging the loyalty of the warriors from Benjamin under his command and promising to make peace on David's behalf with "all Israel," i.e., Ephraim. Joab, under the pretext of a private conversation, draws Abner aside and stabs him in retaliation for Abner's killing, in wartime, of Joab's brother Asahel (2 Sam 3:26–30). The narrator goes to great lengths to distance David from Joab's murder of Abner, the most powerful warrior remaining in the House of Saul. The narrator includes David's avowal of innocence ("I and my kingdom are forever guiltless before YHWH for the blood of Abner"), declares that Joab acted alone, and even adds the text of the elegy that David performed at Abner's funeral (2 Sam 3:28–29; 31–39).

And what of the charge that David had his own son, Absalom, murdered in order to maintain his throne? "Absalom," as Steven McKenzie writes, ". . . forced David to fight him, and even then David ordered leniency toward him. It was Joab, in direct disobedience of this order, who killed Absalom and broke David's heart ([2 Sam] 18:1–19:9)."[15] Once again, maximum distance has been arranged between David and his right-hand man who had eliminated a dangerous rival of his lord.

It is a hall of mirrors. A straightforward reading of Joab's character in 2 Samuel yields the portrait of a score settler, a blood feuder of the Old School, cunning and deadly in personal duels, shrewd and knowing in field tactics. In the hindsight of critical reappraisal, Joab looks more like the fall guy, the loyal general, the royal fixer who took care of all of David's problems and settled all of David's scores, against Abner, Uriah, Absalom, and Amasa, only to be betrayed by his liege in the end.

Maybe there is a place between these alternative readings where they blur into a single messy mix of motivations personal and political, of actions private and public, and operations covert and overt. Whichever interpretation we follow, the end of the story is clear. Joab's deeds, good or bad, do not go unpunished. On his deathbed, according to 1 Kings 2, David draws Solomon to his bedside, a version of a popular Semitic literary genre, the deathbed testimony of a father. David instructs Solomon, in general Deuteronomistic terms, to be virtuous ("Keep [YHWH's] statutes and teachings and commandments and ordinances as written in the teachings of Moses"). Then David gets down to cases.

"Also," David says to Solomon, "you know what Joab, son of Zeruiah, did to me, what he did to the two commanders of the armies of Israel, to Abner . . . and to Amasa. . . .

"He killed them and he shed the blood of warfare in
    peacetime (*bāšālôm*).
. . . Now, you act according to your wisdom (*ḥokmâ*).
Do not let his grey head descend in peace (*bāšālôm*) to
    Sheol." (1 Kgs. 2:5–6)

Though it is difficult to accept reported speech in any ancient
text as an actual transcription, these words are, at the least, worthy
of David, "the sweet psalmist of Israel" (2 Sam 23:1, KJV), the orator
and elegist, speaking in bracketing cadences to the end, casting his
final words in the rhyming parallelism of *bāšālôm* . . . *bāšālôm*, "in
peacetime" . . . "in peace." This speech also reinforces the motif of
Solomon's wisdom, though here *ḥokmâ* assumes the form, not of
judicial discrimination or proverbial artistry, but of the cunning
manipulation of events.

Is this David's voice, the remnants of his reputed poesy still evident in the way he finishes his lines in parallel fashion? If it is
David speaking, do we imagine his motivation to be righteous
vengeance on behalf of these two dead men, or something personal,
the erosion of friendship for to hatred of a servant whose obduracy
eventually rubbed his master the wrong way. Joab had been too un-
feeling in his rebuke of David for grieving over the death of Absalom
and too passionate in his vendettas that complicated David's goal of
winning over former rivals. If we suspect that David was complicit
in all of Joab's extracurricular killings, is David arranging to silence
the sole remaining man who knows where all the bodies, and how
many more, were buried?

Or maybe this is not David's voice speaking, but that of a
Solomonic apologist? In the final days of David's reign, according to
1 Kings 1–2, the royal house was split into camps, each with its
champion prince. Joab and the priest Abiathar sided with David's
son Adonijah, who lost the succession contest to Solomon, supported by Bathsheba, the prophet Nathan, and the priest Zadok. If

this deathbed scene is Solomonic propaganda, then Solomon, in "his wisdom," is absolved of responsibility for the death of Joab, supporter of his rival. The virtuous son was only fulfilling the wish of a dying father.

Regardless of how we view the wheels-within-wheels of the above royal rhetorical construction, the depiction of Joab's death is straightforward. When Joab hears that Solomon has had the prince who had Joab's support, Adonijah, killed, the last *gibbôr* flees, maybe for the first time in his life, to seek sanctuary in what was then the central shrine, the Tent of Yhwh (1 Kgs 2:28–34). Joab grabs the horns of the altar, gaining ritual sanctuary through contact with an inviolate icon. Benaiah, the executioner appointed by Solomon, calls him out. But Joab refuses, takes his stand, and says, "No, here I will die." Solomon must repeat his command; Benaiah is wary of the taboo, but he is a good soldier. He follows his orders.

Joab's fate is emblematic of the *gibbôrîm*. There was no place for the last great warrior from Israel's heroic frontier age in an era of temples, thrones, and royal houses. After Benaiah executes Joab, he brings his body out from the Tent of Meeting for burial. Joab is buried, it says, at his house (2 Kgs 2:34).

The location of Joab's home is never mentioned in the Bible. Joab had first appeared in the story, in 1 Samuel 26, as David roamed the desert area southeast of Jerusalem, between Hebron and the Dead Sea. The note in 1 Kings 2:34 about Joab's burial at his home "in the desert (*bāmmidbar*)," was probably meant literally: that Joab's home was in the very region, the Judean wilderness, where he had initially appeared in the story. Still, symbolically, the location of Joab's grave is fitting. The body of ancient Israel's last warrior, like the *gibbôrîm* in much of Jewish and Christian tradition, belongs *bāmmidbar*, in the wilderness.

DAVID'S MEN

We began this study with an analysis of the lists of David's men in 2 Samuel 21 and 23.[16] In the end, they were all David's men, all the *gibbôrîm*. Their function was to carve out, raid by raid, battle by battle, vendetta by vendetta, duel by duel, the territories of the Davidic-Solomonic kingdom, North and South, and to advance a program that was only realized centuries later in the Persian period: the hegemony of Judahite culture among the community that saw itself as the descendants of the twelve tribes of Israel.[17] Judah's preferred name for the deity, YHWH, would be preserved through taboo; Judahite scribes in the Diaspora and Judah itself would over the course of centuries assemble the story of this people; Judah's central shrine, the Temple on Mount Zion in Jerusalem, would be the supreme sacred space for their culture; Judah's first king, David, would be forever intertwined with the political identity and eschatological hope of the Hebrew people.

In the periodization of the Deuteronomistic History, the warriors belong to *illo tempore*, to that time, to the frontier days. Once Solomon's throne is secure, their usefulness is at an end. Kings, prophets, priests, and scribes would administer and maintain the culture that the *gibbôrîm* hacked out of a wilderness. The *gibbôrîm* belong to that wilderness, the political wilderness of the premonarchical period and the literary wilderness of the book of Judges. But once the dynasty and deity have their houses, the mediations of the warriors are no longer needed. The breath of YHWH will now inspire prophetic speech, not martial deeds.

Again, this is the view of the Deuteronomistic History. And it is a convenient periodization, making a virtue out of necessity. For there is nothing heroic about defeat, unless like Saul at Gilboa or Davy Crockett at the Alamo, it is the penultimate act in a conflict. The *gibbôrîm* in Judges and Samuel, the stuff of legends, remain undefeated, or so the story goes. Biblical historians writing in the

Late Monarchical, Exilic, and Persian periods could not say the same about their own eras. For them, there would be no lost cause, a glorification of defeated warriors. Instead, new forms of heroism emerged.

There are exceptions in Jewish literature from the late biblical period. In the era of the Maccabean revolt, in the second century B.C.E., Judahite statehood was revived for a century. Jewish literature in this period includes the story of Judith, a composite of many of the motifs from the heroic material in Judges. Like Jael in Judges 4–5, the heroine Judith kills an unsuspecting male foreign oppressor in a domestic context.[18] Jael had nursed the Canaanite general Sisera with goat's milk, lulling him to sleep before driving a tent peg through his skull. Judith gains access to the tent of the Persian general Holofernes, waits while he drinks himself to sleep with wine, then beheads him with his own sword.

But the tale of Judith also borrows from the story of Ehud. She is the secret agent on a diplomatic mission, with her secret weapons. Ehud had natural left handedness, Judith had beauty (Jdt 8:7), which allowed them access to a foreign warlord. Ehud provided himself with a specially forged weapon, concealed in his robe, bound to his forearm; Judith's provisions were her kosher food and wine (the same tokens that allowed the Hebrew youths to triumph in one of the Daniel tales in Dan 1), cosmetics, and clothes guaranteed to make her irresistible to Holofernes (and impress the men of her village who saw her depart) (Jdt 10:1–7). In the style of the Ehud story, Judith's progress from her home to the enemy lair and back is noted threshold by threshold: from the city gate of Bethulia (Jdt 10:6–9), down the mountain, through a valley (Jdt 10:10), to the Assyrian camp (Jdt 10:11–16), to Holofernes' tent (multichambered like Eglon's palace), where she assassinates a foreign warlord in his most private chamber; then back through the Assyrian camp, through the valley, up the mountain, until she reaches the gates of Bethulia (Jdt 13:6–11).[19]

But for the most part, the adventure heroes of Second Temple Judahite literature will not be this hard boiled. Daniel and Esther are more typical models of Diaspora heroism. The roots of many genres of contemporary popular literature can be traced to these stories. The Bible is not the font of all Western literature but it is part of it, and it is amazing how many genres of popular literature it preserves. The Esther tale is a kind of spy story (she is the sleeper agent planted in the enemy headquarters until activated by her handler, Mordecai); the Greek Daniel tales (i.e., Susanna and Bel and the Dragon in the Apocrypha) are detective stories.[20] Cleverness, courage, quick thinking, good timing, and faithfulness to Judahite faith allow these beautiful paragons of Judahite youth to rescue their people, humiliate idolaters, and rise from rags to riches in worlds dominated by foreign kings.[21] But these Hellenistic-period secret agents and detectives do not kill. They are soft-boiled heroes, precursors of the protagonists of drawing room mysteries and court-room dramas. The narratives of the *gibbôrîm* of Judges are, in contrast, precursors of stories of a different sort: Ehud of the mission in and out of the impenetrable fortress; Gideon of the mission of a small, elite band against an army; Abimelech of the gangland "wages of sin" story, as rival gangs rid the landscape of each other; and Samson of the outlaw hero who rights an entire crooked career dedicated to "letting it rip," violently and sexually, with a final, single sacrificial act on behalf of the group.

These are broad strokes. Clan warlords and their militias, rene-gade warlords and their gangs of empty men, ritualized duels, random encounters between goatherds and predatory animals: none of these ended the day that Solomon ascended to power, to be re-placed by a state defended by professional armies, the *gibbôrîm* in baronial repose beneath their vines and fig trees. It would be centuries before the clannish warrior-hunters of the Levant with their Oriental style of warfare, with their rural scrimmages, with their feral cunning, became vestigial. Eventually, like other barbarian prisoners-of-war from Southern Europe and Northern Africa, the Western Asian heirs of the *gibbôrîm* were imported by Roman culture to provide urban entertainment, displaying their dueling and hunting skills in imperial coliseums.

The Davidic-Solomonic empire attained neither the aspirations of the monarchical court historians who first chronicled it nor those of the Exilic priestly historians who preserved, amplified, and transformed its heritage in hopes of its restoration. Jerusalem, the Davidic dynasty, the Temple: all fell. But, for weal and for woe, the ideas of the compilers of the biblical primary history still animate our world: chiefly, the idea of a community known as Israel in covenant with a deity known as Yhwh. One goal of this study was to retell a set of biblical adventure stories. For the writer they retain their power both to entertain and to inspire courage: physical, artistic, intellectual, and moral.

I also wanted to erect a small memorial above the literary landscape of the book of Judges. It is there, below the surface, close to bedrock, under all the many mansions built in subsequent centuries on this ancient foundation—attempts to recreate territorial Israels in the Holy Land, in Old World empires, and in New World republics, and the myriad spiritual transformations of these ideas in Judaism and Christianity—that the *gibbôrîm* sleep with their ancestors.

NOTES

1. For the *Retterbuch*, see pp. 7–8.

2. I differ with W. Richter's scheme only in one particular, its ending point. As discussed in chapter 5 I see the Abimelech narrative as a secondary addition to the Gideon cycle. Therefore, I would have the *Retterbuch* end with the terminal formula of the Gideon cycle ("and the land had rest," Judg 8:28).

3. D. Akenson writes that narrative histories issuing from the Exile, such as the Deuteronomistic work, "had served a single purpose: to shore up the Judahist version of what the religion of the Chosen People should be: Yahweh-only in belief, Temple-centred in liturgy, Judah-dominated in ethnicity" (*Surpassing Wonder*, 84).

4. I assume that the promonarchical ending of the book of Judges was appended to the collection either late in the Exilic or early in the Postexilic period, before the hopes for a restored monarchy among the returning Judahites had been tempered.

5. B. Halpern points out that David's defeat of Goliath was not so much an account of an underdog succeeding against all odds but that of the superiority of light artillery over infantry. David does not quixotically engage Goliath on the Philistine's terms. His opponent has a longer reach and superior weapons. David eschews the outdated convention of close dueling, launches his stone from a distance, and fells the giant without being touched (*David's Secret Demons*, 11–13).

6. I am reading the final word of Judg 3:2 as *yādāʿû*, as suggested by the editors of BHS, instead of the MT *yĕdāʿûm*. There is no satisfactory explanation for the final *mêm* in the latter word. If it is a masculine pronominal suffix, then it does not agree with its apparent antecedent, *milḥāmôt*, "wars," in 3:1. It could be, as the notes in BHS suggest, an archaic ("enclitic") *mêm*.

7. M. Coogan, "Joshua," 111.

8. The story in Josh 7:2–26 of the defeat at Ai, which appears to rattle Joshua and reveal his humanity, is an exception.

9. M. Coogan, "Joshua," 111.

10. For more on Joab, see D. Schley, "Joab."

11. 2 Sam 3:39; cf. 2 Sam 16:10; 19:23 (19:22 ET).

12. P. McCarter, "The Apology of David."

13. P. McCarter, "The Apology of David," 499.

14. S. McKenzie has expanded on P. McCarter's scheme in *King David*, 32–35.

15. S. McKenzie, *King David*, 34.

16. See pp. 31–34.

17. Akenson, "Surpassing Wonder," 84.

18. S White, "In the Steps of Jael and Deborah." For Judith in general, see also L. Wills, "Judith."

19. T. Craven describes these symmetrical structures throughout the book of Judith in *Artistry and Faith in the Book of Judith*. Her analysis of Judith's journey from Bethulia to the Assyrian camp and back is on pp. 94–101.

20. L. Wills, speaking of the Susanna narrative, refers to Daniel's "courtroom heroics" (*The Jewish Novel in the Ancient World*, 55).

21. For an analysis of Esther and Daniel as Diaspora heroes, see L. Wills, *Jewish Novel*, and *The Jew in the Court of the Foreign King*.

Bibliography

Abusch, Tzvi. "The Socio-Religious Framework of the Babylonian Witchcraft Ceremony *Maqlû*: Some Observations on the Introductory Section of the Text, Part II." Pp. 467–94 in *Solving Riddles and Untying Knots: Biblical, Epigraphic, and Semitic Studies in Honor of Jonas C. Greenfield*. Ed. Z. Zevit, S. Gitin, and M. Sokoloff. Winona Lake, Ind.: Eisenbrauns, 1995.

Ackerman, Susan. *Warrior, Dancer, Seductress, Queen: Women in Judges and Biblical Israel*. ABRL. New York: Doubleday, 1998.

Akenson, Donald Harman. *Surpassing Wonder: The Invention of the Bible and the Talmuds*. Chicago: University of Chicago Press, 2001.

Aharoni, Yohanan. *The Land of the Bible: A Historical Geography*. Rev. ed. Philadelphia: Westminster, 1979.

Albertz, Rainer. *A History of Israelite Religion in the Old Testament Period*. Trans. John Bowden. OTL. 2 vols. Louisville: Westminster John Knox, 1994.

Alonso-Schökel, Luis. "Erzählkunst im Buche der Richter." *Biblica* 42 (1961): 143–72.

Alter, Robert. *The Art of Biblical Narrative*. New York: Basic Books, 1981.

———. "How Convention Helps Us Read: The Case of the Bible's Annunciation Type-Scene." *Prooftexts* 3 (1983): 115–30.

Amit, Yairah. "The Story of Ehud (Judges 3:12–30): The Form and the Message." Pp. 97–123 in *Signs and Wonders: Biblical Texts in Literary Focus*. Ed. J. Cheryl Exum. Semeia Studies. Atlanta: Scholars Press, 1989.

Anderson, Gary A. *Sacrifices and Offerings in Ancient Israel: Studies in Their Social and Political Importance.* HSM 41. Atlanta: Scholars Press, 1987.

———. "Introduction to Israelite Religion." Pp. 272–83 in *New Interpreter's Bible* 1. Ed. L. Keck. Nashville: Abingdon, 1994.

Anderson, J. K. "Wars and Military Science: Greece." Pp. 679–701 in *Civilization of the Ancient Mediterranean: Greece and Rome* 1. Ed. M. Grant and R. Kitzinger. New York: Charles Scribner's Sons, 1988.

Aristotle. *Aristotle's Poetics.* Trans. S. H. Butcher. New York: Hill and Wang, 1961.

The Assyrian Dictionary of the Oriental Institute of the University of Chicago. Ed. I. J. Gelb et al. Chicago: Oriental Institute, 1956– .

Auerbach, Erich. *Mimesis: The Representation of Reality in Western Literature.* Trans. W. R. Trask. Princeton: Princeton University Press, 1953. Orig. publ. 1946.

Auld, A. Graeme. "Gideon: Hacking at the Heart of the Old Testament." *VT* 39 (1989): 257–67.

Bal, Mieke. *Lethal Love: Feminist Literary Readings of Biblical Love Stories.* Bloomington, Ind.: Indiana University Press, 1987.

———. *Death and Dissymmetry: The Politics of Coherence in the Book of Judges.* Chicago: University of Chicago Press, 1988.

Balsdon, J. P., and A. W. Lintott. "Gladiators, Combatants at Games." *OCD.* 3rd ed. Ed. S. Hornblower and A. Spawforth. Oxford: Oxford University Press, 1996, 637–38.

Barr, James. *The Semantics of Biblical Language.* London: Oxford University Press, 1961.

Barré, Michael. "The Meaning of *pršdn* in Judges III 22." *VT* 41 (1991): 1–11.

Barrera, Julio Trebolle. "Textual Variants in 4QJudg^a and the Textual and Editorial History of the Book of Judges." *RevQ* 54 (1989): 229–45.

———. "4QJudg^a." Pp. 161–64 in *Qumran Cave 4.IX: Deuteronomy, Joshua, Judges, Kings.* Ed. E. Ulrich, F. M. Cross, et al. DJD 14. Oxford: Clarendon, 1995.

Bartlemus, Rüdiger. *Heroentum in Israel und seiner Umwelt: Eine traditionsgeschichtliche Untersuchung zu Gen. 6, 1–4 und verwandten Texten im Alten Testament und der altorientalischen Literatur.* ATANT 65. Zurich: Theologischer Verlag, 1979.

Bartra, Roger. *Wild Men in the Looking Glass: The Mythic Origins of European Otherness.* Trans. C. Berrisford. Ann Arbor, Mich.: University of Michigan Press, 1994.

Bauckham, Richard. "Descent to the Underworld." Pp. 145–59 in *ABD* 2. Ed. D. N. Freedman. New York: Doubleday, 1992.

Baumgartner, Walter. See further, L. Koehler.

Bergman, J., et al. "דבר *dābhar.*" Pp. 84–125 in *TDOT* 3. Ed. G. J. Botterweck and H. Ringgren. Trans. J. Willis and G. Bromiley. Grand Rapids, Mich., 1978.

Bernheimer, Richard. *Wild Men in the Middle Ages: A Study in Art, Sentiment, and Demonology.* Cambridge, Mass.: Harvard University Press, 1952.

Betlyon, John W. "Coinage." Pp. 1076–89 in *ABD* 1. Ed. D. N. Freedman. New York: Doubleday, 1992.

Bier, Carol. "Textile Arts in Ancient Western Asia." Pp. 1567–88 in *CANE* 3. Ed. J. Sasson. New York: Charles Scribner's Sons, 1995.

Birdsall, J. Nelville. "Versions, Ancient (Gothic)." Pp. 803–6 in *ABD* 6. Ed. D. N. Freedman. New York: Doubleday, 1992.

Black, Jeremy, and Anthony Green. *Gods, Demons and Symbols of Ancient Mesopotamia: An Illustrated Dictionary.* Austin: University of Texas Press, 1992.

Blenkinsopp, Joseph. "Some Notes on the Saga of Samson and the Heroic Milieu." *Scripture* 11 (1959): 81–89.

———. "Structure and Style in Judges 13–16." *JBL* 82 (1963): 65–76.

Bloom, Allan. See further, Plato.

Boling, Robert G. *Judges.* AB 6A. Garden City, N.Y.: Doubleday, 1975.

———. "Gideon." Pp. 1013–15 in *ABD* 2. Ed. D. N. Freedman. New York: Doubleday, 1992.

———. "Judges, Book of." Pp. 1107–17 in *ABD* 3. Ed. D. N. Freedman. New York: Doubleday, 1992.

Boni, Margaret Bradford. *The Fireside Book of Favorite American Songs.* New York: Simon and Schuster, 1952.

Boogaart, T. A. "Stone for Stone: Retribution in the Story of Abimelech and Shechem." *JSOT* 32 (1985): 45–56.

Braun, Joachim. *Music in Ancient Israel/Palestine: Archaeological, Written, and Comparative Sources.* The Bible in Its World. Trans. D. Stott. Grand Rapids: Eerdmans, 2002.

Brettler, Marc Zvi. *The Creation of History in Ancient Israel.* London: Routledge, 1995.

Brichto, Herbert C. "Kin, Cult, Land and Afterlife—A Biblical Complex." *HUCA* 44 (1973): 1–54.

Brown, Cecil. *Stagolee Shot Billy.* Cambridge, Mass.: Harvard University Press, 2003.

Brown, Raymond E. *The Birth of the Messiah: A Commentary on the Infancy Narratives in Matthew and Luke.* ABRL. Rev. ed. New York: Doubleday, 1993.

Brueggemann, Walter. *Theology of the Old Testament: Testimony, Dispute, Advocacy.* Minneapolis: Fortress, 1997.

Burkert, Walter. *Greek Religion.* Trans. J. Raffan. Cambridge, Mass.: Harvard University Press, 1985.

———. *Creation of the Sacred: Tracks of Biology in Early Religions.* Cambridge, Mass.: Harvard University Press, 1996.

Burney, C. F. *The Book of Judges and Notes on the Hebrew Text of the Book of Kings.* Library of Biblical Studies. Ed. H. Orlinsky. New York: KTAV, 1970. Repr. of *The Book of Judges,* 1918.

Bynum, David E. "Samson as a Biblical φὴρ ὀρεσκῷος." Pp. 57–73 in *Text and Tradition: The Hebrew Bible and Folklore.* Ed. S. Niditch. Semeia Studies. Atlanta: Scholars Press, 1990.

Camp, Claudia V., and Carole R. Fontaine. "The Words of the Wise and Their Riddles." Pp. 127–51 in *Text and Tradition: The Hebrew Bible and Folklore.* Ed. S. Niditch. Semeia Studies. Atlanta: Scholars Press, 1990.

Clay, Albert T. See further, M. Jastrow.

Clifford, Richard J. *The Cosmic Mountain in Canaan and the Old Testament.* HSM 4. Cambridge, Mass.: Harvard University Press, 1972.

Collon, Dominique. *First Impressions: Cylinder Seals in the Ancient Near East.* Chicago: University of Chicago Press, 1987.

Conrad, Edgar. *Fear Not Warrior: A Study of the ʿal tîrāʾ Pericopes in the Hebrew Scriptures*. BJS 75. Chico, Cal.: Scholars Press, 1985.

Conrad, J. "נכה *nkh*." Pp. 415–23 in *TDOT* 9. Ed. G. J. Botterweck, H. Ringgren, and H.-J. Fabry. Trans. D. Green. Grand Rapids, Mich., 1998.

Coogan, Michael D. *Stories from Ancient Canaan*. Philadelphia: Westminster, 1978.

——. "Joshua." Pp. 110–31 in *NJBC*. Ed. R. E. Brown, J. Fitzmyer, and R. Murphy. Englewood Cliffs, N. J.: Prentice Hall, 1990.

Cowley, A. E. See further, E. Kautzsch.

Craigie, Peter C. *The Problem of War in the Old Testament*. Grand Rapids: Eerdmans, 1978.

Craven, Toni. *Artistry and Faith in the Book of Judith*. SBLDS 70. Chico, Cal.: Scholars Press, 1983.

Crenshaw, James L. "The Samson Saga: Filial Devotion or Erotic Attachment?" *ZAW* 86 (1974): 470–504.

——. *Samson: A Secret Betrayed, a Vow Ignored*. Atlanta: John Knox, 1978.

——. "Samson." *ABD* 5. Ed. D. N. Freedman. New York: Doubleday, 1992, 950–54.

Cross, F. L. *ODCC*. Ed. E. A. Livingstone. 3rd ed. Oxford: University Press, 1997.

Cross, Frank Moore. *Canaanite Myth and Hebrew Epic: Essays in the History and Religion of Israel*. Cambridge, Mass.: Harvard University Press, 1973.

——. "Problems of Method in the Textual Criticism of the Hebrew Bible." Pp. 31–54 in *The Critical Study of Ancient Texts*. Ed. Wendy D. O'Flaherty. Berkeley: University of California Press, 1979.

——. *From Epic to Canon: History and Literature in Ancient Israel*. Baltimore: Johns Hopkins University Press, 1998.

——. *Leaves from an Epigrapher's Notebook: Collected Papers in Hebrew and West Semitic Paleography and Epigraphy*. HSS 51. Winona Lake, Ind.: Eisenbrauns, 2003.

——, and David Noel Freedman. *Studies in Ancient Yahwistic Poetry*.

Biblical Resource Series. 2nd ed. Grand Rapids: Eerdmans, 1997. Orig. publ. 1950.

———. See further, J. T. Milik.

———, and E. Ulrich, eds. *Qumran Cave 4: IX: Deuteronomy, Joshua, Judges, Kings.* DJD 14. Oxford: Clarendon, 1995.

van Daalen, Aleida G. *Simson.* SSN 8. Assen: Van Gorcum, 1966.

Dahood, Mitchell. *Psalms II: 51–100.* AB 17. Garden City, N.Y.: Doubleday, 1968.

———. *Psalms III: 101–150.* AB 17A. New York: Doubleday, 1970.

Dalley, Stephanie. *Myths from Mesopotamia.* Oxford: Oxford University Press, 1989.

———, trans. "The Descent of Ishtar to the Underworld (1.108)." Pp. 381–84 in *COS* 1. Ed. W. Hallo. Leiden: Brill, 1997.

Day, Peggy. "From the Child Is Born the Woman: The Story of Jephthah's Daughter." Pp. 58–74 in *Gender and Difference in Ancient Israel.* Ed. P. Day. Minneapolis: Fortress, 1989.

———. "Why Is Anat a Warrior and Hunter?" Pp. 141–46 in *The Bible and the Politics of Exegesis: Essays in Honor of Norman K. Gottwald.* Ed. D. Jobling et al. Cleveland: Pilgrim Press, 1991.

———. "Anat: Ugarit's 'Mistress of Animals.' " *JNES* 51 (1992): 181–90.

———. "Anat." Pp. 36–43 in *DDD.* Ed. K. van der Toorn, B. Becking, and P. W. van der Horst. 2nd ed. Brill: Leiden, 1999.

Dayagi-Mendels, Michal. "Cosmetics." Pp. 67–69 in *OEANE* 2. Ed. E. Meyers. New York: Oxford University Press, 1997.

Dearman, Andrew. "Historical Reconstruction and the Mesha Inscription." Pp. 155–210 in *Studies in the Mesha Inscription and Moab.* Ed. A. Dearman. Atlanta: Scholars Press, 1989.

Deutsch, Robert and Michael Heltzer. *Forty New Ancient West Semitic Inscriptions.* Tel Aviv/Jaffa: Archaeological Center, 1994.

———. *New Epigraphic Evidence from the Biblical Period.* Tel Aviv/Jaffa: Archaeological Center, 1995.

Dietrich, M., and O. Loretz, and J. Sanmartín, eds. *The Cuneiform Alphabetic Texts from Ugarit, Ras Ibn Hani and Other Places.* Münster: Ugarit-Verlag, 1995.

Driver, S. R. *Notes on the Hebrew Text and Topography of the Books of*

Samuel. 2nd ed. Winona Lake, Ind.: Alpha, 1984. Orig. publ. 1912.

Dumézil, Georges. *The Destiny of the Warrior.* Trans. A. Hiltebeitel. Chicago: University of Chicago Press, 1970.

Eissfeldt, Otto. "Die Rätsel in Jdc 14." *ZAW* 30 (1910): 132–35.

———. *The Old Testament: An Introduction.* Trans. P. Ackroyd. New York: Harper & Row, 1965. From the 3rd Ger. edition, 1964.

Eliade, Mircea. *Rites and Symbols of Initiation.* Trans. W. Trask. New York: Harper & Row, 1958.

Emery, Allan C. "Weapons of the Israelite Monarchy: A Catalogue with Its Linguistic and Cross-Cultural Implications." Ph.D. diss., Harvard University, 1999.

Exum, J. Cheryl. "Literary Patterns in the Samson Saga: An Investigation of Rhetorical Style in Biblical Prose." Ph.D. diss., Columbia University, 1976.

———. "Promise and Fulfillment: Narrative Art in Judges 13." *JBL* 99 (1980): 43–59.

———. "Aspects of Symmetry and Balance in the Samson Saga." *JSOT* 19 (1981): 3–29.

———. "The Theological Dimension of the Samson Saga." *VT* 33 (1983): 30–45.

———. *Tragedy and Biblical Narrative: Arrows of the Almighty.* Cambridge: Cambridge University Press, 1992.

———. "Delilah." Pp. 133–34 in *ABD* 2. Ed. D. N. Freedman. New York: Doubleday, 1992.

———. "Wife of Samson." P. 954 in *ABD* 5. Ed. D. N. Freedman. New York: Doubleday, 1992.

———. *Fragmented Women: Feminist (Sub)versions of Biblical Narratives.* JSOTSupp 163. Sheffield: JSOT Press, 1993.

———, and J. William Whedbee. "Isaac, Samson, and Saul: Reflections on the Comic and Tragic Visions." *Semeia* 32 (1984): 5–40.

Fabry, H.-J. "דל *dal.*" Pp. 208–30 in *TDOT* 3. Ed. G. J. Botterweck and H. Ringgren. Trans. J. Willis and G. Bromiley. Grand Rapids, Mich., 1978.

————. See further, S. Tengström.

Fagles, Robert. See further, Homer.

Filene, Benjamin. *Romancing the Folk: Public Memory and American Roots Music*. Chapel Hill, N.C.: University of North Carolina Press, 2000.

Fontaine, Carole R. See further, C. Camp.

Fontenrose, Joseph. *Orion: The Myth of the Hunter and the Huntress*. Berkeley: University of California Press, 1981.

Foster, Benjamin R., trans., *Before the Muses: An Anthology of Akkadian Literature*. 2 vols. Bethesda, Md.: CDL Press, 1993.

Fowler, Donald. "Lion." P. 811 in *Eerdmans Dictionary of the Bible*. Ed. D. N. Freedman. Grand Rapids: Eerdmans, 2000.

Fowler, Jeaneane D. *Theophoric Personal Names in Ancient Hebrew: A Comparative Study*. JSOTSup 49. Sheffield: JSOT Press, 1988.

Fox, Everett. *The Five Books of Moses*. Schocken Bible 1. Dallas: Word, 1995.

Fraser, George MacDonald. *The Steel Bonnets: The Story of the Anglo-Scottish Border Reivers*. London: Collins Harvill, 1989.

Freedman, David Noel. "Yahweh of Samaria and His Asherah." *BA* 50 (1987): 241–49.

————. See further, F. M. Cross.

Gaster. Theodor H. *Myth, Legend, and Custom in the Old Testament*. New York: Harper & Row, 1969.

Geisel, Theodor Seuss (Dr. Suess). *The Cat in the Hat*. New York: Random House, 1957.

van Gennep, Arnold. *The Rites of Passage*. Trans. M. Vizedom and G. Cafee. London: Routledge, 1960. Orig. publ. 1909.

George, Andrew. *The Epic of Gilgamesh: A New Translation*. New York: Barnes & Noble, 1999.

Gillman, Neil. *The Death of Death: Resurrection and Immortality in Jewish Thought*. Woodstock, Vt.: Jewish Lights, 1997.

Ginzberg, Louis. *The Legends of the Jews*. Trans. H. Szold. 7 vols. Baltimore: Johns Hopkins University Press, 1998. Repr. of *The Legends of the Jews*, 7 vols., 1909–1938.

Gordon, Cyrus H. "Homer and Bible: The Origin and Character of East Mediterranean Literature." *HUCA* 26 (1955): 43–108.

———. *Before the Bible: The Common Background of Greek and Hebrew Civilizations.* New York: Harper & Row, 1962.

Gottwald, Norman K. *The Tribes of Yahweh: A Sociology of the Religion of Liberated Israel, 1250–1050 B.C.* Maryknoll, N.Y.: Orbis, 1979.

Gray, John. *Joshua, Judges and Ruth.* Century Bible. London: Nelson, 1967.

———. *Joshua, Judges, Ruth.* NCB. Grand Rapids: Eerdmans, 1986.

Green, Anthony. "Mischwesen B." *RlA* 8. Ed. D. O. Edzard. Berlin: Walter de Gruyter, 1994, 246–64.

———. See further, J. Black.

Greenberg, Moshe. *Ezekiel 21–37.* AB 22A. New York: Doubleday, 1997.

Greenstein, Edward L. "The Riddle of Samson." *Prooftexts* 1 (1981): 237–60.

Gröndahl, Frauke. *Die Personennamen der Texte aus Ugarit.* Studia Pohl 1. Rome: Pontifical Biblical Institute, 1967.

Gunkel, Hermann. "Simson." Pp. 38–64 in *Reden und Aufsätze.* Göttingen: Vandenhoeck & Ruprecht, 1913.

Gunn, David M. "Joshua and Judges." Pp. 102–21 in *The Literary Guide to the Bible.* Ed. R. Alter and F. Kermode. Cambridge, Mass.: Belknap, 1987.

Halpern, Baruch. *The First Historians: The Hebrew Bible and History.* San Francisco: Harper & Row, 1988.

———. *David's Secret Demons: Messiah, Murderer, Traitor, King.* The Bible in Its World. Grand Rapids: Eerdmans, 2001.

Haynes, Stephen. See further, S. McKenzie.

Heltzer, Michael. See further, R. Deutsch.

Herodotus. *The Histories.* Trans. A. de Sélincourt. New ed. London: Penguin, 1996.

Hobbs, T. R. *A Time for War: A Study of Warfare in the Old Testament.* Old Testament Studies 3. Wilmington, Del.: Michael Glazier, 1989.

Hoffner, Harry A. "A Hittite Analogue to the David and Goliath Contest of Champions?" *CBQ* 30 (1968): 220–25.

Holladay, William. *Jeremiah 1.* Hermeneia. Philadelphia: Westminster, 1986.

————. *The Psalms through Three Thousand Years: Prayerbook of a Cloud of Witnesses*. Minneapolis: Fortress, 1993.

Homer. *The Iliad*. Trans. Robert Fagles. New York: Penguin, 1990.

Hoppe, Leslie. *Joshua, Judges*. Old Testament Message 5. Wilmington, Del.: Michael Glazier, 1982.

Houtman, Cees. See further, K. van der Toorn.

Huehnergard, John. *Ugaritic Vocabulary in Syllabic Transcription*. HSS 32. Atlanta: Scholars Press, 1987.

Hurvitz, Avi. "The Date of the Prose-Tale of Job Linguistically Reconsidered." *HTR* 67 (1974): 17–34.

Iwry, Samuel. "New Evidence for Belomancy in Ancient Palestine and Phoenicia." *JAOS* 81 (1961): 27–33.

Jackson, Kent, trans. "The Language of the Mesha Inscription." Pp. 96–130 in *Studies in the Mesha Inscription and Moab*. Ed. A. Dearman. Atlanta: Scholars Press, 1989.

Jameson, Fredric. *The Political Unconscious: Narrative as a Socially Symbolic Act*. Ithaca, N.Y.: Cornell University Press, 1981.

Janzen, J. Gerald. "A Certain Woman in the Rhetoric of Judges 9." *JSOT* 38 (1987): 33–37.

Jastrow, Morris, and Albert T. Clay. *An Old Babylonian Version of the Gilgamesh Epic*. Yale Oriental Series 4:3. New Haven: Yale University Press, 1920.

Johnson, James Weldon, and John Rosamond Johnson. *The Book of American Negro Spirituals*. New York: Viking, 1925.

Johnson, John Rosamond. See further, James W. Johnson.

Josephus. Trans. H. St. J. Thackeray et al. Loeb Classical Library. 10 vols. Cambridge, Mass.: Harvard University Press, 1926–1965.

Jost, Madeleine. "Pan." P. 1103 in *OCD*. Ed. S. Hornblower and A. Spawnforth. 3rd ed. Oxford: Oxford University Press, 1996.

Kang, Sa-Moon. *Divine War in the Old Testament and in the Ancient Near East*. Berlin: Walter de Gruyter, 1989.

Kautzsch, E., and A. E. Cowley. *Gesenius' Hebrew Grammar*. 2nd English ed. Oxford: Clarendon, 1910.

Keegan, John. *The Face of Battle*. New York: Penguin, 1976.

————. *A History of Warfare*. New York: Vintage, 1993.

Keel, Othmar. *Jahwes Entgegnung an Ijob*. Göttingen: Vandenhoeck & Ruprecht, 1978.

King, Philip J. *Amos, Hosea, Micah—An Archaeological Commentary*. Philadelphia: Westminster, 1988.

————, and Lawrence E. Stager. *Life in Biblical Israel*. Library of Ancient Israel. Louisville: Westminster John Knox, 2001.

Kinsella, Thomas. *The Tain*. Oxford: Oxford University Press, 1969.

Kirk, Geoffrey S. *The Nature of Greek Myths*. London: Penguin, 1974.

Klein, Lillian R. *The Triumph of Irony in the Book of Judges*. JSOTSup 68. Sheffield: Almond Press, 1988.

Koehler, Ludwig and Walter Baumgartner. *The Hebrew and Aramaic Lexicon of the Old Testament*. 5 vols. Trans. and ed. M. E. J. Richardson. Leiden: Brill, 1994.

Kosmala, H. "גבר *gābhar*." Pp. 367–82 in *TDOT* 2. Ed. G. J. Botterweck and H. Ringgren. Trans. J. Willis. Grand Rapids, Mich., 1975.

Kraeling, E. G. "Difficulties in the Story of Ehud." *JBL* 54 (1935): 205–10.

Lemche, Niels Peter. "Kings and Clients: On Loyalty between the Ruler and the Ruled in Ancient 'Israel'." *Semeia* 66 (1994): 119–32.

Levenson, Jon D. *Sinai and Zion: An Entry into the Jewish Bible*. San Francisco: Harper & Row, 1985.

————. *Creation and the Persistence of Evil: The Jewish Drama of Divine Omnipotence*. San Francisco: Harper & Row, 1988.

————. *Esther*. OTL. Louisville, Ky.: Westminster John Knox, 1997.

Lévi-Strauss, Claude. *The Raw and the Cooked: Introduction to a Science of Mythology* 1. Trans. J. and D. Weightman. Chicago: University of Chicago Press, 1969. Orig. Fr. publ. 1964.

Levine, Baruch A. *Numbers 1–20*. AB 4A. New York: Doubleday, 1993.

Lewis, Theodore J. "The Identity and Function of El/Baal Berith." *JBL* 115 (1996): 401–23.

————. "The Rapiuma." Pp. 196–205 in *Ugaritic Narrative Poetry*. SBLWAW 9. Ed. S. Parker. Atlanta: Scholars Press, 1997.

L'Heureux, C. E. "The *yᵉlîdê hārāpā'*—A Cultic Association of Warriors." *BASOR* 221 (1976): 83–85.

Lichtheim, Miriam, trans. "Sinuhe (1.38)." Pp. 77–82 in *COS* 1. Ed. W. Hallo. Leiden: Brill, 1997.

Lincoln, Bruce. *Priests, Warriors, and Cattle: A Study in the Ecology of Religions.* Berkeley: University of California Press, 1981.

Lind, Millard C. *Yahweh Is a Warrior: The Theology of Warfare in Ancient Israel.* Scottsdale, Pa.: Herald Press, 1980.

Lindars, Barnabas. *Judges 1–5: A New Translation and Commentary.* Ed. A. D. H. Mayes. Edinburgh: T. & T. Clark, 1995.

Lintott, A. W. See further, J. P. Balsdon.

Lomax, Alan. *Folk Songs of North America.* New York: Doubleday, 1960.

Lomax, John A., and A. Lomax. *American Ballads and Folk Songs.* New York: Macmillan, 1934.

Loretz, O. See further, M. Dietrich.

Lovell, John. *Black Song: The Forge and the Flame.* New York: Macmillan, 1972.

MacDonald, John. "The Status and Role of the Naʿar in Israelite Society." *JNES* 35 (1976): 147–70.

Machinist, Peter. "The Epic of Tukulti-Ninurta I: A Study in Middle Assyrian Literature." Ph.D. diss., Yale University, 1978.

Makiya, Kanan. *The Rock: A Tale of Seventh-Century Jerusalem.* New York, Vintage, 2001.

Marcus, Greil. *Mystery Train: Images of America in Rock 'n' Roll Music.* 4th rev. ed. New York: Penguin, 1997.

———. *Invisible Republic: Bob Dylan's Basement Tapes.* New York: Henry Holt, 1997.

Margalith, Othniel. "Samson's Foxes." *VT* 35 (1983): 224–29.

———. "Samson's Riddle and Samson's Magic Locks." *VT* 36 (1986): 225–34.

———. "More Samson Legends." *VT* 36 (1986): 397–405.

———. "The Legends of Samson/Heracles." *VT* 37 (1987): 63–70.

Margolis, Max L., ed. *The Holy Scriptures.* Philadelphia: JPS, 1917.

Marks, Richard G. "Dangerous Hero: Rabbinic Attitudes Toward Legendary Heroes." *HUCA* 54 (1983): 181–94.

Martin, James D. *The Book of Judges.* CBC. Cambridge: Cambridge University Press, 1975.

Mastin, B. A. "Was the *šālîš* the Third Man in the Chariot?" Pp. 125–54 in *Studies in the Historical Books of the Old Testament*. VTSup 30. Ed. J. A. Emerton. Leiden: Brill, 1979.

Mattingly, Gerald. "Moabite Religion and the Mesha' Inscription." Pp. 211—38 in *Studies in the Mesha Inscription and Moab*. Ed. A. Dearman. Atlanta: Scholars Press, 1989.

Mayer-Opificius, R. "Simson, der sechslockige Held?" *UF* 14 (1982): 149–51.

Mayes, A. D. H. *Judges*. OTG. Sheffield: JSOT Press, 1985.

———. "Deuteronomistic History." *Dictionary of Biblical Interpretation*. Ed. J. Hayes. 2 vols. Nashville: Abingdon, 1999, 1:268–73.

Mazar, Amihai. "The Iron Age I." Pp. 258–301 in *The Archaeology of Ancient Israel*. Ed. A. Ben-Tor. Trans. R. Greenberg. New Haven: Yale University Press, 1992.

Mazar, Benjamin. "The Military Elite of King David." *VT* 13 (1963): 310–20.

McCarter, P. Kyle. *1 Samuel*. AB 8. Garden City, N.Y.: Doubleday, 1980.

———. "The Apology of David." *JBL* 99 (1980): 489–504.

———. *2 Samuel*. AB 9. New York: Doubleday, 1984.

———. "Pieces of the Puzzle." *BAR* 22/2 (1996): 39–43, 62–63.

———. "Over the Transom: Three New Arrowheads." *BAR* 25/3 (1999): 42–43.

McCombs, Davis. *Ultima Thule*. Yale Series of Younger Poets 94. New Haven: Yale University Press, 2000.

McKenzie, Steven L. "Deuteronomistic History." Pp. 160–68 in *ABD* 2. Ed. D. N. Freedman. New York: Doubleday, 1992.

———. *King David: A Biography*. New York: Oxford University Press, 2000.

———, and Stephen Haynes. *To Each Its Own Meaning: An Introduction to Biblical Criticisms and Their Application*. Rev. ed. Louisville: Westminster John Knox, 1999.

Meek, Theophile J., trans. "The Code of Hammurabi." Pp. 163–80 in *Ancient Near Eastern Texts Relating to the Old Testament*. Ed. James P. Pritchard. 3rd ed. Princeton: Princeton University Press, 1969.

Meier, S. A. "Destroyer." Pp. 240–44 in *DDD*. Ed. K. van der Toorn, B. Becking, and P. W. van der Horst. 2nd ed. Brill: Leiden, 1999.

Mendenhall, George E. "The Census Lists of Numbers 1 and 26." *JBL* 77 (1958): 52–66.

Milgrom, Jacob. *Numbers*. JPS Torah Commentary. Philadelphia: JPS, 1990.

Milik. J. T. "An Unpublished Arrow-head with Phoenician Inscription of the 11th–10th Century B.C." *BASOR* 143 (1956): 3–6.

———, and F. M. Cross. "Inscribed Arrowheads from the Period of the Judges." Pp. 303–8 in *Leaves from an Epigrapher's Notebook: Collected Papers in Hebrew and West Semitic Paleography and Epigraphy*. HSS 51. Winona Lake, Ind.: Eisenbrauns, 2003.

Millard, Alan. "How Reliable is Exodus?" *BAR* 26/4 (2000): 51–57.

Miller, Maxwell. "Moab and the Moabites." Pp. 1–40 in *Studies in the Mesha Inscription and Moab*. Ed. A. Dearman. Atlanta: Scholars Press, 1989.

Miller, Patrick D., and J. J. M. Roberts. *The Hand of the Lord: A Reassessment of the "Ark Narrative" of 1 Samuel*. The Johns Hopkins Near Eastern Studies. Baltimore: Johns Hopkins University Press, 1977.

Milton, John. "Samson Agonistes." Pp. 531–93 in *John Milton: Complete Poems and Major Prose*. Ed. Merritt Y. Hughes. Indianapolis: Odyssey, 1957.

Mobley, Gregory. "Samson, the Liminal Hero: A Comparative Study of Judges 13–16 and Ancient Near Eastern Heroic Tradition." Ph.D. diss., Harvard University, 1994.

———. "The Wild Man in the Bible and the Ancient Near East." *JBL* 116 (1997): 217–33.

Moore, George Foot. *A Critical and Exegetical Commentary on Judges*. ICC. Edinburgh: T. & T. Clark, 1895.

Moran, William L. "Ovid's *Blanda Voluptas* and the Humanization of Enkidu." *JNES* 50 (1991): 121–27.

Moscati, Sabatino, and Anton Spitaler, Edward Ullendorff, Wolfram von Soden. *An Introduction to the Comparative Grammar of the Semitic Languages*. Porta Linguarum Orientalium. Wiesbaden: Otto Harrassowitz, 1980.

Münger, S. "Ariel." *DDD*. 2nd ed. Ed. K. van der Toorn, B. Becking, and P. W. van der Horst. Brill: Leiden, 1999, 88–89.

Naʿaman, Nadav. "The List of David's Officers (*šālîšîm*)." *VT* 38 (1988): 71–79.

Naveh, Joseph. *Early History of the Alphabet*. 2nd rev. ed. Jerusalem: Magnes Press, 1987.

Nel, Philip. "The Riddle of Samson (Judg. 14, 14. 18)." *Biblica* 66 (1985): 534–45.

Niditch, Susan. *Underdogs and Tricksters: A Prelude to Biblical Folklore*. San Francisco: Harper & Row, 1987.

———. "Samson as Culture Hero, Trickster, and Bandit: The Empowerment of the Weak." *CBQ* 52 (1990): 608–24.

———. *War in the Hebrew Bible: A Study in the Ethics of Violence*. New York: Oxford University Press, 1993.

Noth, Martin. *Die israelitischen Personennamen im Rahmen der gemeinsemitischen Namengebung*. Stuttgart: W. Kohlhammer, 1928.

———. *The Deuteronomistic History*. JSOTSup 15. 2nd ed. Sheffield: JSOT Press, 1981. Orig. Ger. publ., *Überlieferungsgeschichtliche Studien*, 1943.

O'Connell, Robert H. *The Rhetoric of the Book of Judges*. VTSup 63. Leiden: Brill, 1996.

O'Connor, Michael Patrick. "Judges." Pp. 132–44 in *NJBC*. Ed. R. E. Brown, J. Fitzmyer, and R. Murphy. Englewood Cliffs, N. J.: Prentice Hall, 1990.

———. See further, B. Waltke.

del Olmo Lete, G. "Deber." Pp. 231–32 in *DDD*. Ed. K. van der Toorn, B. Becking, and P. W. van der Horst. 2nd ed. Brill: Leiden, 1999.

Olrik, Axel. "Epic Laws of Folk Narrative." Pp. 129–41 in *The Study of Folklore*. Ed. Alan Dundes. Englewood Cliffs, N.J.: Prentice-Hall, 1965. Orig. publ. 1909.

Olson, Dennis T. "The Book of Judges." Pp. 721–888 in *New Interpreter's Bible* 2. Ed. L. Keck. Nashville: Abingdon, 1998.

Otzen, Benedikt. "בהל *bhl*." Pp. 3–5 in *TDOT* 2. Ed. G. J. Botterweck and H. Ringgren. Trans. J. Willis. Grand Rapids, Mich., 1975.

Palmer, A. Smythe. *The Samson Saga and its Place in Comparative Religion*. New York: Arno Press, 1977. Orig. publ. 1913.

Pardee, Dennis, trans. "The Ba'lu Myth (1.86)." Pp. 241–74 in COS 1. Ed. W. Hallo. Leiden: Brill, 1997.

Parker, Simon B. "Aqhat." Pp. 49–80 in *Ugaritic Narrative Poetry.* SBLWAW 9. Ed. S. Parker. Atlanta: Scholars Press, 1997.

Pedersen, Johannes. *Israel: Its Life and Culture* 3–4. London: Oxford University Press, 1940.

Plato. *The Republic of Plato.* Trans. Allan Bloom. 2nd ed. New York: Basic Books, 1991.

Polzin, Robert. *Moses and the Deuteronomist: A Literary Study of the Deuteronomic History, Part 1: Deuteronomy, Joshua, Judges.* Bloomington, Ind.: Indiana University Press, 1980.

Pope, Marvin. *Song of Songs.* AB 7C. Garden City, N.Y.: Doubleday, 1977.

Puech, E. "Lioness." Pp. 524–25 in *DDD.* Ed. K. van der Toorn, B. Becking, and P. W. van der Horst. 2nd ed. Brill: Leiden, 1999, 524–25.

von Rad, Gerhard. *Holy War in Ancient Israel.* Trans. and ed. M. Dawn. Grand Rapids: Eerdmans, 1991. Ger. Orig., *Der Heilige Kreig im alten Israel,* 1958. 3rd ed.

Reiner, Erica. "City Bread and Bread Baked in Ashes." Pp. 116–20 in *Languages and Areas: Studies Presented to George V. Bobrinskoy.* Chicago: University of Chicago Press, 1967.

Reinhartz, Adele. *"Why Ask My Name?": Anonymity and Identity in Biblical Narrative.* New York: Oxford University Press, 1998.

Richter, Wolfgang. *Traditionsgeschichtliche Untersuchungen zum Richterbuch.* BBB 18. Bonn: Peter Hanstein, 1963.

———. *Die Arbeitungen des "Retterbuches" in der deuteronomistischen Epoche.* BBB 21. Bonn: Peter Hanstein, 1964.

Rilke, Rainer Maria. *Duino Elegies.* Trans. Edward Snow. Bilingual edition. New York: North Point Press, 2000.

Roberts, J. J. M. See further, P. Miller.

Sanmartín, J. See further, M. Dietrich.

Sasson, Jack. "Who Cut Samson's Hair? (And Other Trifling Issues Raised by Judges 16)." *Prooftexts* 8 (1988): 333–46.

———. *Jonah.* AB 24B. New York: Doubleday, 1990.

Schachter, Albert. "Heracles." Pp. 684–86 in *OCD*. Ed. S. Hornblower and A. Spawforth. 3rd ed. Oxford: Oxford University Press, 1996.

Scheiber, A. "Samson Uprooting a Tree." *JQR* 50 (1959–60): 176–80.

———. "Further Parallels to the Figure of Samson the Tree-Uprooter." *JQR* 52 (1961–62): 35–40.

Schley, Donald G. "The *šālîšîm*: Officers or Special Three-Man Squads?" *VT* 40 (1990): 321–26.

———. "David's Champions." Pp. 49–52 in *ABD* 2. Ed. D. N. Freedman. New York: Doubleday, 1992.

———. "Joab." Pp. 852–54 in *ABD* 3. Ed. D. N. Freedman. New York: Doubleday, 1992.

Schloen, J. David. *The House of the Father as Fact and Symbol: Patrimonialism in Ugarit and the Ancient Near East*. Studies in the Archaeology and History of the Levant 2. Winona Lake, Ind.: Eisenbrauns, 2001.

Seward, Desmond. *The Monks of War: The Military Religious Orders*. London: Penguin, 1972.

Shupak, Nili. "New Light on Shamgar ben 'Anath." *Biblica* 70 (1989): 517–25.

Silberman, Neil A. *The Hidden Scrolls: Christianity, Judaism, and the War for the Dead Sea Scrolls*. New York: G. P. Putnam's Sons, 1994.

Slotki, Judah J. "Judges." Pp. 152–318 in *Joshua and Judges*. Soncino Bible. Ed. A. Cohen. London: Soncino Press, 1950.

Smith, Mark S. "Anat's Warfare Cannibalism and the West Semitic Ban." Pp. 368–86 in *The Pitcher is Broken: Memorial Essays for Gösta W. Ahlström*. JSOTSup 190. Ed. S. Holloway and L. Handy. Sheffield: Sheffield Academic Press, 1995, 368–86.

———. "The Baal Cycle." Pp. 81–180 in *Ugaritic Narrative Poetry*. SBLWAW 9. Ed. S. Parker. Atlanta: Scholars Press, 1997.

Soggin, J. Alberto. *Judges*. Trans. J. Bowden. OTL. Philadelphia: Westminster, 1981.

Stager, Lawrence E. "The Archaeology of the Family in Ancient Israel." *BASOR* 260 (1985): 1–35.

———. "Forging an Identity: The Emergence of Ancient Israel." Pp. 90–131 in *Oxford History of the Biblical World*. Ed. M. Coogan. New York: Oxford University Press, 1998.

———. "Jerusalem and the Garden of Eden." *ErIsr* 26 (Cross Vol.) (1999): 183*–94*.

———. "The Shechem Temple: Where Abimelech Massacred A Thousand." *BAR* 29/4 (2003): 26–35, 66–69.

———. See further, P. King.

Steinthal, H. "The Legend of Samson." Pp. 392–446 in *Mythology Among the Hebrews*. Ignaz Goldziher. Trans. R. Martineau. London: Longmans, Green, and Co., 1877.

Sternberg, Meir. *The Poetics of Biblical Narrative: Ideological Literature and the Drama of Reading*. Bloomington, Ind.: Indiana University Press, 1985.

Stokes, G. T. "Ulfilas." Pp. 1059–60 in *A Dictionary of Christian Biography*. Ed. W. Smith and H. Wace. 4 vols. London: John Murray, 1887.

Tate, Marvin. *Psalms 51–100*. WBC 20. Dallas: Word, 1990.

Tengström, S., and H.-J. Fabry. "חלף *chālaph*." Pp. 432–35 in *TDOT* 4. Ed. G. J. Botterweck and H. Ringgren. Trans. D. Green. Grand Rapids, Mich., 1980.

Tidwell, N. L. "The Philistine Incursions into the Valley of Rephaim (2 Sam. vv. 17ff.)." Pp. 190–212 in *Studies in the Historical Books of the Old Testament*. VTSup 30. Ed. J. A. Emerton. Leiden: Brill, 1979.

van der Toorn, Karel and Cees Houtman. "David and the Ark." *JBL* 113 (1994): 209–31.

Trible, Phyllis. *Texts of Terror: Literary-Feminist Readings of Biblical Narratives*. OBT. Philadelphia: Fortress, 1984.

Turner, Victor W. *The Ritual Process: Structure and Anti-Structure*. Chicago: Aldine, 1969.

Ulrich, Eugene. See further, F. M. Cross.

Uehlinger, C. "Leviathan." Pp. 511–15 in *DDD*. Ed. K. van der Toorn, B. Becking, and P. W. van der Horst. 2nd ed. Brill: Leiden, 1999.

Van Dam, Cornelis. *The Urim and Thummim: A Means of Revelation in Ancient Israel*. Winona Lake, Ind.: Eisenbrauns, 1997.

de Vaux, Roland. "Single Combat in the Old Testament." Pp. 122–35 in *The Bible and the Ancient Near East.* Trans. D. McHugh. Garden City, N.Y.: Doubleday, 1971.

———. *Ancient Israel: Its Life and Institutions.* Biblical Resource Series. Trans. J. McHugh. Grand Rapids: Eerdmans, 1997; repr. of *Ancient Israel,* 2 vols., 1961.

Walls, Neal H. *The Goddess Anat in Ugaritic Myth.* SBLDS 135. Atlanta: Scholars Press, 1992.

Waltke, Bruce K., and Michael Patrick O'Connor. *An Introduction to Biblical Hebrew Syntax.* Winona Lake, Ind.: Eisenbrauns, 1990.

Webb, Barry. *The Book of the Judges: An Integrated Reading.* JSOTSup 46. Sheffield: JSOT Press, 1987.

Weber, Max. *Ancient Judaism.* Translated and ed. H. H. Gerth and D. Martindale. New York: Free Press, 1952. Orig. publ. 1917–1919.

Wehr, Hans. *Arabic-English Dictionary.* Ed. J. M. Cowan. Ithaca, N.Y.: Spoken Language Services, 1976.

Weisman, Ze'ev. *Political Satire in the Bible.* Atlanta: Scholars Press, 1998.

Wellhausen, Julius. *Prolegomena to the History of Ancient Israel.* Gloucester, Mass.: Peter Smith, 1973. Repr. of *Prolegomena to the History of Ancient Israel,* trans. J. S. Black and A. Enzies, 1885; Ger. Orig., *Prolegomena zur Geschichte Israels,* 2nd ed., 1883.

Wenning, Robert, and Erich Zenger. "Der siebenlockige Held Simson: Literarische und ikonographische Beobachtungen zu Ri 13–16." *BN* 17 (1982): 43–55.

Westenholz, Joan Goodnick. *Legends of the Kings of Akkade: The Texts.* Mesopotamian Civilizations 7. Winona Lake, Ind.: Eisenbrauns, 1997.

White, Sidnie Ann. "In the Steps of Jael and Deborah: Judith as Heroine." Pp. 5–16 in *"No One Spoke Ill of Her": Essays on Judith.* Ed. James C. VanderKam. SBLEJL 2. Atlanta: Scholars Press.

Wiedemann, Thomas. *Emperors and Gladiators.* London: Routledge, 1992.

Wiggermann, F. A. M. "Exit *TALIM!*: Studies in Babylonian Demonology, I." *JEOL* 27 (1981–82): 90–105.

———. *Babylonian Prophylactic Figures: The Ritual Texts.* Amsterdam: Free University Press, 1986.

———. "Mischwesen A." *RlA* 8. Ed. D. O. Edzard. Berlin: Walter de Gruyter, 1994, 222–45.

Willesen, F. "The Philistine Corps of the Scimitar from Gath." *JSS* 3 (1958): 327–35.

Wills, Lawrence M. *The Jew in the Court of the Foreign King.* HDR. Minneapolis: Fortress, 1990.

———. *The Jewish Novel in the Ancient World.* Myth and Poetics. Ed. Gregory Nagy. Ithaca, N.Y.: Cornell University Press, 1995.

———. "Judith." Pp. 1075–1183 in *New Interpreter's Bible* 3. Ed. L. Keck. Nashville: Abingdon, 1999.

Wilson, John A., trans. "An Egyptian Letter." Pp. 475–79 in *Ancient Near Eastern Texts Relating to the Old Testament.* Ed. James B. Pritchard. 3rd ed. Princeton: Princeton University Press, 1969.

Wilson, Robert R. *Prophecy and Society in Ancient Israel.* Philadelphia: Fortress, 1980.

Wyatt, N. "Qeteb." Pp. 673–74 in *DDD.* Ed. K. van der Toorn, B. Becking, and P. W. van der Horst. 2nd ed. Brill: Leiden, 1999, 673–74.

Xella, P. "Resheph." *DDD.* 2nd ed. Ed. K. van der Toorn, B. Becking, and P. W. van der Horst. Brill: Leiden, 1999, 700–03.

Yadin, Yigael. *The Art of Warfare in Biblical Lands.* 2 vols. New York: McGraw-Hill, 1963.

Younger, K. Lawson, trans. "Ninurta-Kudurrī-Uṣur—Suḫu Annals # 2 (2.115B)." Pp. 279–82 in *COS* 2. Ed. W. Hallo. Leiden: Brill, 2000.

Zakovitch, Yair. חיי שמשון (*The Life of Samson*) (Hebrew). Jerusalem: Magnes Press, 1982.

———. "∪ and ∩ in the Bible." *Semeia* 32 (1984): 107–14.

Zenger, Erich. See further, R. Wenning.

Author Index

Biblical Reference Index

Page numbers are in *italic* type.

Subject Index